RED ALERT·
Hurtling
Into
Eternity

*Interpreting Today's Headlines
in Light of Bible Prophecy*

HERBERT EDGAR DOUGLASS

Pacific Press® Publishing Association
Nampa, Idaho
Oshawa, Ontario, Canada
www.pacificpress.com

Editing by Ken McFarland
Cover design by Steve Lanto
Cover resources from Dreamstime.com
Page design by Page One Communications

The author assumes full responsibility for the accuracy of all facts and quotations as cited in this book.

All scripture quotations, unless otherwise indicated, are taken from The New King James Version, copyright © 1979, 1980, 1982 by Thomas Nelson Inc., Publishers.

Scripture quotation from *The Message*. Copyright © by Eugene H. Peterson, 1993, 1994, 1995, 1996, 2000, 2001, 2002. Used by permission of NavPress Publishing Group.

Scriptures marked NCV quoted from The Holy Bible, New Century Version, copyright 1987, 1988, 1991 by Word Publishing, a division of Thomas Nelson, Inc. Used by permission.

Scripture quotations marked NIV are from the HOLY BIBLE, NEW INTERNATIONAL VERSION®. Copyright © 1973, 1978, 1984 by International Bible Society. Used by permission of Zondervan Publishing House. All rights reserved.

"Though all the winds of doctrine were let loose to play upon the earth, so Truth be in the field, we do ingloriously, by licensing and prohibiting, to misdoubt her strength. Let her and Falsehood grapple: who ever knew Truth put to the worse in a free and open encounter?"—John Milton

"But what matter," said Charmides, "from whom I heard this?" "No matter at all," I replied: "for the point is not who said the words, but whether they are true or not."—Socrates

Library of Congress Cataloging-in-Publication Data
Douglass, Herbert E.
  Red alert : hurtling into eternity : interpreting today's headlines in
light of Bible prophecy / Herbert Edgar Douglass.
     p. cm.
  ISBN 13: 978-0-8163-2488-0 (pbk.)
  ISBN 10: 0-8163-2488-3 (pbk.)
  1. Bible—Prophecies—End of the world. 2. End of the world—Biblical
teaching. 3. Seventh-day Adventists—Doctrines. I. Title.
  BS649.E63D68 2011
  236'.9—dc22
                                                                2011007453

11 12 13 14 15 • 5 4 3 2 1

Other Books by Herbert Edgar Douglass

If I Had One Sermon to Preach (editor, plus intro)—1972

Why I Joined—1973

What Ellen White Has Meant to Me (editor, plus intro)—1973

We Found This Truth—1974

Perfection: The Impossible Possibility (co-author)—1975

Why Jesus Waits—1976

Jesus—The Benchmark of Humanity (co-author)—1977

Parable of the Hurricane—1977

Faith, Saying Yes to God—1978

The End—1979

How to Survive the 80s (co-author)—1982

Rediscovering Joy—1994

Messenger of the Lord (college/seminary textbook)—1998

How to Survive in the 21st Century—2000

Should We Ever Say, "I Am Saved"?—2003

God At Risk—2004

Feast Days—2006

They Were There (stories of E.G.W.'s visions and the people affected)—2006

Truth Matters—An Evaluation of Rick Warren's Purpose-Driven Ministry–2006

Never Been This Late Before—2006

Dramatic Prophecies Predicted by Ellen White—2007

Love Finds a Way (a devotional)—2007

A Fork in the Road—2008

The Jesus Difference—2008

The Heartbeat of Adventism: The Great Controversy Theme in the Writings of Ellen White—2010

Dedication

To Norma, my God-fearing soulmate, without guile;
And to our children, friends forever:
Janelle, Herb III, Reatha, Randy, Vivienne Sue, Donna, Chip, Judy,
With whom we will march into the kingdom together.

Contents

Preface

I never intended to write this book—at least, not so soon.

Instead, I have been researching another book that would keep step with *Heartbeat of Adventism: The Great Controversy Theme in the Writings of Ellen White,* recently published. In some way, that next book would be an unfolding of the Great Controversy Theme written for young people in a conversational style. No subject is more motivating than getting the character of God right, so that clarity on that central issue can directly help a young person make his or her core decisions in this turbulent world.

But for the last six months, events happening in about every area—political, religious, social, and financial, as well as disasters in the natural world—seemed to overwhelm me. Many sources of news come through my computer every day, almost every minute. Some say that I am a news junkie. Perhaps so, as I always seem to want to know what's happening in the world "right now!"

For years, I have kept bulging files on these key topics, and every once in a while, I empty them into another book. But this year, those files became swamped, pleading to be disgorged—and so this book.

But this time, the compulsion became overwhelming. Sometimes I feel that I am swimming in five lanes at once. And *Red Alert* seemed to galvanize me night and day, in between finishing off *Heartbeat* and fulfilling a number of speaking appointments.

An author usually writes because people are asking questions. The chapters in this book are limited answers to questions I have been hearing, loud and clear.

My purpose in these twelve chapters covering tremendously important issues is to introduce the reader, maybe for the first time, to God's loving warning about future events and their impact on each person in this world. To be willingly ignorant about Satan's final deceptions will be to fall for a believable lie and lose eternal life. The stakes could not be higher. Anyone willing to take the time can know for sure what is planned—what's just ahead!

What may seem today to be just another everyday occurrence could have eternal consequences. In fact, what we are looking at today are the storm signals for the Most Perfect Storm this world has ever faced.

Herbert Edgar Douglass
Lincoln Hills, California
February 15, 2011

CHAPTER ONE

THEME:

> The mother of Jesus will become a worldwide phenomenon, revered by more than Roman Catholics before the end of time.

The Reappearance of Mother Mary

In 1990, St. Dominic's in Colfax, California, was the magnet for hundreds of cars driving in, day after day, to behold what most thought they saw—the image of Mary, the mother of Jesus. About four miles from Colfax is Weimar Center of Health and Education, and some of us there were entranced by the sincerity, reverence, and devotion of faithful Catholics, who—week after week—traveled many miles to see the "image." That is, until a physics professor explained the phenomenon to be a reflection of sunlight on a new lighting fixture. No more traffic jams.

Colfax was simply one of many sites around the world where crowds journey, and increasingly so into the twenty-first century, to see what was advertised as an appearance of the mother of Jesus. Hundreds of thousands of pilgrims flocked to Nancy Fowler's farm in Conyers, Georgia—every month from October 13, 1990 to May 13, 1994; then continuing annually each October 13 through 1998—to hear Fowler's "message to America" from the Virgin Mary. On Holy Hill, at the spot on the hill where a crucifix stood, plastic bottles were filled with "holy water" from the local well. Many priests were available to provide absolution for one's sins. Lines of those awaiting their turn were long.[1]

Modern Roman Catholics might look back enviously at Europe's golden age of pilgrimage. But in fact, the golden age is now, reports Philip Jenkins:

---

1. *U.S. News & World Report*, October 27, 1997.

The sheer scale of modern European pilgrimage is startling. The world's largest Marian shrine is Guadalupe in Mexico, which attracts 10 million visitors a year, but several European centers draw pilgrims on nearly that scale. And just since the 1970s, those numbers have grown substantially. Lourdes, which drew about a million visitors each year in the 1950s, now records closer to 6 million annually (50,000 might pass through on a quiet day). Each year, Jasna Góra in Czestochowa, Poland, attracts 4 or 5 million to see a picture of the Virgin Mary supposedly drawn from life by St. Luke the Evangelist. Each year, around 15 percent of Poles make a pilgrimage to some site. Four million believers visit the site of Mary's apparition at Fátima in Portugal. Europe as a whole has probably 500 images of the Black Virgin, and many are venerated at pilgrimage sites like Altötting in Bavaria and Montserrat in Spain.[2]

In Bosnia, an estimated thirty million pilgrims have visited Medjugorje since the apparitions of the Blessed Virgin Mary began in 1981.[3] Visiting Medjugorje is a tough challenge, involving many hours by bus over war-torn roads.

In Sabana Grande, Puerto Rico, where the Virgin Mary reportedly appeared more than fifty years ago, multiplied thousands come from all over the world—so popular that preparations are underway to build a 305-foot statue of Mary on a 1,200-foot base, giving the eventual structure a total height of approximately 1,500 feet.[4]

In 1997, *Newsweek* ran a cover story on the Virgin Mary:

> In many ways, the 20th century has belonged to Mary. From almost every continent, visionaries have reported more than 400 "apparitions" of the Virgin—more than in the previous three centuries combined. . . . Taken together, these visions point to what the Marian Movement believes is a millennial "Age of Mary."[5]

These countries are not predominately Catholic. For example, apparitions are reported from Japan to Africa, from Korea to Australia, from Iraq to Israel, from Egypt to Syria, and even deep within Russia and among the peoples of India. Interesting—they are all allegedly being visited by a woman who calls herself Mary, the Queen of Heaven, Our Lady.

2. *Christian Century,* May 16, 2010.

3. Wayne Weible, *The Final Harvest* (Brewster, MA: Paraclete Press, 1999), xiv.

4. Steve Beauclair, "Skyscraper Statue Slated for Sabana Grande: $42 million Virgin Mary Part of Mystical City," *Caribbean Business,* Feb. 26, 1998, Late News cover story.

5. Kenneth L. Woodward, "Hail, Mary," *Newsweek,* August 25, 1997, 50.

Robert Faricy, quoted in the book *Queen of the Cosmos*, states:

Never in the history of Christianity has the Blessed Virgin Mary appeared to so many people over so long a period of time with such regularity. Moreover, it seems that the apparitions at Medjugorje have ushered in a new Marian age. There are reports of her appearing everywhere.[6]

Evangelicals Rediscovering Mary

But the reemergence of the Virgin Mary is not only an attraction for Roman Catholics. The cover story for *Time*, March 23, 2005, entitled "Hail, Mary," focused on the extraordinary emphasis on Mary within the Protestant world. Some of these developments include the increased emphasis on feminism and the role of the divine feminine (think *Red Tent* and *The Da Vinci Code*) and the remarkable interest within Protestantism in the practices and texts of the Christian church's first fifteen hundred years that was immersed in Marianism. "Ancient-modern" is the catchphrase.

For about three hundred years, the Protestant world, while clearly emphasizing that the Virgin Mother was indeed the mother of Jesus, regarded any further emphasis as being sheer "Mariolatry"—the elevation of Mary to a status approaching Christ's. (Their emphasis was to forestall any attempt to suggest that Jesus was not preexistent, that He was only an ordinary baby.)

However, "the times, they are a-changing"! For instance, Brian Maguire, pastor of Westminster Presbyterian Church in Xenia, Ohio, made news in 2005 by combining an emphasis on Mary, as well as Jesus, in his Easter remarks. He joined the day of the Annunciation (when the angel Gabriel told Mary that she would give birth to the Messiah) with his Easter celebration.[7] Maguire called it a "beautiful, poetic opportunity." After all, he said, Mary was "the first and the last disciple to reach out during his [Christ's] life."[8]

But Beverly Gaventa, a professor of New Testament literature at Princeton, portrays Mary as the victim of "a Protestant conspiracy: theologically, liturgically, and devotionally." In other words, Protestants drag her out for a few weeks in December and then pack her in the crèche for the rest of the year, so disdainful are they of the reverence many believe is due her.[9]

---

6. Jan Connell, *Queen of the Cosmos* (Brewster, MA: Paraclete Press, 1990), 4.

7. The Day of Annunciation is celebrated on March 25, precisely nine months before Christmas, December 25.

8. *Christianity Today*, December 1, 2003.

9. *Time*, May 13, 2005.

Arguments on behalf of Mary have sprung up like dandelions in the last ten years. Note *Christianity Today* (December 2003), which featured an extended article, "The Blessed Evangelical Mary," by Timothy George, Dean at Beeson Divinity School, Samford University, in Birmingham, Alabama.

Speaking as a convinced Evangelical, George asked some searching questions:

> The question remains: does Protestantism have a place for the Blessed Virgin Mary? . . . Without compromising the Reformation principles of *sola gratia, sola fide,* and *sola scriptura,* can we understand and honor Mary in ways that are scripturally based and evangelically motivated? Are we to be included among those of every generation who call Jesus' mother "blessed"? Protestants are right to be concerned about these issues, especially when such extreme devotion to Mary remains unchecked at a popular level. But in reacting to Catholic excesses, have we gone to the other extreme? Must nearly everything we say about Mary be couched in the language of dissent and disbelief? The fact is, evangelicals often say less about Mary than the New Testament does. She is seldom mentioned in our sermons or worship services, except for her honorary appearance in the annual Christmas pageant.[10]

But the real message we are getting—a river flowing with increasing volume—is the departure of well-known leaders in politics and academia to a fully embraced Catholic Church. It's not that odd these days in theological circles. Last year a string of theologians left their Protestant denominations for the Church of Rome. The list includes three Lutherans—Reinhard Hütter and Bruce Marshall, theologians at Methodist seminaries (Duke and Southern Methodist), and Mickey Mattox, a Luther scholar at Marquette; two Anglicans—Rusty Reno of Creighton and Douglas Farrow of McGill University; and a Mennonite—Gerald Schlabach of St. Thomas University.[11]

---

10. *Christianity Today,* December 1, 2003.

11. "All six all have strong connections to mainline institutions and several were involved in official ecumenical conversation at high levels. They are also relatively young, poised to influence students and congregations for several decades. They more or less fit the description 'postliberal' in that they accept such mainline practices as historical criticism and women's ordination while wanting the church to exhibit more robust dogmatic commitments. All of them embrace what Mattox describes as an 'evangelical, catholic and orthodox' vision of the church. They could not see a way to be all those things within mainline denominations." http://www.catholiceducation.org/articles/printarticle.html?id=2252.

But perhaps these men and women of the present day and recent past got more front-page attention: Nicole Kidman, Tony Blair, Anne Marie, Gary Cooper, Jeb Bush, Graham Greene, Frances Kydd (mother of Princess Diana), T. S. Eliot, Senator Sam Brownback, and Bob Novak. Or perhaps David Pendleton, Adventist pastor/lawyer/state representative in Hawaii.

Why are these folk, especially Evangelicals, converting to Roman Catholicism? Scott McKnight researched thirty Evangelicals who had converted to the "Mother" church and concluded: (1) Certainty, rejecting the "doctrinal mayhem" and "choose-your-own-church" syndrome of Protestantism. (2) History, desiring connection to the entire history of the Christian church and not just the period since the Reformation. (3) Unity, seeking refuge in the perceived unity of the Roman Catholic Church. (4) Authority, doctrinal issues now settled, no longer trying to sort through the various interpretations of Protestant theologians and pastors. (5) Becoming Catholic, after reading massive amounts of research and Catholic books.[12]

Brad Wilcox adds his reasons for this exodus of Protestants to Rome:

The collapse of Protestant morality in American culture, the centrifugal drift of evangelical Protestantism, and the socioeconomic mobility of evangelical Protestants have all played key roles.[13]

Tim Perry writes that some of the emerging dialogue between Catholics and Evangelicals over Mary became possible because of a deepening interest in "the ecumenism of the trenches," such as common concerns over abortion and rapid developments in biotechnology, embryology, and gerontology—alliances that previously did not exist.[14]

Mary, the Model for All Mothers—a Protestant View

Elva McAllaster wants Protestants to think about Mary on Mother's Day—she is "an archetypal mother: to the mother within whose flesh Divinity became flesh."[15]

She points out that since the Reformation, "Protestants have tended, in their scorn for Madonna-worship, to ignore what all Christians can learn from her."

Some of the points Protestants can learn:

First, we note the total submission to God's will for her personal life expressed in Luke 1:38: "Behold the handmaid of the Lord; be it

---

12. http://www.theologicalstudies.org/page/page1572353.htm.
13. http://www.catholiceducation.org/articles/printarticle.html?id=2252.
14. Tim Perry, "Evangelicals and Mary," in *Theology Today*, July 2008.
15. *Christianity Today*, May 12, 1972. http://www.christianitytoday.com/ct/2000/mayweb-only/56.0ahtml.

unto me according to thy word." [16]

Think of the thoughts whirling through her head—surely uncertainty and fear of misunderstanding. But note her response, so accepting. Of course, she had no idea of how rough the donkey ride would be from Nazareth to Bethlehem or what it would really mean to see soldiers nail her Son to rough posts. Every Christian mother should take note: with all the decisions to be made in a very earthy routine, in listening to the pruning and guiding of the Holy Spirit, what could be a more appropriate response—"Be it unto me according to thy word."

Second, Luke 2:51 suggests that *Mary found and understood the roles of authority and responsibility with in God's plan:* "He went down with them, and came to Nazareth, and was subject unto them. . . ." [17]

She knew her Son was divine (she learned that in the Annunciation). Yet as her Son, the Divine One would be "subject unto" her and Joseph. Mary was a role model of a disciplining parent. What could that mean? When to wake Him up, when and how to feed Him, when to tell Him to get water at the village well or get the lumber for His father's shop, when to help with the common chores of the house! All this is quite contrary to much of the parent-child relationship in homes today—when it seems that from birth the child rules the parents, and it gets worse in the teen-age years!

Next, *she was a meditating mother.* The record continues in Luke 2:51: "His mother kept all these sayings in her heart." [18]

Surely most mothers today with all the hurried, harried, materialistic expectations, desires, demands of modern living would do well to ponder often God's actions in their own lives. In other words, how often does anyone these days take time to ponder the words of a sermon or a treasured book being read in fits and starts? Or to cultivate an awareness of God's presence, even as we pull weeds or talk with the neighbors?

Mary was, furthermore, one who gave leadership to the Christian community in its communal prayer. Among the scriptural allusions to her, one of the strangely neglected ones is Acts 1:14; in their preparation for Pentecost, the disciples in the upper room "continued with one accord in prayer and supplication, with the women, and Mary the mother of Jesus." [19]

One fact is obvious—the disciples were not praying their heavenly Fa-

16. Ibid. Emphasis added.
17. Ibid. Emphasis added.
18. Ibid. Emphasis added.
19. Ibid.

ther through her. She was a suppliant with the others. But can you imagine what her very presence must have meant to everyone? Think about the vitality, urgency, joy and faith that she added. Wow!

Every home and church needs people who know how to "supplicate" and add courage and vitality to the group. Such opportunities everywhere cry out for reproductions of women (and men) like Mary.[20]

Yes, Protestants could do well to remember and emulate Mary's virtues even today.

Mary and Muslims/Islam

Now we are getting very close to where we all are, no matter what country we are in. Any way we look at Muslim expansion and political consequences in most every nation in the perceived Christian world, the Muslim presence has changed the landscape in the twenty-first century.

Many questions are asked, especially by those who think in terms of this earth's last days. How does this unprecedented world power fit into biblical prophecies? In many countries, it has become a Roman Catholic/Muslim issue.

How the Roman Catholic Church, with its mighty political influence, will relate to the astonishing rise of Muslim political influence should be of great interest to all.

Do we have any clue as to how the Roman Church is already planning to overcome Muslim antagonism? Much in every way!

Malachi Martin, consummate Vatican insider and intelligence expert, wrote in his incomparable *The Keys of This Blood* (1991) that the future of Roman Catholics and the Islamic world was one of Pope John Paul II's highest concerns:

> In reckoning the future of Islam, Pope John Paul takes into account that as a genuinely religious faith, it preserves certain fundamental truths that the Holy Spirit reveals to all people of good will, and that, in God's providence, Islam can be a threshold from which its adherents can be prepared to accept the only historical revelation made by God in this world. There will come a day, John Paul believes, when the heart of Islam—already attuned to the figures of Christ and of Christ's Mother, Mary—will receive the illumination it needs.[21]

A few years earlier at Vatican II, it was agreed that "the plan of

---

20. Ibid.

21. Malachi Martin, *The Keys of This Blood* (New York: Simon & Schuster, Inc., 1990), 285.

salvation also includes those who acknowledge the Creator, in the first place amongst whom are the Moslems; these profess to hold the faith of Abraham, and together with us they adore the one, merciful God, mankind's judge on the last day."[22]

That same Vatican II document suggested that "everyone, even idol worshippers, will eventually come under the saving umbrella of the Roman Catholic Church—everyone, that is except Protestants."[23]

How does all this fit? Bishop Fulton J. Sheen, one of the first religious speakers to appear on TV in the 1950s, attracted my attention with his platform finesse and almost incredible ability to translate theological jargon for every listener. Sheen was a prolific, brilliant writer. One of his most acclaimed books was *The World's First Love*.[24] In this book he focused his attention on how Mother Mary would be the meeting place for the conversion of the Muslim world:

> The Qu'ran, which is the Bible for the Muslims, has many passages concerning the Blessed Virgin. First of all, the Qu'ran believes in the Immaculate Conception, and also in her Virgin Birth. . . . When Mary is born, the mother says: "And I consecrate her with all of her posterity under thy protection, O Lord, against Satan!" . . . The Qu'ran has also verses on the Annunciation, Visitation, and Nativity. Angels are pictured as accompanying the Blessed Mother and saying, "Oh, Mary, God has chosen you and purified you, and elected you above all the women of the earth." In the nineteenth chapter of the Qu'ran there are 41 verses on Jesus and Mary. There is such a strong defense of the virginity of Mary here that the Qu'ran, in the fourth book, attributed the condemnation of the Jews to their monstrous calumny against the Virgin Mary.
>
> Mary, then, is for the Muslims the true Sayyida, or Lady. The only possible serious rival to her in their creed would be Fatima, the daughter of Mohammed himself. But after the death of Fatima, Mohammed wrote: "Thou shalt be the most blessed of all women in Paradise, after Mary."
>
> In a variation of the text, Fatima is made to say, "I surpass all the women, except Mary."

22. Justin Flannery, O.P. gen. ed., *Vatican Council II: The Conciliar and Post Conciliar Documents*, rev. ed. (Northport, NY: Costello Publishing, 1988), vol. 1, 367. Cited in Dave Hunt, *A Woman Rides the Beast* (Eugene, OR: Harvest House Publishers, 1994), 293.

23. Ibid., Dave Hunt.

24. Fulton Sheen, *The World's First Love* (San Francisco, CA: Ignatius Press, 1952).

This brings us to our second point namely, why the Blessed Mother, in the 20th century, should have revealed herself in the insignificant little village of Fatima [Portugal], so that to all future generations she would be known as "Our Lady of Fatima." Since nothing ever happens out of Heaven except with a finesse of all details, I believe that the blessed Virgin chose to be known as "Our Lady of Fatima" as a pledge and a sigh of hope to the Muslim people, and as an assurance that they, who show her so much respect, will one day accept her divine Son too.

Evidence to support these views is found in the historical fact that the Muslims occupied Portugal for centuries. At the time when they were finally driven out, the last Muslim chief had a beautiful daughter by the name of Fatima. A Catholic boy fell in love with her, and for him she not only stayed behind when the Muslims left, but even embraced the faith. The young husband was so much in love with her that he changed the name of the town where he lived to Fatima. This, the very place where our lady appeared in 1977 bears a historical connection to Fatima, the daughter of Mohammed.

The final evidence of the relationship of Fatima to the Muslims is the enthusiastic reception the Muslims in Africa, India, and elsewhere gave to the pilgrim statue of Our Lady of Fatima. Muslims attended the church service in honor of our Lady, they allowed religious processions and even prayers before their mosques, and in Mozambique, the Muslims who were unconverted, began to be Christian as soon as the statue of our Lady of Fatima was erected.

Missionaries in the future will, more and more, see that the apostolate among the Muslims will be successful in the measure that they preach Our Lady of Fatima. Mary is the advent of Christ, bringing Christ to the people before Christ himself is born. In an apologetic endeavor, it is always best to start with that which people already accept. Because the Muslims have a devotion to Mary, our missionaries should be satisfied merely to expand and to develop that devotion, with the full realization that Our Blessed Lady will carry the Muslims the rest of the way to her divine Son. She is forever a "traitor," in the sense that she will not accept any devotion to herself, but will always bring anyone who is devoted to her to her divine Son. As those who love devotion to her lose belief in the divinity of Christ, so those who intensify devotion to her gradually acquire that belief. . . .

The Muslims should be prepared to acknowledge that, if Fatima must give way in honor to the Blessed Mother, it is because she is different from all the other mothers of the world and that without Christ she would be nothing.

World's Spiritual Mother Who Intercedes for All Humanity

Newsweek, August 25, 1997, had a cover story featuring the petition drive to have the Pope make formal the definition of the fifth Marian dogma—that Mary is "Mediatrix of all Graces, Co-redemptrix and Advocate."[25]

Every Catholic is bound to believe an *ex cathedra*[26] declaration of the Pope—if doubted or rejected, it would be the same as rejecting the declared word of God that has the same authority as if God himself had declared it in person.

By these three titles for Mary, the Roman Catholic Church means that salvation for *everyone* is obtained through Mary and not directly from Jesus. That the Catholic Church for many years has been teaching all this is an undeniable fact—but it has never been formally declared *ex cathedra.*

Many examples through the centuries can be cited, but Pope John Paul II was surely the pope who often emphasized Mary's role as "co-redemptrix." He made the phrase *totus tuus* ("totally hers") as his papal motto. During his General Audience of September 8, 1982, Pope John Paul II greeted the sick with, "Mary, though conceived and born without the taint of sin, participated in a marvelous way in the suffering of her divine Son, in order to be *Co-Redemptrix* of humanity."[27]

Mary's work was to be our co-redemptress, and to mediate for us together with Christ, but of course in subordination to Him. . . . By a special title, there we call her co-redemptress. . . . She is our spiritual Mother in heaven, and she fulfills the duties of a Mother winning for us by her intercession that grace of Christ which is life to our souls and which, please God, will mean eternal life in the end.[28]

The petition drive mentioned in the *Newsweek* article was promoted by Professor Mark Miravalle of Franciscan University in Steubenville, Ohio,

25. The first four Marian dogmas are (1) That Mary is the "Mother of God"; (2) Mary was "Ever-Virgin"; (3) Mary was herself "immaculately conceived"; (4) Mary was assumed bodily into Heaven and crowned "Queen of Heaven and Earth."
26. "Out of the chair," here used as a papal declaration considered as dogma.
27. Insegnamenti di Giovanni Paolo II, I, V/3 (1982), 404.
28. *Redemptoris Mater,* encyclical of Pope John Paul II, March 25, 1987. See *Radio Replies*, Second Volume, by Leslie Rumble, M.S.C. and Charles Mortimer Carty, printed by Radio Replies Press, St. Paul, Minn., #674, 162.

during a 1993 Marian conference at the university. It asks the pope to make ex cathedra officially that Mary is co-redeemer. The petition says, "If this were done, she would be a vastly more powerful figure, something close to the fourth member of the Holy Trinity and the primary female face through which Christians experience the divine."

Miravalle's petition received support from Mother Teresa, 440 bishops, Cardinal John O'Conner, and 41 other cardinals. What is surprising is that by the end of 2000, more than six million signatures from 148 countries reached the Vatican. The primary driving force behind this unprecedented surge is the Catholic mission of ecumenism—*the uniting of all Christians and all the world under one head.*[29] More about this later!

Mary and the Flag of European Unity

Daily, I receive an article from ZENIT news agency.[30] At times I find this Catholic news agency very relevant and thus useful. Its December 7, 1999, article #ZE99120707 got my attention, and I filed it away for future use.

December 8 is a very special day for Europe: in 1955, on that day, the European Ministers' delegates officially adopted the European flag designed by Arsene Heitz, who today is an octogenarian artist in Strasbourg. The decision was taken following the 1950 European Council's (one of the predecessors of today's European Union) convocation of a competition to design the flag of the newborn European Community. Among many other artists, Heitz presented several designs, and one was chosen: 12 stars on a blue background.

Recently Heitz revealed to a French magazine the reason for his inspiration. At that time he was reading the history of the Blessed Virgin's apparitions in Paris' Rue du Bac, known today as the Virgin of the Miraculous Medal. According to the artist, he thought of the 12 stars in a circle on a blue background, exactly the way it is represented in traditional iconography of this image of the Immaculate Conception. In the beginning, Heitz saw it as a flight of fancy, among the many that run through an artist's imagination; but the idea caught his attention, to the point that it became the subject of his meditation.

According to Javier Paredes, Professor of Contemporary History at

29. Cardinal Luis Aponte Martinez, http://www.fifthmariandogma.com/index.php?option=com_content&view=article&id=247.
30. ZENIT's objective is to inform us about the "world seen from Rome," to view the modern world "through the messages of the Pope," and to tell about the "happenings of the Catholic Church."

the University of Alcala in Spain, in statements sent to *Zenit*, "Heitz listens to God in his interior; in other words, he prays with his heart and his head. He says he is profoundly religious and devoted to the Virgin, to whom he never misses praying a daily Rosary, together with his wife. Because of this, he believes the inspiration not only from his artistic talents, but from the silent voices that Heaven always speaks to men of good will, among whom Heitz can undoubtedly be numbered. He is an artist who, virtually at the end of his life and at the zenith of his career, can proclaim with the guarantee of authenticity that he recalls that moment, that he is interested in very few but very important things, that he regards himself as a man who loves the whole world, but especially the Blessed Virgin, who is our Mother."

Numerous pictures (icons) through the years depict the Virgin Mary as the "woman" of Revelation 12:1—"Now a great sign appeared in heaven: a woman clothed with the sun, with the moon under her feet, and on her head a garland of twelve stars." Many are the references supporting this belief in Catholic periodicals.[31]

On this kind of evidence, Catholics appear justified in believing the European Union (EU) flag is a tribute to Mary. The Euro Flag was officially adopted on December 8, 1955, on the Feast of The Immaculate Conception of Mary. On September 2, 1958, Archbishop Montini (later Pope Pius XII) dedicated a statue of "Our Beloved Lady, Ruler of Europe."

The Papal Nuncio in Brussels, Monsignor Karl-Josef Rauber, described the EU as "a Catholic confederation of States."[32] Pope Paul VI declared that it is "the Catholic faith that made Europe."[33] In the Jesuit publication *America Magazine,* the president of the EU was referred to as "a bearer of the torch first lit by the Catholic architects of European unity."[34]

Pope John XXIII, likewise, speaking of his interest in a United Europe said it would become "the greatest Catholic superstate the world has ever

---

31. For example, Ted and Maureen Flynn, *The Thunder of Justice* (Sterling, VA: MaxKol Communications, Inc., 1993), 5, 14, 30, 99, etc.

32. *European Institute of Protestant Studies,* http://www.ianPaisley.org/article.asp?ArtKey=eu4.

33. http://www.tomorrowsworld.org/cgi-bin/tw/tw-mag.cgi?.

34. Adrian Hilton, *The Principality and Power of Europe* (Rickmansworth, Hertfordshire, England: Dorchester House Publications, 1997), 160.

known."[35]

This brief overview of a developing supranational superstate, in which EU citizens have no voting rights that can alter EU legislation, was almost beyond imagination even sixty years ago. The fact that this planned political reality is not yet apparent to many Europeans seems to be proof of the brilliance of its execution and of the strange docility, perhaps ignorance, of the majority of Europeans.

Mary, Spiritism, and World Peace

This section could easily be a book by itself. References relating to how the Virgin Mary will intervene amidst last-day tumult mount up like fallen leaves in a New England October! I can only paint with a broad brush.

In 1991, to the Marian Movement of Priests, Mary is reported as saying:

> Soon, I will come, my children! Soon, I will be in your midst with a great light. I will enlighten the entire world. Many souls will cry because they did not listen to my call. . . . I will pass above everyone in a cloud and everyone will see me. What will become of those who insulted me and made a laughing stock of me? . . . I will come soon, my sons, to travel through the entire world. I will give a great sign in the sky for those who will still want to be saved. All those who have recourse to me, who have a look of repentance, this will be sufficient to save them.[36]

A few years ago, anything in this chapter would have been called fantasy—a flight of wild imagination. If anyone had said that the Virgin Mary would take on worldwide importance, he or she would have been laughed to scorn. Times have changed.

Pictures of the weeping Madonna (Mary) are on the front cover of national news magazines. Countless tens of thousands visit her shrines throughout the world, as mentioned earlier. Books are being written about her personal appearances. She gives inspirational messages; warns of coming events; and speaks of the end of the world, the horror of last-day events, and how to find peace and security in her personal presence.[37]

---

35. "[A united Europe will be] the Greatest Catholic superstate the world has ever known . . . the greatest single human force ever seen by man," Pope John XXIII. www.liebreich.com/LDC/HTML/Europe/04-Religion.html. "Forty years ago, Pope John XXIII predicted that the new Europe would become 'the greatest Catholic super state the world has ever known,'" www.revivalscotland.com/jesuit_europe.html.

36. http://www.biblebelievers.com/tetlow/queenofall01.html.

37. Read Michael H. Brown's *The Final Hour* (Guthrie, OK: Faith Publishing Co.), 1997.

If we ask the question, What would cause the world to welcome the Virgin Mary as God's last-day envoy? the answer would be PEACE. If she brought peace to this world, who would not love her? Only those who know the real future, as revealed in the Bible's Big Picture!

But think! What if Mary worked out a peace plan for Israel and her Arab neighbors that all concerned suddenly saw was absolutely workable—and they applied her counsel? What if Mary reconciled Protestants and Catholics in Northern Ireland? What if Mary projected a plan for Serbs (Greek Orthodox) and Croats (Roman Catholic) and Bosnians (Muslim) that startled them with its simplicity? What if North Korea and South Korea were given a peace plan that neither dreamed of before Mary presented it? What if Mary worked through the pope of Rome to bring Jews, Catholics, Muslims, Buddhists, Hindus, and others to a peace table, with a plan that stunned everyone with its startling freshness?

What if she walked across the Hudson River in New York City, with every news camera in the world broadcasting the event in living color, heading for the United Nations building to lay out these peace plans?

Who in the world, on any continent, would dare to speak against the Virgin Mary? That person would be targeted as an enemy of the human race.

What then do we do with *this* prediction?

Fearful sights of a supernatural character will soon be revealed in the heavens, in token of the power of miracle-working demons. The spirits of devils will go forth to the kings of the earth and to the whole world, to fasten them in deception, and urge them on to unite with Satan in his last struggle against the government of heaven. By these agencies, rulers and subjects will be alike deceived. . . . They will perform wonderful miracles of healing and will profess to have revelations from heaven contradicting the testimony of Scripture.[38]

As spiritualism more closely imitates the nominal Christianity of the day, it has greater power to deceive and ensnare. Satan himself is converted, after the modern order of things. He will appear in the character of an angel of light. Through the agency of spiritualism, miracles will be wrought, the sick will be healed, and many undeniable wonders will be performed. And as the spirits will profess faith in the Bible, and manifest respect for the institutions of the church, their work will be accepted as a manifestation of divine power.

The line of distinction between professed Christians and the un-

---

38. Ellen G. White, *The Great Controversy*, 624.

godly is now hardly distinguishable. Church members love what the world loves and are ready to join with them, and Satan determines to unite them in one body and thus strengthen his cause by sweeping all into the ranks of spiritualism. Papists, who boast of miracles as a certain sign of the true church, will be readily deceived by this wonder-working power; and Protestants, having cast away the shield of truth, will also be deluded. Papists, Protestants, and worldlings will alike accept the form of godliness without the power, and they will see in this union a grand movement for the conversion of the world and the ushering in of the long-expected millennium.[39]

Note how the key words—peace, millennium, Spiritualism (Spiritism)—are used in this paragraph and also in many, many accepted messages of the Virgin Mary. I find all this remarkable. To me, this is Satan's masterpiece: Satan stops all wars and conflicts (or it appears so) in his final plan to control the earth. And for all those in the world watching their TV sets, Mary has done it all. Who wouldn't love her? The prayers for world peace have been answered!

To top it off, Jesus Himself seems to appear, to support His mother Mary! What could be more convincing? "As the crowning act in the great drama of deception, Satan himself will personate Christ."[40]

But what happens when our friends in China, or France, or New York City learn of people who believe that this stunning, dazzling Lady of Peace and Light is not the Virgin Mary—that the "glorious appearing" of Jesus, too, is but the work of impersonating demons? All the furies pent up in emotionally exhausted minds and hearts will be unleashed. Words are inadequate to describe the hatred and fury the whole world will heap upon those who deny what seems so right to the eyes and ears of the world's multitudes.

The Lord said that the day will come when His people will be "hated by all nations for my name's sake" (Matt. 24:9). This prophecy has not yet been fulfilled—*it will be before the end of time, just before He returns.*

What causes this hatred? The world will not tolerate any opposition to the Virgin Mary. She brought them peace. Everybody loves her—except those who expose her.

But there is more . . .

---

39. Ibid., 588, 589.
40. Ibid., 624.

CHAPTER TWO

THEME:

> Jesus will return after this planet has endured an *unprecedented, exponential* rise of disasters, natural and man-made. Note "unprecedented" and "exponential"!

The Birth Pangs of Mother Nature

Not much is more important than "birth pangs"!

All mothers know what I am talking about! All fathers worth their salt should, as well! I really don't think parents ever lose the excitement when birth pangs begin, amidst the concern, of course, for mother and the child about to be born.

Remember wondering if the baby will wait until we finish the crib or paint the walls! What about the car—is the tank full?

How many minutes between the "pangs"? Who's counting? What? Five minutes? Let's get in the car! Now! And so it goes, baby after baby. At least, in developed countries. Elsewhere, birth may happen on the street or in a private hut where men are not allowed.

Jesus surely understood all this when He said, in reference to the future just preceding the end of the world, that such signs as wars, famines, pestilences, and earthquakes were only "the beginning of sorrows" (Matthew 24:5–8). "Sorrows" is a translation of the Greek word for "birth pangs." Now, every mom and dad gets the point, without having a college class in Greek exegesis!

Every mom tells us—as the "labor pains" come *closer together*—that they become more *intense.* All these signs were clearly understood ahead of time, because the parents took their Lamaze instructor seriously! Jesus told us that His followers in the "last days" will catch the increasing tempo of events, even as a wise mother and father should.

In Matthew 24 and 25 and Luke 21, wars, earthquakes, hurricanes, pestilences, and floods are presented as "the *beginning* of sorrows" (Matthew 24:8). In other words, these are not, in themselves, specific signs of *the end* of the world. On one hand, they are signs that the world is *not* getting better and better, as social progressives and evolutionists want to say.

Jesus did not leave us with a guessing game. He said to note the increasing frequency and intensity of these natural disasters.

However, He also compared the last days of planet Earth to the last days before Noah entered the ark (verses 37–39). People will be so used to troubles and the latest inventions that the prevailing mood will actually be an optimistic picture of the future![40] How could that be? More about that coming up!

And He gave us another clue—His return would be delayed, as noted in the delay in the Bridegroom's appearance at his wedding (25:5).

Going back to those familiar signs—I, with most of you, for too long have only romanticized these words: "Famines will increase. Pestilences will sweep away thousands. Dangers are all around us from the powers without and satanic workings within, but the *restraining power of God*

---

40. "Come when it may, the day of God will come unawares to the ungodly. When life is going on in its unvarying round; when men are absorbed in pleasure, in business, in traffic, in money-making; when religious leaders are magnifying the world's progress and enlightenment, and the people are lulled in a false security—then, as the midnight thief steals within the unguarded dwelling, so shall sudden destruction come upon the careless and ungodly, 'and they shall not escape' [1 Thess. 5:3]," Ellen White, *The Great Controversy,* 38. "Christ declares that there will exist similar unbelief concerning His second coming. As the people of Noah's day 'knew not until the Flood came, and took them all away; so,' in the words of our Saviour, 'shall also the coming of the Son of man be.' Matthew 24:39. When the professed people of God are uniting with the world, living as they live, and joining with them in forbidden pleasures; when the luxury of the world becomes the luxury of the church; when the marriage bells are chiming, and all are looking forward to many years of worldly prosperity—then suddenly as the lightning flashes from the heavens, will come the end of their bright visions and delusive hopes." White, *The Great Controversy,* 338, 339. See also chapter 11 of this book: "Intoxicating Optimism Dangerous to One's Health."

is now being exercised."[41] We previously had no way of relating to these words, any more than young wives can relate to what their mothers said about "birth pangs"! But the time comes when mothers-to-be gasp, "Now I know what you mean!" The mother's contractions must increase in an exponential way, or the baby will never be born alive.

So it is in the end times: "These wonderful manifestations will be *more and more frequent and terrible* just before the second coming of Christ and the end of the world, as signs of its speedy destruction."[42]

"More frequent and terrible!" "Birth pangs!" The truth is, Jesus will return after this planet has endured an *unprecedented, exponential rise* of natural disasters; note—*unprecedented and exponential!*

The Exponential Curve

The line of an exponential curve arcs in an upward trajectory and is described in terms of multiplication, in contrast to the slanting upward path of a straight line, best described in terms of addition. We see this curve in many areas of the scientific and financial worlds. For example, think of the interest on savings in your bank account. If you want to know how much $100,000 will become in ten years at 8 percent simple interest, you can draw an upwardly slanted straight line, adding $8,000 the first year, $8,000 the second year, etc. In ten years you would have $80,000 earned interest (that is, you would now have $180,000). In thirty years, you would have $340,000.

But if you were earning compound interest at 8 percent, you would not have a predicted straight line of $8,000 per year but a line that would slope up continually, always trending more toward vertical. At the end of the second year, you would own $117,349 (not $116,000); at the end of the third year, $127,121 (not $124,000); and at the end of the fourth year, $137,708, (not $132,000). After thirty years, you would have $1,102,027. Compare!

How does this apply to last-day events? All the awful catastrophes of the past will be repeated but in exponential rapidity, much like the mother's labor in childbirth! Can anyone deny that, in most respects, hurricanes, floods, famines, pestilences, national debt, personal debt, bankruptcies, moral degradation, depletion of water aquifers, energy consumption, civil wars, international crises, and so on, are increasing with astonishing speed? Most people live with the sense that everything is out of control, compared to the life we lived even twenty-five years ago, and there seems to be no way to turn back the clock. The escalator, either down or up, seems to go faster every day and with every news broadcast.

---

41. White, *Last Day Events*, 27.
42. Ellen White, *Patriarchs and Prophets*, 109; emphasis added.

And almost everyone has the lurking feeling that they cannot get off that escalator!

The impact of events is heightened when the latest disaster is wired into our offices or living rooms through CNN or FOX News in living color. Instantly, we are fed the reporter's hype, and this constant feed gives us the feeling that events are happening more rapidly than ever, that we are surrounded with distress, and that life has never happened like this before. Our perceptions are only adding to the reality around us.[43] We need to realize that our scientific equipment today can detect, calculate, and compare all these events far more accurately and exhaustively than even twenty years ago, never mind a hundred years in the past. So are disasters actually increasing, or are we simply detecting and measuring events more accurately?

Earthquakes

For a fast overview, the largest earthquakes of all time are as follow's:

▶ Chile, May 22, 1960, 9.5

▶ Sumatra, Indonesia, December 26, 2004, 9.3

▶ Prince William Sound, Alaska, March 28, 1964, 9.2

▶ Aleutian Islands, March 9, 1957, 9.1

▶ Kamchatka, Russia, November 4, 1952, 9.0

▶ Ecuador, January 31, 1906, 8.8

▶ Chile, February 27, 2010, 8.8

▶ Aleutian Islands, February 4, 1965, 8.7

▶ Lisbon, Portugal, November 1, 1755, 8.7

▶ Sumatra, Indonesia, March 28, 2005, 8.7

▶ India-China border, August 15, 1950, 8.6

▶ Kamchatka, Russia, February 3, 1923, 8.5[44]

The Lisbon earthquake has probably had more press than any of the others. Christian peoples of different churches, at that time, saw in the Lisbon earthquake the fulfillment of New Testament prophecies. Lisbon was a beautiful city, and the vast European population was astonished by

---

43. I am well aware of some who declare that our "perceptions" are due to better, worldwide communications and that we only "feel" that everything is worse. And true, death tolls are, marvelously, fewer in modern tornadoes, hurricanes, floods, and other disasters, because we have achieved remarkable improvements in early warning systems.

44. http://www.epicdisasters.com/index.php/site/comments/the_world'sworstfloods.

the shocking devastation and afraid of what it might portend. Perception ruled, and for Europe, "it was the worst ever."

Floods

Throughout history, floods have proved to be the deadliest natural disasters, mainly due to high population densities near rivers. That all ancient civilizations, as well as almost every city in the United States, rose around a river is no accident. Not all flood victims die in the initial floodwaters. Disease and famine that follow often kill more than the floodwaters themselves. In the following lists, flooding disasters primarily caused by typhoons or hurricanes have been excluded.[45]

The Yellow River (China) has an almost unspeakable record of flood deaths, ranging from 500,000 (1938) to 1.0–3.7 million (1931). The Netherlands has had its share, ranging from 50,000 (1287) to 10,000 (1421).

The deadliest U.S.A. floods, excluding hurricane-caused flooding, are as follows:

▸ Johnstown, PA (1889), 2,200

▸ Mississippi Valley (1937), 1,100

▸ Ohio River (1913), 700

▸ Santa Paula, CA (1928), 450 (dam broke)

▸ Rapid City, SD (1972), 237

▸ Kansas City, MO (1903) 200

▸ Mississippi Valley (1912), 200

▸ Willow Creek, OR (1903) 200

▸ Man, WV (1972), 118 (dam collapsed)

▸ Loveland, CO (1976) 139[46]

While I am writing this chapter (August 30, 2010), I have my eye on Pakistan, which is having its own epic disaster. The *Washington Post* today reports that

> One month after monsoon rains caused flooding in the northern mountains, relief efforts were still in emergency mode. On Sunday the Indus River, surging at 40 times its normal volume, breached levees. . . . Evidence is growing that the river's path of destruction has stunted, if not annihilated, social and economic systems across Pakistan. . . .

---

45. Ibid.
46. Ibid.

Unlike the deadly jolt of the 2005 earthquake that previously ranked as Pakistan's gravest natural disaster, the flooding metastasized like a cancer, submerging an area nearly as large as Florida. With much of the south still underwater, assessing the damage remains guesswork. Where the waters have receded, officials banter about figures in the sums of millions and billions of dollars. . . .

The floods killed about 1,600 people. More than 17 [some say, 21] million have been affected, and nearly 5 million of those lack shelter, officials said. At least 800,000 were still stranded in isolated areas this week, the U.N, reported. Many may never be able to return home, relief officials said.[47]

What can I say? No wonder millions around the world today are living in fear, as predicted by our Lord: "Men's hearts failing them from fear and the expectation of those things which are coming on the earth" (Luke 21:26).

Pestilence (Disease)

An epidemic occurs when a disease spreads beyond a local population. A pandemic happens when the epidemic reaches worldwide proportions. However, to know exactly how many died in most of the world's epidemics or pandemics is impossible.

The Great Influenza (1918–1919) has been called the "deadliest plague in history."[48] Fifty to one hundred million people were killed in a six-month period. These numbers are staggering, when we consider that the world's population at that time was just 1.9 billion! A similar outbreak today would kill 350 million people in six months![49]

The AIDS epidemic, when comparing deaths caused by influenza, malaria, and other diseases, is still among the worst plagues of all time. Since 1981, it has claimed twenty-five million people. Worst of all, these deaths were entirely preventable. AIDS is not transmitted through the air, food, or water but through human behaviors.[50]

New strains of food poisoning continue to keep the U.S. Centers for Disease Control and Prevention very busy. Several trends have converged to create a perfect storm of danger in the food supply. For one example among many, think *Escherichia coli* O157:H7, the product of the evolution of a common food pathogen into an ultra-dangerous strain. Common *E. coli* lives in the gut of most mammals. Almost all forms are

47. *Washington Post*, August 20, 2010.
48. "Epic Disasters," in http://www.epicdisasters.com/tenworstepidemics.php.
49. Ibid.
50. Ibid.

harmless; some are actually necessary for health. It wasn't until the 1970s that a deadly version, *E. coli* O157:H7, emerged that causes kidney damage and death.

The O157:H7 strain can cause bloody diarrhea and dehydration. The very young, seniors, and people with weak immune systems are the most vulnerable. In children, *E. coli* O157:H7 may lead to a severe, sometimes fatal kidney disease called HUS (hemolytic-uremic syndrome).[51]

Another global bacteria that has become exponentially dangerous is the multi-drug resistant XDR tuberculosis strain. "Our own body defenses will have to defend us," wrote Drs. Handysides and Landless in 2007.

> The HIV population is at immense risk. . . . The inability to control this form of tuberculosis with medication, coupled with millions unable to fight it, means that the potential for its becoming even more of a problem is immense.[52]

"A Safer Future," a 2007 World Health Organization (WHO) report, warned of high risk of global epidemic from new diseases that are emerging at a "historically unprecedented" rate. Since the 1970s, the WHO has identified thirty-nine new diseases, including Ebola, SARS, bird flu, Nipah virus, and Marburg hemorrhagic fever.[53]

Chronically Hungry People

In June 2009, for the first time, the number of chronically hungry people worldwide is greater than 1 billion! This was an increase of 11 percent in one year![54] Jacques Diouf, director-general of the U.N. Food and Agriculture Organization (FAO) said, "Worsening hunger in the last three years largely stems from economic shocks," and "neither drought, nor floods or disastrous harvests can be held to blame this time." Further, the world's food system is "fragile and vulnerable," and the "situation goes beyond traditional humanitarian dimensions. It calls for a new world food order."[55]

Volcanoes

Following is a list[56] of the world's worst volcanic eruptions, as measured by death toll:

1. Mount Tambora, Indonesia, April 10–15, 1816: 92,000. The

51. *USA Today,* October 31, 2006.

52. *Adventist World-NAD,* October 2007.

53. http://www.washingtonpost.com/wp-dyn/content/article/2007/10/16/AR2007101601392.

54. www.fao.org/news/story/0/item/20568/icode/en/.

55. Ibid.

56. http://www.epicdisasters.com.

concussion from the explosion was felt as far as a thousand miles away. Mount Tambora, more than 13,000 feet tall before the explosion, was reduced to 9,000 feet, after ejecting more than 93 cubic miles of debris into the atmosphere. The effects of the eruption were felt worldwide: 1816 became known as the "year without a summer" because of the volcanic ash in the atmosphere that lowered worldwide temperatures.

2. **Mount Pelee,** West Indies, April 25–May 8, 1902: 40,000. The primary eruption, on May 8, completely destroyed the city of Saint Pierre, killing 25,000. The only survivors were a man held in a prison cell and a man who lived on the outskirts of the town. Several ships also were destroyed, with all hands lost.

3. **Mount Krakatoa,** Indonesia August 26–28, 1883: 36,000. The sound of the explosion was the loudest ever documented and was heard as far away as Australia. Interestingly, it's probable that no one died in the initial explosion. The casualties all came from the resulting tsunami.

4. **Nevado del Ruiz,** Columbia, November 13, 1985: 23,000. A small eruption of the Nevado del Ruiz volcano melted part of the volcano's ice cap, creating an enormous mudslide that buried the city of Armero, killing 23,000.

5. **Mount Unzen,** Japan, 1792: 12,000–15,000. The eruption of Mount Unzen was followed by an earthquake, which collapsed the east flank of the dome. The resulting avalanche created a tsunami which killed 12,000 to 15,000 in nearby towns.

6. **Mount Vesuvius,** Italy, April 24, A.D. 79: 10,000+. Probably one of the most famous eruptions of all time, it completely destroyed Pompeii and Herculaneum. The eruption, which is said to have lasted nineteen hours, buried Pompeii under ten feet of volcanic ash.

7. **The Laki Volcanic System,** Iceland, June 8, 1783–February 1784: 9,350. Nearly a year of constant eruptions created a dusty volcanic haze that created massive food shortages, resulting in the deaths.

8. **Mount Vesuvius,** Italy, December 1631: 6,000. Mount Vesuvius has erupted more than a dozen times since it destroyed the towns of Pompeii and Herculaneum.

9. **Mount Kelut,** Indonesia, May 19, 1919: 5,110. Most of the casualties, apparently, were the result of mudslides.

10. **Mount Galunggung,** Java, Indonesia, 1882: 4,011.

One of the two worst volcanic eruptions in the United States of America was **Mount St. Helens,** Washington State, May 18, 1980, resulting in fifty-seven deaths. The eruption created a debris avalanche about 0.7 cubic miles in volume, destroyed more than two hundred homes, and lowered the mountain from 9,677 feet to 8,363 feet.

Then there was **Novarupta, Alaska,** 1911, zero fatalities (prior to Alaskan statehood). This was the largest volcanic explosion of the twentieth century—ten times more powerful than the eruption of Mount St. Helens. It ejected 9.2 square miles of debris.

Hurricanes/Cyclones

Most of the deadliest hurricanes[57] have occurred in southeastern Asia and India, where flooding from tropical cyclones or hurricanes have wreaked havoc in low-lying, highly populated areas.

The deadliest hurricane on record (November 12, 1970) struck East Pakistan (Bangladesh), flooding the low-lying areas. At least five hundred thousand deaths were blamed on the storm, with some estimates rising as high as one million.

The next worst hurricanes worldwide are as follows:

▶ Bengal, India, 1737 (300,000)

▶ Haiphong, Vietnam, 1881 (300,000)

▶ Bengal, India, 1876 (200,000)

▶ Bombay, India, 1882 (At least 100,000)

▶ Burma (Myanmar), 2008 (100,000+ and still being counted).

Our perceptions are increasingly based, not on the dreadfulness of nature's fury, but on the mounting human catastrophe. In January 2005, Andrew C. Revkin wrote in *The New York Times,* during the aftermath of the tsunami that scoured shores in the Far East, resulting in over two hundred and thirty thousand deaths:

> But unimaginable as it may seem, future catastrophes may be far grimmer. Many more such disasters—from earthquakes and volcanic eruptions, to floods mudslides and droughts—are likely to devastate countries already hard hit by poverty and political turmoil. The world has already seen a sharp increase in such "natural disasters"—from about 100 per year in the early 1960s to as many as 500 per year by the early 2000s, said Daniel Sarewitz, a professor of science and society at Arizona State University.

> But it is not that earthquakes and tsunamis and other such calamities have become stronger or more frequent. What has changed is where people live and how they live there, say many experts who study the physics of such events or the human response to their aftermath.[58]

In other words, the casualty lists and the formidable, increasing financial

---

57. http://www.epicdisasters.com.

58. Andrew C. Revkin, *The New York Times,* January 2, 2005.

costs really get our attention. *Thus, for all practical purposes, natural disasters surely seem more frequent and more intense—and that is what snares the attention of the modern mind.*

Weird Weather

Most of us can recall the Flood of 1993—the twentieth century's worst and the most devastating in modern U.S. history. Primarily along the Mississippi and Missouri Rivers and their feeder rivers and streams, at least forty-eight people were killed, causing between $15 billion and $20 billion in damage. More than 15 percent of the contiguous United States, including twenty million acres and at least seventy-five towns, were inundated, and fifty thousand homes destroyed.[59]

In August 2010, the San Julián Fish Farm in the Santa Cruz Department [state] of Bolivia lost fifteen tons of fish in the extreme cold that overtook the Southern hemisphere that year. Scientists say that this extreme cold is the biggest ecological disaster Bolivia has ever known. Blame is assigned to a mass of Antarctic air that settled over southern South America for most of July. The prolonged cold was linked to the death of about five hundred and fifty penguins along the coast of Brazil and thousands of cattle in Paraguay and Brazil, as well as hundreds of people.[60]

What has been the response? Reasons given show that the old rubber band of Climate Change stretches out to fit most any circumstance. No longer called Global Warming, the rubber band covers everything unusual. Anyone who studies the statistics and graphs, however, realizes that the temperatures on this planet have been much hotter and much colder as centuries have moved on.

As I write, floods in China and Pakistan and droughts in Russia remind me that natural disasters have always existed—but the perceptions of people bombarded with hour-by-hour TV coverage call out, "It's never been this bad before!" We have to remember that Jesus said, "All this is the *beginning* of sorrow"! Greater events are happening that are not getting our attention as much as the latest natural disaster.

I highlight all this to emphasize that severe weather—plus all kinds of weather disasters—fits exactly with what Jesus said would occur, but He also noted that these are but the beginning of birth pangs. We live on a tired planet, and evil has done its best to control weather patterns to bring frustration and death to millions. Satan will do anything to keep our minds off the real events that are even now converging in these last of the last days.

---

59. http://geography.about.com/library/misc/blcenturyworst.htm.
60. http://www.nature.com/news/2010/100827/full/news.2010.437.html.

Water Crisis

Most everyone knows that a catastrophic water shortage could prove an even greater threat to mankind than soaring food prices or the exhaustion of energy reserves. Lord Stern, the World Bank's former chief economist, said governments have been slow to accept the awful truth that usable water is running out—chiefly because fresh rainfall is not enough to fill the underground water tables. "Water is not a renewable resource."[61]

That is, it is not renewable in the sense we can "make" more of it. The supply is pretty much constant and finite; the increasing demand is the big variable.

A Goldman Sachs report said, "Demand for water continues to escalate at unsustainable rates. At the risk of being called alarmist, we see parallels with Malthusian economics. Globally, water consumption is doubling every twenty years. By 2025, it is estimated that about one third of the global population will not have access to adequate drinking water."[62]

Weather Modification

What I find most interesting is the unparalleled sense of urgency to find some way that hurricanes could be tricked into dispersing, that earthquakes could be disarmed (by nuclear explosions?), and floodwaters held back (by, say, mountains of dirt?), and so on.

After World War II, nothing seemed beyond reach for science—after all, the atom had been split, and men had landed on the moon. China, for example, sent rockets, anti-aircraft guns, and aircraft to pelt the sky with chemicals. Result: lots of experience, but very little rain. The idea of hauling icebergs to hurricane-prone waters to cool off the southern Atlantic Ocean didn't work. All kinds of possibilities were considered doable. In 2005, the Air Force said that it simply did not want to meddle with Mother Nature.

Doomsday Predictions

It is hard to go through the news each day and not find someone talking about "apocalypse now"! For instance, Kari Huus, an MSNBC reporter, wrote in 2005 (what would she say today?) that for "many who await Judgment Day, the writing is on the wall." She refers to the "Rapture Index" that many Protestants use as they look forward to the day when Jesus will secretly "rapture" His saints from earth, leaving the world in the hands of Antichrist to endure the severe awfulness of seven years of great world distress. Then comes Armageddon, when God comes back to

---

61. http://www.tradeobservatory.org/headlines (June 10, 2008).
62. Ibid.

defeat Satan, followed by Judgment Day.[63]

I remember May 2000, when the moon, sun, and five planets were in close alignment. Doomsday howlers predicted devastating tidal waves and earthquakes, but the only disaster was caused by the ILOVEYOU computer virus! Really now! Doomsday proclaimers have a way of not living up to the expectations they raise!

Scores of Web sites interpret current events through the prism of biblical passages. For instance, Abbaswatchman.com explains how hurricanes, tsunamis, Israel-Arab tensions, and so on, are fulfilling prophecies and that we are in the final moments of world history. One of the chief purveyors of the imminence of the Rapture has been the Left Behind books and films, on which Tim LaHaye and Jerry B. Jenkins have made a fortune.

The reporter quotes Stephen O'Leary, an expert on apocalyptic thinking and an associate professor at the University of Southern California, who says:

> It's a very traditional way of coming to terms with disaster. In one sense it's as old as the hills . . . but there is a recent uptick of this kind of thinking. . . . You don't have to be a religious believer to think that we're headed for disaster.[64]

In the last ten years we have seen and heard certain terms that can be very confusing, such as, "settled science"—often a term that betrays the scientific method in favor of politics or money or both; or "denier," hurled at anyone who looks for truth amidst an ocean of "settled science."

Once thought to be the discovery to help end food shortages worldwide, Bayer now admits, of GMO (genetically modified organisms), that these are out of control![65] The cry from environmentalists is that all outdoor field trials or commercial growing of GEO (genetically engineered organism) crops must be stopped before our agriculture is irreversibly contaminated. Greenpeace welcomed a federal jury award of $2 million to two Missouri farmers after their rice crop was contaminated with an experimental variety of rice that Bayer CropScience was testing in 2006. But the same issues have continued, with elevation of damages. Some successes have been achieved in regulating GMO/GEO, but much remains that concerns environmentalists. The challenge for science is to improve the safety of GMO/GEO practices, since so much of the world would benefit from more productive crops.

63. Kari Huus, http://www.msnbc.com, updated 10/19/2005 9:02:07 P.M., ET.

64. Ibid.

65. Bayer's Defense lawyer, as reported in *Bloomberg News*, November 4, 2009.

We are surrounded with many bright people who believe that our Lord's prophecies of Matthew 24 and those of other biblical writers are fast fulfilling. Our job is to make sure that we are reading those prophecies correctly. Our responsibility is to make sure that we see all these noteworthy "signs" through the lens of the Big Picture that we call the "Great Controversy Theme." Otherwise, we may find ourselves among the foolish who see in each "sign" the signal of our Lord's imminent[66] return—or we join those who reject the whole idea of useful "signs" and thus turn our backs on the Big Picture that has a direct relationship to each of our lives.

Disaster Fatigue

Although not surprising, it has nonetheless been stunning to note the typical fantastic outpouring of charitable giving, at least in the United States. But when the numbers are too big to fathom, when disasters pile up like snowflakes in a whopper snowstorm, charities are now seeing what they call "donor fatigue." Ironically, the more bad news there is, the less likely people will maintain their giving.

The differences in giving for the 2005 Asian tsunami and the Hurricane Katrina devastation, when compared to the more recent Pakistan disaster that killed over eighty thousand people, generates a pitiful contrast. Too much, too often. Sad but understandable. These truly are unprecedented times.

Here I am trying to close out this book, and I read a recap of 2010 in language that I hesitate to use! "This was the year the Earth struck back" wrote the Associated Press, noting that natural disasters claimed more lives in 2010 than terrorism has in the last forty years combined.[67]

"2010's world gone wild!" was the lead into an article that said: "The term '100-year event' really lost its meaning this year. . . . While the Haitian earthquake, Russian heat wave, and Pakistani flooding were the biggest killers, deadly quakes also struck Chile, Turkey, China, and Indonesia in one of the most active years in decades. . . . After strong early year blizzards, nicknamed Snowmageddon, paralyzed the U.S. mid-Atlantic and record snowfalls hit Russia and China, the temperature turned to broil. . . . The year may go down as the hottest on record worldwide. . . . Northern Australia had the wettest May-October on record, while the southwestern part of that country had its driest spell on record. And parts of the Amazon River basin struck

---

66. *Imminence* means "at any time." *Nearness* means not necessarily imminent but soon.

67. http://www.cbsnews.com (December 20, 2010).

by drought hit their lowest water levels in recorded history."[68]

A volcano in Iceland paralyzed air traffic for days in Europe, disrupting travel for more than 7 million people. . . . A nearly 2-pound hailstone 8 inches in diameter fell in South Dakota in July to set a U.S. record. The storm that produced it was one of seven declared disasters for that state this year! In the United States, FEMA declared a record number of major disasters, 79 as of Dec. 23—the average year has 34.[69]

Before I close out a look back over the year 2010, I shake my head at what's happening to my beloved British Isles, where more than a week's worth of stranded passengers in its airports are still waiting for the planes to be free to come in and go out. Besides the deep snow, weather forecasters see no letup for at least another month of subzero temperatures—the coldest since records began in 1910.[70]

Whew!

---

68. http://apnews.nyway.com/article/20101219/D9K734E81.html.
69. Ibid.
70. *The Daily Mail Recorder*, December 17, 2010.

CHAPTER THREE

THEME:

Jesus will return not after the world gets better and better but after it comes close to destroying itself.

The World's Bloodiest Century

The Doomsday Clock is a symbolic clock face maintained since 1947 by the board of directors of the *Bulletin of the Atomic Scientists* at the University of Chicago. The closer the clock is to midnight, the closer the world is estimated to be to global disaster. As of July 2010, the Doomsday Clock read 11:54 P.M. Since its creation, the time on the clock has changed nineteen times.[71]

Originally, the analogy represented the threat of global nuclear war, but since 2007 it has also reflected the potential impact of new developments in climate-changing technologies, the life sciences, and nanotechnology that could inflict irrevocable harm.

Suitcase Nukes

Of course, all it would take to move those hands yet again would be a nuclear catastrophe perpetrated by a terrorist in or from any country. Who knows who has these suitcase bombs?

In his fascinating book *Al Qaeda: Brotherhood of Terror,* Paul L. Williams—an FBI consultant on international terrorism—describes, among

---

71. Indianapolis, IN: Alpha Books—Penguin, 2002.

many scary events, how al Qaeda bought at least three "suitcase nukes" in the late 1990s.[72] One of the purchases was from KGB agents in 1998, for $30 million.

Williams writes that by 1990 Osama bin Laden had hired hundreds of atomic scientists from the former Soviet Union for $2,000 a month who worked in a highly sophisticated and well-fortified laboratory in Kandahar, Afghanistan.

Suitcase nukes are not really suitcases at all, but suitcase-size nuclear devices. The weapons can be fired from grenade or rocket launchers or detonated by timers. A bomb placed in the center of a metropolitan area would be capable of instantly killing hundreds of thousands and exposing millions of others to lethal radiation.[73]

In addition, al Qaeda has chemical weapons from North Korea and Iraq (Hussein era), such as anthrax spores, sarin, botulism biotoxin, and Ebola.[74]

EMP Nuclear Bomb

Senator John Kyl (R-AZ) wrote in the *Washington Post* in April 2005:

An electromagnetic pulse (EMP) attack on the American homeland, said one of the distinguished scientists who testified at the hearing, is one of only a few ways that the United States could be defeated by its enemies—terrorist or otherwise. And it is probably the easiest. A single Scud missile, carrying a single nuclear weapon, detonated at the appropriate altitude, would interact with the Earth's atmosphere, producing an electromagnetic pulse radiating down to the surface at the speed of light. Depending on the location and size of the blast, the effect would be to knock out already stressed power grids and other electrical systems across much or even all of the continental United States, for months if not years.

Few if any people would die right away. But the loss of power would have a cascading effect on all aspects of U.S. society. Communication would be largely impossible. Lack of refrigeration would leave food rotting in warehouses, exacerbated by a lack of transportation as those vehicles still working simply ran out of gas (which is pumped with electricity). The inability to sanitize and distribute water would quickly threaten public health, not to mention the safety of anyone in the path of the inevitable fires, which would rage unchecked. And as we have seen in areas of natural and other

72. http://www.wnd.com/?pageId=23172.

73. Ibid. See also *U.S. News & World Report,* April 17, 1995.

74. Joseph Farah, http://www.WorldNetDaily.com, April 4, 2005.

disasters, such circumstances often result in a fairly rapid breakdown of social order. . . .

This threat may sound straight out of Hollywood, but it is very real. CIA Director Porter Goss recently testified before Congress about nuclear material missing from storage sites in Russia that may have found its way into terrorist hands, and FBI Director Robert Mueller has confirmed new intelligence that suggests al Qaeda is trying to acquire and use weapons of mass destruction. Iran has surprised intelligence analysts by describing the mid-flight detonations of missiles fired from ships on the Caspian Sea as "successful" tests. North Korea exports missile technology around the world; Scuds can easily be purchased on the open market for about $100,000 apiece.

A terrorist organization might have trouble putting a nuclear warhead "on target" with a Scud, but it would be much easier to simply launch and detonate in the atmosphere. No need for the risk and difficulty of trying to smuggle a nuclear weapon over the border or hit a particular city. Just launch a cheap missile from a freighter in international waters—al Qaeda is believed to own about 80 such vessels—and make sure to get it a few miles in the air.

The Sept. 11 commission report stated that our biggest failure was one of "imagination." No one imagined that terrorists would do what they did on Sept. 11. Today few Americans can conceive of the possibility that terrorists could bring our society to its knees by destroying everything we rely on that runs on electricity. But this time we've been warned, and we'd better be prepared to respond.[75]

In a speech delivered to Hillsdale College National Leadership Seminar on the topic, "America's War Against Islamic Terrorism," on January 24, 2005, Frank J. Gaffner, Jr. described how the EMP would detonate. Three components would each have specific assignments, with the total effect of impairing or destroying all communication throughout the United States. Any rogue nation or group would be virtually impossible to deter, at least at this moment.[76]

The Commission to Assess the Threat reported that our country has "very little redundancy . . . built into America's critical infrastructure. There is, for example, no parallel 'national security power grid' built to provide greater resiliency than the civilian grid. America's critical infrastructure has scarcely any capacity to spare in the event of disruption—

75. Senator John Kyl (R-AZ), *Washington Post,* April 2005.

76. *Imprimis,* vol. 34, no. 6.

even in one part of the country (recall the electrical blackout that crippled the northeastern U.S. for just a few days in 2003), let alone nationwide."[77]

Review of a Century of Incredibly Awful Wars

I was prepared to review all the earthly hell that this planet has gone through in the last century. The statistics were staggering. But I ended up with this shorter review, comparing, at times, with other war periods just for contrast. The numbers below include civilians and soldiers.

World War II (1939–1945) topped them all. Some of us lived through those years. Others of our families and friends did not. Can anyone really imagine what sixty-two million deaths mean? Or fifteen million in World War I (some say sixty-six million when the victims of Spanish Flu are added in)?

But we also should not forget these wars:

▸ The Russian Civil War (1919–1921) with its 5,000,000–9,000,000

▸ The Korean War (1950–1953) with its 2,500,000–3,500,000

▸ The Vietnam War (1949–1975, with its 2,300,000–3,100,000

▸ The Iraq-Iran War (1980–1988) with its 1,000,000

And on it goes—many millions more! Think of the scores of civil wars that killed their many millions! Even the Falklands War (1982) with its one thousand deaths.

Just going over the individual battles would galvanize our senses, such as these:

▸ Battle of Stalingrad (1942–1943), 1,800,000

▸ Siege of Leningrad (1941–1944), 1,500,000

▸ Battle of Okinawa (1945), 150,000

▸ Battle of the Bulge (1944–1945), 38,000

▸ Battle of Iwo Jima (1945), 29,000[78]

And again, the list goes on ...

In many places in this crazy world, young people have been born, grown up, and never have known a day without some kind of bloodshed, actual or threatened.

I know some could say that we have always had wars. *But never a century like the most recent!* At no other time has war reached epidemic proportions. Seems as if John the Revelator wrote an amazing portrayal of our day: "The nations were angry. . . . The time has come for destroying those who destroy the earth" (11:18).

---

77. Ibid.

78. *Wikipedia,* list of wars and disasters by death toll.

Interesting, too, is that we cannot really turn our back on the Cold War. Near our home in Lincoln, California, less than two miles away, a Titan I missile in 1962 was action-ready in its 160-foot-deep silo, with its 32,000 cubic yards of concrete, 90 miles of cables, 300 tons of piping, and 1,800 separate supply items. One of three Titan I sites surrounding Beale Air Force Base, it was prepared for the worst. Of course, an enemy would know where to find these sites, and if targeted, Lincoln, California, would be no more!

But the bases were deactivated in 1965. However, their memory lives on in a new battle—this time between the Lincoln Public Works Department and the Army Corps of Engineers. Why? Toxic contaminants in the groundwater! The argument is over which government agency is responsible.

Tailor-Made Martyrs

The world probably has never seen anything like it! The roster of nearly 250 names ranges from a thirteen-year-old Syrian boy who died fighting the Americans in Fallujah, Iraq, to the reigning kung fu champion of Jordan, who sneaked off to wage war by telling his family he was going to a tournament.

Some clamored to follow the terrorist "heroes" of September 11, 2001, finding in Iraq an "easy" way to join them. Al Qaeda Web sites "hail death in Iraq as the inspiration for a new generation of terrorists in much the same way that Afghanistan attracted Muslims eager to fight against the Soviet Union in the 1980s."[79]

Unintended consequences!

We all could write a book on "unintended consequences." The ubiquitous syringe, for example. Or DVDs.

Think too about computers, Web sites, Blackberries, iPhones—all providing instant communication! And especially consider how terrorists use the Web world as the base of their operations. Those who know al Qaeda say that every other al Qaeda member carries a laptop computer, along with a Kalashnikov.[80]

Al Qaeda suicide bombers and ambush units depend on the Web for training and tactical support. Why? The Internet offers anonymity and flexibility, with near impunity. Terrorist activity is a "Web-directed" phenomenon, as long-time State Department expert Dennis Pluchinsky puts it.[81]

They not only have a massive online library of training materials but also online experts to answer questions on message boards. Anyone, anywhere, can learn how to obtain ricin poison, create a bomb from com-

79. Susan B. Glasser, *Washington Post,* May 15, 2005.
80. Steve Coll and Susan B. Glasser, *Washington Post,* August 7, 2005.
81. Ibid.

mercial chemicals, learn how to sneak through Syria into Iraq, or how to shoot a U.S. soldier. These messages are spread around the World Wide Web in "Arabic, Urdu, Pashto and other first languages of jihadist volunteers."[82]

Earlier, terrorists had to go to Yemen or Sudan or Afghanistan to train, but no more. They now find it safer to have all the information needed anywhere, as long as they have a computer, privacy, and anonymity. No longer must these terrorists carry blueprints, plans, and pictures in their suitcases, as long as they have their computer.

In other words, terrorists have, in the Internet, "an open university for jihad," says Reuven Paz, head of the Project for the Research of Islamist Movements in Israel. "The main audience are the younger generation in the Arab world . . . one big *madassa* on the Internet."[83]

Role of Religion in Civil Unrest and War

I remember well the hideous pictures and awful stories of the "killing fields of Rwanda" in 1994. Here we are, fifteen years later, and the elements of terror still exist, though muted.

Rwanda is a symbol of the undercurrents of distrust and hate that continue to flow between generations in places such as the following:

- Afghanistan (extreme Talibans vs. everyone else)
- Bosnia (Serbian Orthodox, Roman Catholics, Muslims)
- Côte d' Ivoire (Muslims, Christian, indigenous)
- Cyprus (Christians, Muslims)
- East Timor (Christians, Muslims)
- India (animists, Hindus, Muslims, Sikhs, Christians)
- Indonesia (Christians, Muslims)
- Kashmir (Hindus, Muslims)
- Kosovo (Orthodox Catholics, Muslims)
- Kurdistan (Christians, Muslims)
- Macedonia (Orthodox Catholics, Muslims)
- Middle East (Jews, Muslims, Christians)
- Nigeria (Christians, Animists, Muslims)
- Northern Ireland (Protestants, Catholics)
- Pakistan (Sunni, Shi'ite Muslims)

---

82. Ibid.
83. Ibid.

▶ Philippines (Christians, Muslims)

▶ Russia Chechnya (Russian Orthodox, Muslims)

▶ South Africa (Animists, Witches, Christians)

▶ Sri Lanka (Buddhists, Hindus)

▶ Sudan (animists, Christians, Muslims)

▶ Tibet (Buddhists, Communists)

▶ Uganda (Animists, Christians, Muslims)

Nancy Gibbs reported in *Time*, May 16, 1994, that a missionary told her "there are no devils left in hell. They are all in Rwanda." She watched the swollen rivers, not from rain only, but from the burden of bodies or pieces of them—men and boys cut down while protecting their women, women cut down in their hiding places, and babies with no marks on them, thrown into the rivers to drown.

Aid workers estimated that anywhere from one hundred thousand to three hundred thousand Rwandans died in the civil war between the Hutu and the Tutsi *in the previous month.* But Rwanda is only one tragedy among others in Africa and elsewhere that defines barbarism in the late twentieth and early twenty-first centuries—defying the rest of the world to try to do something about the horror.

What was more than interesting is the fact that the obvious tribal hatred clouded another "get even" opportunity—*moderate* members of the Hutu government who had been working on relieving the tensions with the Tutsi were the first to die from the hands of the "hard-liners" in the first few hours! Politics and genocide made for a frightful several weeks!

The roads and paths into surrounding countries (Uganda, Zaire, Burundi, Tanzania) were crowded by almost two million Rwandans (that is, those still alive) out of a population of about 8.1 million

But what got my real and lasting attention was one significant paragraph:

If the Rwanda catastrophe was more than a simple tribal meltdown, it also showed signs of being the kind of conflict that scholars warn will haunt the world for decades to come. These wars are not started by statesmen or fought by armies or ended by treaties. The tribal skirmishes recall the wars of the Middle Ages, when religion and politics and economics and social conflicts all messily intertwined.[84]

Religious and racial struggles are ancient and visceral. The hate virus lurks in most every mind and heart not being transformed by the Holy

---

84. "Why? The Killing Fields of Rwanda," *Time*, May 16, 1994.

Spirit. Quickly, human interactions turn into oppressed versus oppressor. International wars often start with struggles within countries—examples abound.

When Kalashnikov machine guns are as available as chewing gum, when young men and women are trained to hate, when economic insecurity seems to extend forever, when religion and race are powder kegs to be used whenever other alternatives fail—any nation, anywhere, better watch out!

Iran's Apocalyptic Prophet

Whatever happens anywhere these days happens everywhere else, because everything is connected to everything else.

Think of the dire pronouncements of the current president of Iran, Mahmoud Ahmadinejad, beginning with his first speech to the United Nations in 2005. This is the man who has said on numerous occasions that the State of Israel should be wiped off the map of the world. During that 2005 speech, he claims to have been in an aura of light and felt a change in the atmosphere, during which time no one present could blink their eyes.

In that speech, which was his international debut, the Iranian president was expected to offer conciliatory proposals to defuse the nuclear crisis that his country had restarted. But the assembly was astonished with his apocalyptic language of a struggling Iran amidst the evil Western powers that were promoting "terror" and imposing the "logic of the dark ages."

But it got worse. He ended his speech with the messianic appeal to God "to hasten the emergence of your last repository, the Promised One, that perfect and pure human being, the other one that will fill this world with justice and peace."[85]

What did this all mean? Ahmadinejad is devoted to the "Hidden Imam." The 12th Imam, supposedly a direct descendant of the Prophet Mohammed, is seen as having divine stature, as are each of the succession of sons.[86]

The 12th Imam will supernaturally appear just before the Day of Judgment. He will rule over the Arabs and the world for seven years. He will eradicate all tyranny and oppression, bringing harmony and total peace. At that time, the Imam will have prayer in Mecca, with Jesus at his side. *But, his return will be preceded by cosmic chaos, war, and bloodshed.*

---

85. " 'Divine Mission' Driving Iran's New Leader," *The Telegraph,* January 24, 2006.

86. "12th Imam—Anointed Ruler?" http://www.allaboutpopularissues .org/12th-imam.htm.

After this cataclysmic confrontation with evil and darkness, the 12th Imam will lead the world into universal peace.[87]

Further, Ahmadinejad believes that the influence of these events will be to hasten the return of the 12th Imam. When this man has his hands on nuclear weapons with hated enemies in sight, many in the world have reason to worry. Imagine provoking chaos to hasten the time when the world will finally be at peace!

Hang on—much more remains to think about!

---

87. *The Telegraph*, op. cit.; emphasis added.

CHAPTER FOUR

THEME:

Jesus will return after this world has had its worst economic collapse, ever!

When the World Is Broke!

I have been trying to start this chapter for many days, but I keep getting put off—the incoming news of financial stress and gloom does not stop! Makes me wonder if I will ever finish this book! The galloping future arriving in the present seems to overtake me!

I keep my news Web sites on day and night. I lived through last century's very worst depression from 1929–1940 (saved by World War II) and several recessions since. I have seen the stock market go through the roof several times (with equally astonishing sell-offs).

I have never, however—and neither has anyone else—seen such a colossal hemorrhage of debt and deficit as is now smothering not only the United States but all other sovereign nations. More financial red bleeding has taken place in the last twenty months *than in all the preceding years (in the United States) from George Washington to President Reagan!* [88]

Five years ago, I wrote about this problem in an earlier book,[89] just a few months prior to the housing bubble crash (and all its spreading,

---

88. "In the first 19 months of the Obama administration, the federal debt held by the public increased by $2.5260 trillion, which is more than the cumulative total of the national debt held by the public that was amassed by all U.S. presidents from George Washington through Ronald Reagan." CNSNEWS.com, September 1, 2010; emphasis added.

89. *Never Been This Late Before* (Roseville, CA: Amazing Facts, 2006), 29–43.

octopus-tentacled consequences), of which former Federal Reserve Chairman Paul Volker had said:

> Under the placid surface, there are disturbing trends: huge imbalances, disequilibria, risks—call them what you will. Altogether the circumstances seem to me as dangerous and intractable as any I can remember, and I can remember quite a lot.[90]

About the same time, David Walker, comptroller general of the United States, said that the United States can be likened to Rome before the fall of the empire. Its financial condition is "worse than advertised," and it has a "broken business model. It faces deficits in its budget, its balance of payments, its savings—and its leadership."[91]

Of course, we heard other dogs barking in the barnyard. But they seemed so contrary to so-called "reality." On February 18, 2007, Mark Trahant, editor of the *Seattle Post-Intelligencer* editorial page, under the title "Our credit democracy is nearing bankruptcy," wrote:

> These are the best times ever. A new report by the Mortgage Bankers Association brags that we Americans are demonstrating "the greatest and wildest availability of mortgage finance in our nation's history, which in turn has made possible record homeownership rates."
>
> The bankers call it the credit democracy: The wonderful era when nearly everybody could borrow freely with few documents, lighter restrictions and self-proclaimed income.

Then Trahant ended his editorial:

> And these numbers reflect a strong economy, the best times ever. We'd better pray it stays that way. Our credit democracy is at risk of bankruptcy.

How many heard that dog barking in the barnyard?

Not many months later, the value of our homes plummeted, stocks on Wall Street got chopped off at the knees, and cushy retirement nest eggs for so many evaporated.

All this reminds me of Lewis Carroll's *Through the Looking Glass*[92] and his Red Queen's Race:

> The Queen kept crying "Faster!" but Alice felt she could not go faster, though she had no breath to say so. The most curious part of the thing was that the trees and the other things round them

---

90. *Strategic Investment*, May 1, 2005.

91. *USA Today*, November 14, 2005.

92. *Alice's Adventures in Wonderland & Through the Looking Glass* (New York: New American Library, Signet Classic, 2000), 146, 147.

never changed their places at all: however fast they went, they never seemed to pass anything. "I wonder if all the things moved along with us?" thought poor puzzled Alice. And the Queen seemed to guess her thoughts, for she cried, "Faster! Don't try to talk!"

Not that Alice had any idea of doing that. She felt as if she would never be able to talk again, she was getting out of breath: and still the Queen cried, "Faster! Faster!" and dragged her along. "Are we nearly there?" Alice managed to pant out at last.

"Nearly there!" the Queen repeated. "Why, we passed it 10 minutes ago! Faster!" And they ran on for a time in silence, with the wind whistling in Alice's ears, and almost blowing her hair off her head, she fancied.

"Now! Now!" cried the Queen. "Faster! Faster!" And they went so fast they seemed to skim through the air, hardly touching the ground with their feet, till suddenly, just as Alice was getting quite exhausted, they stopped, and she found herself sitting on the ground, breathless and giddy. The Queen propped her against a tree, and said kindly, "You may rest a little now."

Alice looked round her in great surprise. "Why, I do believe we've been under this tree the whole time! Everything's just as it was!"

"Of course it is," said the Queen. "What would you have it?"

"Well, in our county," said Alice, still panting a little, "you'd generally get to somewhere else—if you ran very fast for a long time, as we've been doing."

"A slow sort of country!" said the Queen. "Now, here, you see, it takes all the running you can do, to keep in the same place. If you want to get somewhere else, you must run at least twice as fast as that!"

The moral? Most every man or woman alive feels that they must run faster just to stay even, in balancing their personal budgets! The same for Mr. Bernanke and the Federal Reserve—Bernanke has become America's Red Queen!

Somehow through the past twenty-five years, the United States and most other developed nations have been enjoying the anesthetic of financial fantasy. People have come to believe that they can build heaven on earth, where, thanks to the ever-improving miracles of central banking—with its endless supply of paper money—as well as medical science, higher education, and cosmetic surgery, they can spend all their money and still grow richer and prettier. Wall Street magic will make them wealthier. The health industry's products will make them healthier. However, too many have discovered that their rock-candy mountains indeed melt under the weight of mortgage payments and credit card deficits that remain after the party is over.

To put all this in another way: It takes a *negative* savings rate, *expanding credit* to incredible levels, and *excessive* government spending *just to stand in one spot!* It doesn't take an MBA from Stanford to figure out that the Red Queen had it just right: " 'Here, you see, it takes all the running you can do, to keep in the same place. If you want to get somewhere else, you must run at least twice as fast as that!' " And that is exactly what most families in the United States are doing—going farther and faster into debt just to stand still in the same place.

Alice Was Learning

But Alice learned something more that we all will learn, sooner or later. She was on her way to the Garden of Live Flowers:

"I should see the garden far better," said Alice to herself, "if I could get to the top of that hill: and here's a path that leads straight to it—at least, no, it doesn't do *that* . . . (after going a few yards along the path, and turning several sharp corners), . . . but I suppose it will at last. But how curiously it twists! It's more like a corkscrew than a path! Well, *this* turn goes to the hill, I suppose—no, it doesn't! This goes straight back to the house! Well, then, I'll try it the other way."

And so she did: wandering up and down, and trying turn after turn, but always coming back to the house, do what she would. Indeed, once, when she turned a corner rather more quickly than usual, she ran against it before she could stop herself.[93]

Lesson No. 1: In Alice's world, as in our world, forward movements ultimately and most often take people back to their starting point; and rapid movements, whether in Wonderland or in the twenty-first century, can cause very abrupt stops.

Lesson No. 2: Alice found a way out, but financial and political leaders today are trapped with unintended consequences. Most countries are in the same fix as the United States: We can choose between hyperinflation (continue the same policies that got us where we are today) and deflation (slow down the economy with higher interest rates plus reduction in government spending).

The problem before the Federal Reserve Bank is the same as Alice's—if we cannot run fast enough, our economy will implode (deflate). But if

---

93. Ibid., 139.

we run too fast, the value of the dollar (in precarious shape now) will be sharply devalued. Foreign governments may yank their billions out of the U.S. treasury; federal and state governments will have no choice but to rapidly increase taxes and swiftly reduce Medicare, grants, and other governmental assistance programs. Life as we have known it for half a century will come to a halt, abruptly!

Well, neither Paul Volcker nor David Walker were chairmen of the House or Senate committees that promoted the Alice in Wonderland "credit democracy"! We all are learning through tough experience what the mirage of "credit democracy" can do in just a few years!

The Big Picture

I think that you who have read this far are beginning to realize that each chapter in this small volume focuses on one of the remarkable forces converging on a not-too-distant future. None of these chapters is disconnected from the others. Each chapter's stream of developing events only adds to the global dimension of that final focus when all the world will be totally involved—and where no one may hide.

As we are seeing in this chapter, one of those fast-moving currents is the astonishing, startling global meltdown of once-solid national economies.

Have we been asleep? What has happened that suddenly shocked every developed country the world over, as if all this were only a bad dream?

Not a bad dream for the average American family. Census bureau data highlights that the typical household's income was trimmed significantly in the last decade, the worst for American families in "at least half a century."[94] How to cope? Many Americans reverted to the old-fashioned way—by merging households: The number of multifamily households rose 11.6 percent from 2008 to 2010, while the total number of households rose only 0.6 percent.[95]

The number of people living in poverty has climbed to 14.3 percent of Americans, "with the ranks of working-age poor reaching the highest level since at least 1965."[96]

Sovereign nations (Greece, Portugal, Spain, Iceland), teeter on the edge of bankruptcy (meaning they have run out of money to pay their liabilities)! Banks totter, and some fall almost overnight because of crazy lending policies without supporting assets.

For instance:

---

94. "Lost Decade for Family Income," *Wall Street Journal,* September 17, 2010.

95. Ibid.

96. *The Washington Post,* September 16, 2010.

Think about Fannie Mae and Freddie Mac—taxpayer losses from the government seizure of these two financial giants "could reach nearly $400 billion" but could be mitigated by forcing banks that sold bad loans to repay these two giants. Maybe! That is a lot of money!

What went wrong? A number of cascading steps, *all taken with the hope of increasing the number of American families owning their own homes.* Very good for winning votes!

In 1999, Fannie Mae came under pressure from the Clinton Administration to expand mortgage loans to low- and moderate-income borrowers by increasing the ratios of their loan portfolios in distressed inner city areas designated in the CRA (Community Reinvestment Act) report of 1977.[97]

In 2000, because of a reassessment of the housing market by HUD (Department of Housing and Urban Development), anti-predatory lending rules were put into place that disallowed risky, high-cost loans from being credited toward affordable housing goals. In 2004, however, these rules were dropped, and high-risk loans were again counted toward affordable housing goals.[98]

The intent was that Fannie Mae's enforcement of the underwriting standards they maintained for standard conforming mortgages would also provide a safe and stable means of lending to buyers who did not have prime credit. As Daniel Mudd, then president and CEO of Fannie Mae, testified in 2007, that agency's underwriting requirements drove business into the arms of the private mortgage industry, who marketed aggressive products without regard to future consequences:

> We also set conservative underwriting standards for loans we finance to ensure the homebuyers can afford their loans over the long term. We sought to bring the standards we apply to the prime space to the subprime market with our industry partners primarily to expand our services to underserved families.

> Unfortunately, Fannie Mae-quality, safe loans in the subprime market did not become the standard, and the lending market moved away from us. Borrowers were offered a range of loans that layered *teaser rates, interest-only, negative amortization* and payment options and low-documentation requirements on top of floating-rate loans. In early 2005 we began sounding our concerns about this "layered-risk" lending. For example, Tom

97. *Los Angeles Times*, September 16, 2010.
98. Carol D. Leonnig, "How HUD Mortgage Policy Fed the Crisis," *Washington Post*, June 10, 2008.

Lund, the head of our single-family mortgage business, publicly stated, "One of the things we don't feel good about right now as we look into this marketplace is more homebuyers being put into programs that have more risk. Those products are for more sophisticated buyers. Does it make sense for borrowers to take on risk they may not be aware of? Are we setting them up for failure? As a result, we gave up significant market share to our competitors."[99]

Alex Berenson of *The New York Times* reported in 2003 that Fannie Mae's risk is much larger than is commonly held.[100]

On September 10, 2003, the Bush Administration recommended the most significant regulatory overhaul in the housing finance industry since the savings and loan crisis. Under the plan, a new agency would be created within the Treasury Department to assume supervision of Fannie Mae. *The New York Times* reported that the plan was an acknowledgment by the administration that oversight of Fannie Mae and Freddie Mac is broken. *The Times* also reported Democratic opposition to Bush's plan:

> "These two entities—Fannie Mae and Freddie Mac—are not facing any kind of financial crisis," said Representative Barney Frank of Massachusetts, the ranking Democrat on the Financial Services Committee. "The more people exaggerate these problems, the more pressure there is on these companies, the less we will see in terms of affordable housing."[101]

The rest is history. At least we know, or should, how to avoid playing politics with the laws of simple accounting and centuries of lending to secured borrowers. I replay all this to illustrate how easily political forces directly drive the country's finances, meaning the financial well-being of the average citizen. It could just as easily happen again, when any group creates a crisis that is too useful to overlook.

Whenever we try to work our way through the various highs and lows of the financial world, I return constantly to some very wise words written in 1909:

> There are not many, even among educators and statesmen, who comprehend the causes that underlie the present state of society. Those who hold the reins of government are not able to solve the problem of moral corruption, poverty, pauperism, and increasing

99. http://www.fanniemae.com/media/2007. Emphasis added.

100. http://www.nytimes.com/2003/08/07/business/07LEND.html.

101. Stephen Labaton, "New Agency Proposed to Oversee Freddie Mac and Fannie Mae," September 31, 2003.

crime. They are struggling in vain to place business operations on a more secure basis.[102]

Competing economic philosophies permeate countries, here and elsewhere. Politicians, no matter their affiliation, aim at pleasing the most voters with their policies—policies that inevitably face their own built-in judgment day, as we have seen in the last few years.

Great Depression Myths

For instance, some of the elements, in the haunting fog that continues to confuse many, especially Americans, are the myths surrounding the Great Depression in the United States and worldwide (1929–1941). One terror engendered by the Great Crash is that economic contractions could occur at any time without warning. Other myths: that the free market economy was responsible, and that only government intervention brought America's economic recovery! One might as well believe that Little Red Riding Hood would win the New York State Lottery or Alice found her Wonderland!

In a nutshell, however, the awful Great Depression was foreshadowed by the irresponsible monetary and fiscal policies of the U.S. government in the late 1920s and early 1930s. Murray Rothbard, in his *America's Great Depression*, catalogued how the Fed bloated the money supply by more than 60 percent from mid 1921–1929—and how this easily available credit drove interest rates down, pushing the stock market to dizzying heights and giving us the "Roaring Twenties."[103]

All this led to a dramatic contraction of the money supply. Between August 1929 and March 1933, the money supply shrank by one third—seismic incompetence.[104]

Men such as Bernard Baruch and Joseph Kennedy saw the party coming to an abrupt end and bought bonds and gold and became multimillionaires.[105]

To the miscalculation of the Federal Reserve, add the short-sighted Smoot-Hawley Tariff (1930) that closed the borders to foreign goods and

---

102. Ellen White, *Testimonies for the Church*, vol. 9 (Nampa, ID: Pacific Press® Publishing Association, 1909), 13.

103. Murray Rothbard, *America's Great Depression* (Kansas City, MO: Sheed and Ward, Inc., 1975), 89.

104. Milton Friedman and Anna Jacobson Schwartz, *A Monetary History of the United States, 1867–1960* (New York: National Bureau of Economic Research, 1963; ninth paperback printing by Princeton University Press, 1993), 411–415.

105. Lindley H. Clark Jr., "After the Fall," *The Wall Street Journal*, October 26, 1979, 18.

ignited a vicious international trade war—resulting in the hammering of industries such as auto production and the devastation of American agriculture (no importing of vital items and no market for farm products). Further, add the Revenue Act of 1932, wherein tax rates soared—personal, corporate, gasoline, and postal rates sucked whatever money was left out of American hands.

What did the change of administration in 1933 do? Only multiplied the financial recklessness! The Great Depression, to which our present financial crisis is persistently likened, changed the world forever. Out of it came the Keynesian intellectual revolution, an entirely new framework for governing the banking system.

After one year as Roosevelt's Director of the Budget, Lewis W. Douglas resigned, angered by his boss's abandonment of his campaign promises. He saw the rise of a government monster. He made it plain that the United States was facing a momentous choice:

> Will we choose to subject ourselves—this great country—to the despotism of bureaucracy, controlling our every act, destroying what equality we have attained, reducing us eventually to the conditions of impoverished slaves of the state? Or will we cling to the liberties for which man has struggled for more than a thousand years? It is important to understand the magnitude of the issue before us. . . . If we do not elect to have a tyrannical, oppressive bureaucracy controlling our lives, destroying progress, depressing the standard of living . . . then should it not be the function of the Federal government under a democracy to limit its activity to those which a democracy may adequately deal, such for example as national defense, maintaining law and order, protecting life and property, preventing dishonesty, and . . . guarding the public against vested special interest?[106]

In so many ways, seen and unseen, American life was changed forever. For instance, the National Labor Relations Act in 1935 became organized labor's Magna Carta. Hans Seinholz wrote:

> This law revolutionized American labor relations. It took labor disputes out of the courts of law and brought them under a newly created Federal agency, the National Labor Relations Board, which became prosecutor, judge, and jury, all in one. . . . The U.S. thereby abandoned a great achievement of Western civilization, equality under the law. . . . Anything an employer might do in self-defense

---

106. From *The Liberal Tradition: A Free People and a Free Economy*, by Lewis W. Douglas, as quoted in "Monetary Central Planning and the State, Part XIV: The New Deal and Its Critics," by Richard M. Ebeling, in *Freedom Daily*, February 1998, 12.

became an "unfair labor practice" punishable by the Board.[107]

When World War II began, unemployment in the United States was still in excess of 17 percent. And the Treasury was underwater beyond anyone's expectation. Perhaps Roosevelt's own Treasury Secretary, Henry Morgenthau, said it best in his diary:

> We have tried spending money. We are spending more than we have ever spent before and it does not work. . . . We have never made good on our promises. . . . I saw after eight years of this Administration we have just as much unemployment as when we started . . . and an enormous debt to boot.[108]

I have devoted an unusual amount of space in reviewing the history of the United States for the past eighty years, not only because I have lived through these years, but because so much of our recent history is terrifyingly comparable to the 1930s. *The same federal decisions, the same unforeseen results, the same economic distress, but with even greater consequences.*

It seems so hard these days to realize that we can't spend ourselves out of debt. That debt is only a symptom—spending is the disease. Especially when it is somebody else's money!

My only question: Have we gone too far down the road of passing legislation that promises and pleases those voters whose hands and mouths are in the federal trough?

I am reminded of the Egyptians, around 1600 B.C. who created the image of a serpent devouring its own tail. Hundreds of years later, the Greeks gave the serpent a name: "Ouroboros." Some call the image a symbol of nature throughout the universe—creation out of destruction, life out of death—the Ouroboros eats its own tail to sustain its life.

To me, the Ouroboros is a symbol of what has happened in developing countries everywhere—homeowners were feeling "full" with the refinancing of their homes, pulling out equity for a new car, a swimming pool, more vacations, and the latest facial or tummy tuck. But they were eating their own tail to stay financially alive, until reality set in.

But the tail is getting bigger. Some of this new form of gorging on the tail of the United States is the astounding rise of the "cult of the victim." In the last seventy years, young people have been taught that their government should pay the bills of anyone afflicted by hardship. The "cult of the victim" permeates political action and social expectation of western civilization—a remarkable tsunami overtaking traditional values

---

107. Hans F. Stenholm, "The Great Depression," *The Freeman,* April 1975, 212, 213.

108. John Morton Blum, *From the Morgenthau Diaries: Years of Crisis, 1928–1938* (Boston: Houghton Mifflin Company, 1959), 24, 25.

and common sense. So many people have been taught that every manifestation of even perceived misfortune, incompetence, or underachievement might become a financial asset! After decades of government funding to subsidize failure and/or irresponsibility, we teach young people that failure can also become a personal asset!

What is the future of those caught in this "cult of the victim"? Their cries will not go away, especially when many have been excused for years in their schools, with inflated grades and unwarranted diplomas. Or excused for a dozen "reasons" when unwilling to take jobs that required hard work. When the government runs out of money or ideas to maintain the "cult of the victim," blood will flow in the streets. Or when public unions hold their cities, states, and nations hostage to pay stupendous pensions. Check some European countries today! Or some states within the United States! We're broke!

Entitlement Cult

The same reasoning can be applied to the "entitlement cult." Americans in the last generation have been taught that life has "always been this way"—the government exists to provide for every facet of their lives. For nearly two hundred years, not so! But today many, rich and poor, depend on the government for all kinds of services known as "entitlements."

That is why a balanced budget is an elusive phantom. The problem is that people rationalize that they have paid for their entitlements! But in reality, most entitlement beneficiaries will receive far more than they ever paid into the system. This includes Social Security and Medicare, but few want to know the truth. The money they are receiving is only borrowed to be paid back by the next generation—and that only by increased taxation. The Ouroboros is eating its own tail.

Kevin D. Williamson calls the "entitlement bubble"—the bust that is going to be a "nightmare."[109] All he tried to do was to remind us that our national debt liability is around $130 trillion, not the $14.7 trillion that our present administration tries to emphasize (if that were a trifle). These numbers mean very little, even to accountants, but they are very real promises that will come due one of these days—with no cash with which to keep the promise of Social Security[110] for many baby boomers and others.

The bust? When our politicians realize that the economic survival of

---

109. *National Review* online, September 16, 2010.

110. Just a reminder: there is no trust fund into which Social Security payments made today are being kept. The so-called fund is simply an unfunded liability for the United States government, an account without a dime in it.

this country depends on reducing the decades of entitlements, including Social Security as we know it today—then this nation will get a taste of what France and Greece and others are now facing: the rage of young and old in the streets of America, demanding what they have become used to. But the public treasury is broke!

Adding to the mystery of how badly or how confused the American economy has become, think about a request by *Bloomberg News* to the Federal Reserve to disclose the recipients of more than $2 trillion of emergency loans from U.S. taxpayers![111] This is on top of the TARP $700 billion! The central bank loans don't have the oversight safeguards that Congress imposed upon the TARP.

> "If they told us what they held, we would know the potential losses that the government may take and that's what they don't want us to know," said Carlos Mendez, a senior managing director at New York-based ICP Capital LLC, which oversees $22 billion in assets.[112]

Congress is demanding more transparency from the Fed and Treasury on the bailout, most recently during December 10, 2008, hearings by the House Financial Services committee, when Representative David Scott, a Georgia Democrat, said Americans had "been bamboozled."[113]

Fiat Money

I don't have the space to examine one of the legacies of the Roosevelt New Deal and the Nixon Shock (1971)—the abandonment of the gold standard in favor of fiat money (legal tender, especially paper currency, authorized by a government but not based on or convertible into gold or silver.) What does this all mean? Any government can print as many more "dollars" as they want, but when they do, the value of the "dollar" goes down. We call that inflation! Not good for those who save or those on fixed incomes. That is why our look into the future has instability written all over it! And also, reasons for panic, as the unsettling gets worse here in the United States, as well as any country elsewhere.

No wonder Alan Greenspan, once the heralded former Federal Reserve chairman, caused a buzz when he warned at the Council on Foreign Relations on September 15, 2010, that "fiat money has no place to go but

---

111. Mark Pittman, "Fed Refuses to Disclose Recipients of $2 Trillion," *Bloomberg News*, December 8, 2008.

112. Ibid.

113. Ibid.

gold."[114] The dollar dropped to a new low, and spot gold was up almost $7.00 immediately. Just a sample of more to come.

For example, when governments (such as Greece, Ireland, Portugal— and the United States in the near future) face defaults on their government bonds (federal or state) or guaranteed pension funds, etc., amidst the burden of aging populations and the difficulty of increasing tax revenue, they will pay back these debts to their stakeholders (average citizens or anybody else who invests in "the sure thing" of the U.S. government) with devalued fiat money. Exactly as occurred in Weimar Germany in the early 1930s, when workers got paid but rushed to the store with wheelbarrows full of cash to buy food before the prices were marked up daily.

Street Riots

For months now, in fact, for several years from time to time, we hear and see on twenty-four-hour cable TV the clash of police with organized mobs in cities usually considered the best in western culture. France and Greece come to mind, especially during this extreme financial meltdown when sovereign nations (not corporations) are defaulting on their contractual agreements with public workers and others.

Just this morning, I note the anger that austerity is prompting in Europe—the showcase of modern socialism:

> Painful cuts by overspending EU countries come head to a head with mounting social anger on Wednesday [September 28, 2010] when labor leaders call angry workers onto streets right across the continent.

> Set for its largest Europe-wide protest for a decade is Brussels where labor leaders are planning to bring 100,000 people from 30 countries to say "No to austerity!"[115]

The protest—the biggest such march since 2001, when eighty thousand people spilled into the EU capital—is being held to coincide with a plan to fine EU governments running up deficits.

Millions of jobs fell off the European map in the global downturn, and many more are set to be squeezed, as governments axe public spending.

In Spain, where trade unions called a general strike on September 19, 2010, unemployment has more than doubled, with one in five workers jobless as of the most recent July. Madrid, in consequence, began looking at a drastic overhaul of its labor legislation to ease flex-time and hiring and firing. Pensions were frozen, wages cut for civil servants, and VAT (value added tax) rose.

---

114. http://www.nysun.com/editorials/greenspans-warning-on-gold/87080/.
115. *The Economic Times*, September 29, 2010.

Portugal's leading labor confederation, the CGTP (English: General Confederation of the Portuguese Workers), which is close to the Communists, called protests in Lisbon and Porto.

Poland's main unions, Solidarity and OPZZ (English: All-Poland Alliance of Trade Unions), expected "several thousand" at a protest outside government headquarters.[116]

Similar marches were scheduled in Greece, Ireland, Italy, Latvia, and Serbia, with labor leaders across the board clamoring for growth and protesting, as they saw it, the injustice of workers paying for the errors of the financial sector.

All this is pent-up fury on the part of labor unions that have been infiltrated for decades by socialistic/communistic bullies. I have reason to assure you that the United States should be forewarned.

Hyperinflation

Obviously, you are wondering how all these world jitters are going to affect you and your pocketbook. Obviously, everything we have been lightly reviewing is not something long ago and far away. Obviously, everyone still reading this book will soon feel and see how all this global financial crisis directly affects them—where it hurts the most.

On November 8, 2010, The National Inflation Association released its report about its projection for future U.S. food price increases, due to the massive monetary inflation being created by the Federal Reserve's $600 billion "quantitative easing" (a.k.a. fiat money being printed without anything to back it up—talk about Orwellian language!).

The report noted that despite cotton rising by 54 percent, corn rising by 29 percent, soybeans rising by 22 percent, orange juice rising by 17 percent, and sugar rising by 61 percent during the months of September and October alone (2010), these huge commodity price increases had yet to pass along to the retail customer. But that is not likely to remain the case.

The NIA projected that the average U.S. grocery store will soon enough be asking $11.43 for one ear of corn, $23.05 for a 24-oz. loaf of wheat bread, $62.21 for a 32-oz. package of Domino granulated sugar, $24.31 for a 43-fl. oz. container of soy milk, $45.71 for a 64-fl. oz. container of Minute Maid orange juice, and so on. They also project that by the end of the current decade, a plain white men's cotton T-shirt at Wal-Mart will cost $55.57.[117]

No End in Sight

Some 279 banks have failed since September 25, 2008, when Washington

116. Ibid.

117. http://inflation.us/foodpriceprojections.pdf.

Mutual became the biggest bank failure on record.[118] Standard & Poor's reported that "in the second quarter of this year, the Federal Deposit Insurance Corporation increased its number of problem banks by 6% to 829"![119]

Why does the liquidation of banks matter? Cutbacks in banks mean fewer banking choices, lower interest rates on savings accounts, and lost jobs (that can be measured in the tens of thousands)!

Suicides Rise

Study is ongoing in trying to find the cause for the rise of middle-aged suicides in the United States. Normally, middle-aged people are usually a low risk for suicides, but baby boomers are checking this trend. Unemployment rates in the United States rose between 2000 and 2003, and at the same time, middle-ages suicide rates increased rapidly. In addition, rates of bankruptcy significantly increased between 1991 and 2007, with personal financial consequences.[120]

No wonder the Merriam-Webster's 2010 Word of the Year was "austerity."[121]

But not all is "austere" and imploding. Hardly! Think of a UAE (United Arab Emirates) $11 million Christmas tree! That's right, a single tree—not another hotel! A ritzy Muslim emirate of Abu Dhabi unveiled a forty-foot (thirteen-meter) "tree" bedecked with necklaces, earrings, and other jewelry draped around the tree's branches. It holds a total of 181 diamonds, pearls, emeralds, sapphires, and other precious stones. A special seven-day package, priced at $1,000,000, includes a private butler and a chauffeur-driven Baybach luxury car at guest disposal, as well as a private jet available for trips to other countries in the region. Something to write home about![122]

I am only tapping into the surface of issues that are confronting Americans as a bad dream—a nightmare, for too many. I will wrap up this chapter with predictions from two remarkable economists who were laughed off the public stage in 2006—but not anymore: Gerald Celente and Nouriel Roubini.

Gerald Celente, Renowned Predictor

First—Gerald Celente, CEO of Trends Research Institute, is renowned for his accuracy in predicting future world and economic events—often

---

118. *Wall Street Journal,* September 27, 2010.

119. Ibid.

120. Reuters, September 27, 2010.

121. AP, *The Washington Post,* December 20, 2010.

122. http://www.breitbard.com/article.php?id:CNG 12/16/20.

by sending chills down the spines of those who stand long enough to listen. He predicted the 1987 stock market crash and the fall of the Soviet Union, the 1997 Asian Currency Crisis, the subprime mortgage collapse, and the massive devaluation of the U.S. dollar.

In November 2007 he told the UPI that the following year would be known as "The Panic of 2008," adding that giants would tumble to their deaths (think Lehman Brothers, Bear Stearns, and so on).

Regarding America's future in 2008:

"There will be a revolution in this country. It's not going to come yet, but it's going to come down the line and we're going to see a third party and this was the catalyst for it: the takeover of Washington, D.C., in broad daylight by Wall Street in this bloodless coup. And it will happen as conditions continue to worsen.

"The first thing to do is organize with tax revolts. That's going to be the big one because people can't afford to pay more school tax, property tax, any kind of tax. You're going to start seeing those kinds of protests start to develop. [Is anyone thinking Tea Parties?]

"It is going to be very bleak. Very sad. And there is going to be a lot of homeless, the likes of which we have never seen before. Tent cities are already sprouting up around the country and we're going to see many more.

"We're going to start seeing huge areas of vacant real estate and squatters living in them as well. . . . It's going to come as a shock and with it, there's going to be a lot of crime. And the crime is going to be a lot worse than it was before because in the last 1929 Depression, people's minds weren't wrecked on all these modern drugs— over-the-counter drugs, or crystal meth or whatever it might be. So, you have a huge underclass of very desperate people with their minds chemically blown beyond anybody's comprehension."[123]

Nouriel Roubini, Dr. Doom

Next, Nouriel Roubini, the fifty-one-year-old widely known as "Dr. Doom." In 2007, Roubini had been the object of derision in the economics community as he prophesied a U.S. housing market crash, financial crisis, and partial collapse of the banking sector. Today, as an adviser to governments and central bankers and much feted in the media, he's well aware of the power of being right.

"In my line of business your reputation is based on being right,"

123. Paul Joseph Watson, "Celente Predicts Revolution, Food Riots, Tax Rebellions by 2012," http://www.infowars.com/?p=5938.

he says. "The publicity is just noise. Certainly with a global crisis, the dismal scientists are having some prominence, even if most of the economics profession actually failed to predict it."

Roubini continued:

"The crisis is not over; we are just at the next stage. This is where we move from a private to a public debt problem. . . . We socialized part of the private losses by bailing out financial institutions and providing fiscal stimulus to avoid the great recession from turning into a depression. But rising public debt is never a free lunch, eventually you have to pay for it."[124]

In late May 2010, markets around the world began dropping, due partly to problems in Greece and the Eurozone. Roubini believed Greece is just the first of a series of countries standing on the brink:

"We have to start to worry about the solvency of governments. What is happening today in Greece is the tip of the iceberg of rising sovereign debt problems in the eurozone, in the UK, in Japan and in the US. This . . . is going to be the next issue in the global financial crisis."[125]

The future: "In the US there is a lack of bipartisanship between Democrats and Republicans, in Germany Merkel has just lost the majority in her legislature, in Japan you have a weak and ineffective government, in Greece you have riots and strikes," he says. "The point is that a lot of sacrifices will have to be made in these countries but many of the governments are weak or divided. It is that political strain that markets are worried about. . . . If you're pushing through austerity while there is growth that's one thing, but if you're pushing it through while the recession is deepening, politically that is harder to sell. And the eurozone doesn't just need fiscal consolidation but also structural reform to increase productivity and restore competitiveness."[126]

Roubini is adamant that the great recession is not over. But a temporary economic pick-up, which would convince governments that reform is unnecessary, could bring its own problems.

"People asked me why I saw there was a bubble and my question was why others didn't. During the bubble everybody was benefiting and losing a sense of reality," he says. "And now, since there is the

---

124. Jonathan Sibun, "Nouriel Roubini Said That the Bubble Would Burst and It Did. So What Next?" May 23, 2010, http://www.telegraph.co.uk/finance/economics/7756684/Nouriel-Roubini-said-the-bubble-would-burst-and-it-did.-So-what-next.html.

125. Ibid.

126. Ibid.

beginning of economic recovery—however bumpy that might be—in some sense people are already starting to forget what happened two years ago. Banks are going back to business as usual and bonuses are back to levels that are outrageous by any standards. There is actually a backlash against even moderate reforms that governments are trying to pass."[127]

Reform, Roubini insists, is necessary, recovery or not. "We are still in the middle of this crisis and there is more trouble ahead of us, even if there is a recovery. During the great depression the economy contracted between 1929 and 1933, there was the beginning of a recovery, but then a second recession from 1937 to 1939. If you don't address the issues, you risk having a double-dip recession and one which is at least as severe as the first one."[128]

Roubini has built his reputation on such forecasts. So, given that the real reputation builder was forecasting the crisis, has he been one of the few to enjoy the troubled times of the past few years?

"We are witnessing the worst global economic crisis in the last 60 to 70 years and for an economist that offers an opportunity," he says. "So it has been interesting, but the damage financially and economically has been so severe and so many people have suffered. Anybody involved has to bear that in mind."[129]

I know you are asking, "What does all this have to do with our chapter's ominous theme: Jesus will return after this world has had its worst economic collapse, ever?"

I have no personal crystal ball. But I can read words from certain authors that I have learned to respect and to believe. And the words of Jesus have always been validated in life as I have known it.

Luke reported that Jesus said, regarding the closing days of earth history immediately preceding His return, "And there will be signs . . . on the earth distress of nations, with perplexity . . . men's hearts failing them from fear and the expectations of those things which are coming on the earth" (Luke 21:25, 26).

Hello!

John the revelator is describing a last-day scenario in which the economy of the world and the world's merchants is to play a significant role in international turmoil. The future is galloping into us! The main theme of Revelation 18 is the collapse of the world's economy:

The fruit that your soul longed for has gone from you, and all the

---

127. Jonathan Sibun, May 23, 2010, http://www.telegraph.co.uk/finance/economies/7756684.
128. Ibid.
129. Ibid.

things which are rich and splendid have gone from you, and you shall find them no more at all. The merchants of these things, who became rich and splendid, have gone from you, and you shall find them no more at all . . . . For in one hour such great riches came to nothing. . . . For in one hour she is made desolate (verses 14–19).

Before These Words Go to the Publisher

I couldn't finish this chapter without including the latest uproar throughout the Arab world following the Tunisian revolution that sent their leader packing and plunging the country into tumult.

The head of the Arab League, Amr Moussa, told the region's leaders on January 19, 2011, "The upheaval in Tunisia is linked to deteriorating economic conditions throughout the Arab world, warning them that their people's anger has reached unprecedented heights."

In impassioned remarks, Amr Moussa told an Arab economic summit in Egypt that "the Arab soul is broken by poverty, unemployment and general recession."

He was referring to the thousands who have demonstrated in Jordan, Egypt, Sudan, Oman, Libya, and Yemen recently over the economic situation in their respective countries, some explicitly in solidarity with the Tunisians.

The Saudi commentator Turki al-Dakhail, writing in the *Al-Watan Daily*, "called for the Arab regimes to end the 'starvation' of their nations.

"The systematic starvation of people in Tunisia led to an uprising and anger of the people," al-Dakhail wrote. "Starving your dog will force him to eat you up."[130]

Future Scenario

Perhaps some are asking, "What does an economic collapse have to do with the Second Advent?" Answer: The coming international economic meltdown, coupled with natural disasters, will drive governments to find scapegoats for the escalating calamities.

The religious card will be played. Something like this will be said, perhaps by the president of the United States: "We are in an enormous crisis. We need unity as never before. We need to restore our common values, our religious roots. We need fewer divisions, less hate talk. In fact, we are going to outlaw any group talking negatively about anyone else. This is a time to come together and fulfill the American dream. Remember, 'Righteousness exalts a nation.' Let's restore peace to our communities, at least for one day of the week. Let's restore America to the way it used to be."

Bingo! Sunday will be the day of choice, and the plea for tolerance and

---

130. *USA Today*, January 19, 2011 (Associated Press).

national unity will trump all negative talk about anyone's sexual orientation, ethnic origin, or religious beliefs.

So what? someone may ask. These unprecedented conditions we have been reviewing in these pages will soon compel frightened citizens to enact strict government laws that will evaporate the basic freedoms on which this country was founded. For instance, no longer will it be permissible to argue for which day is the Sabbath or to point out who changed it—that will be considered intolerant, divisive, and subject to rapid, legal incarceration. Think Canada today!

Bottom line—such a time will come, when loyal, patriotic citizens will not be able to buy or sell. And if they continue to be divisive with their appeal to freedom, as guaranteed in the Constitution, Revelation 13 comes into play. Verse 15 predicts that the law will say they should be killed! We are not there yet, but the stage is surely being set. Really, it has never been this late before!

Does anyone still doubt the accuracy of the predictions in Revelation 13 and 18 that we have just reviewed, and *Testimonies*, volume 9, page 13?

In this chapter, we have briefly flown over the current economic/political distress primarily in the United States. Only a fool is saying, "All is well!" But the United States. comprises only part of the world's predicaments.

In our next chapter we will focus on the quiet, though extraordinary methods being used to globalize all aspects of our lives, no matter what country we may live in. "All the world is a stage, and all the men and women merely players," Shakespeare said so well in "As You Like It." Never before in earth's history has planet Earth become such a world theater! Yes, we all are "bit" players! For the world to be bankrupt, "when great riches came to nothing"—that is still ahead.

CHAPTER FIVE

THEME:
> Jesus will come after the world has finally crafted its New World Order, with not only a world government but a world religion.

The Almost Invisible Arms of Globalization

We noted briefly that the interlocking of international banking and business would likely cause the coming financial collapse of nations around the world. The shivering halt to the worldwide mania that "good times" will last forever (even on borrowed money) was made more probable by the steel spider web of globalization. What happens in one country, as we have been experiencing since 2008, causes a developing ripple in others.

WARNING: For years I was one of the many who dismissed those who seemed obsessed with the various "conspiracy theories," such as UFOs, the "New World Order," Bilderbergers, or the Illuminati. But times do change, especially when I learned that the term *conspiracy theory* was created by a government think tank back in the 1960s to de-rate and ridicule anything not broadcast by the official news media on the evening news.[132] It dawned on me that sometimes, we actually have to believe what they say. In other words, "follow the money," or "read their lips," or "believe the unbelievable."

The tentacles of the coming financial disaster (outlined earlier) are now being linked with other kinds of interlocking global strategies—strategies, often religious, that also include the whole world. Here, we can only tease with several observations. More later!

---

132. Jim McCanney, http://www.jmccanneyscience.com.

New World Order

Most of us remember President George Herbert Walker Bush's State of the Union address before the U.S. Congress on January 29, 1991. A few days before, Congress had voted for war against Iraq. In his speech, Bush said:

"What is at stake is more than one small country, it is a big idea—*a new world order*, where diverse nations are drawn together in common cause to achieve the universal aspirations of mankind: peace and security, freedom, and the rule of law. Such is a world worthy of our struggle, and worthy of our children's future!"[133]

A "new world order"! For some Americans, that sounded like something describing millennial bliss! However, the phrase "new world order" has been used hundreds of times by highly placed leaders in education, industry, banking, the media, and politics—*but they were careful to keep it off the front pages of newspapers or round-the-clock cable TV.* To footnote all this would make another book! For example, in a subterfuge way, it became the mantra during the 1960s–1980s for those pushing "values clarification" and "outcome-based education"—a veritable seismic shift in the public school system in the United States.

On July 26, 1968 (Associated Press report), Nelson Rockefeller pledged in his run for the presidency that "as President, he would work toward international creation of a *new world order.*" In 1968, Rockefeller published his book *The Future of Federalism,* a compelling outline of his mantra, *new world order,* maintaining that the older order is crumbling and that there is a "new and free order struggling to be born." He went on to say that at present there was:

"[A] fever of nationalism . . . [but] the nation-state is becoming less and less competent to perform its international political tasks. . . . These are some of the reasons pressing us to lead vigorously toward the true building of a *new world order* . . . [with] voluntary service . . . and our dedicated faith in the brotherhood of all mankind. . . . Sooner perhaps than we may realize . . . there will evolve the basis for a federal structure of the free world" (emphasis added).

In 1975, in the United States, thirty-two senators and ninety-two representatives signed "A Declaration of Interdependence"—written by the distinguished historian Henry Steele Commager—that stated, "We must join with others to bring forth a *new world order.* . . . Narrow notions of national sovereignty must not be permitted to curtail that obligation."[134]

133. http://www.infoplease.com (Famous Presidential Speeches).
134. http://www.co-intelligence.org/DeclarationsOfInterdep.html. Emphasis added.

Marjorie Holt, Maryland congresswoman and a strong proponent of American sovereignty, refused to sign this Declaration of Interdependence. She stated that the document "calls for the surrender of our national sovereignty to international organizations. It declares that our economy should be regulated by international authorities. It proposes that we enter a 'new world order' that would redistribute the wealth created by the American people."[135]

In his address to the United Nations on December 7, 1988, Mikhail Gorbachev called for mutual consensus: "World progress is only possible through a search for universal human consensus as we move toward a *new world order*."[136]

On May 12, 1989, President George H. W. Bush stated that the United States is ready to welcome the Soviet Union "back into the *world order*."[137]

On September 11, 1990, months before the Gulf War began, President Bush emphasized his strategy: "The crisis in the Persian Gulf offers a rare opportunity to move toward an historic period of cooperation. Out of these troubled times. . . *a new world order* can emerge in which the nations of the world, east and west, north and south, can prosper and live in harmony. ... Today the *new world* is struggling to be born."[138]

A remarkable peek into how all this gets quietly circulated into the bloodstream of wide-awake Americans was revealed by David Rockefeller at the Trilateral Commission in June 1991. Sixty-five prestigious members of government, labor, academia, the media, military, and the professions from nine countries heard David Rockefeller say:

"We are grateful to the *Washington Post, The New York Times, Time Magazine,* and other great publications whose directors have attended our meetings and respected their promises of discretion for almost 40 years.

"It would have been impossible for us to develop our plan for the world if we had been subjected to the lights of publicity during those years. But the world is now more sophisticated and prepared to march towards a world government. The supranational sovereignty of an intellectual elite and world bankers is surely preferable to the national auto-determination practiced in past centuries."[139]

135. http://en.wikipedia.org/wiki/Marjorie Holt.
136. http://astro.temple.edu/~rimmerma/gorbachev_speech_to_UN.htm. Emphasis added.
137. http://www.threeworldwars.com/nwo-timeline2.htm.
138. http://www.presidency.ucsb.edu/ws/?pid=18820. Emphasis added.
139. http://quotes.liberty-tree.ca/quote/david_rockefeller_quote_103d. Emphasis added.

It might take a couple of deep breaths and several re-reads of that paragraph to grasp what Rockefeller is revealing.

As if on cue, *Time* magazine published on July 20, 1992, Strobe Talbot's *The Birth of the Global Nation,* in which he wrote:

> All countries are basically social arrangements. . . . No matter how permanent or even sacred they may seem at any one time, in fact they are all artificial and temporary. . . . Perhaps national sovereignty wasn't such a great idea after all. . . . But it has taken the events in our own wondrous and terrible century to clinch the case for *world government.*

Talbot was soon appointed to be the number two person behind Warren Christopher, Secretary of State, where he continued his sharp focus.

"Global Governance"

In the mid-1990s something interesting happened! One rarely heard the term *new world order.* But a new slogan emerged: "global governance."

What does *globalization* or *global governance* mean? In short, we are expanding the obvious human connectedness to a truly global level. On one hand, we think of Christianity essentially as a global faith. On the other, we all sense something has happened in the last ten to twenty years that no one really dreamed of fifty years ago.

Think Internet, cell phones, cable news, GPS systems, superfast airplanes, and other new technology.

Unforeseen problems: the blur of time and the "fast-life"; reality merged with the virtual; families melting down; gender confusion; job insecurity; religion merged with spirituality; consumerism; growing numbers of the homeless and identity-less; novelty trumping wisdom, and so on.[140]

The State of the World Forum, in the fall of 1995, held its meeting at the Presidio in San Francisco, attended by the who's who of the world, including Margaret Thatcher, Maurice Strong, George H. W. Bush, and Mikhail Gorbachev. The term *global governance* was now being used instead of *new world order.*[141]

Forum participants, viewing reality through the new paradigm filter of "global governance," saw national sovereignty as incompatible with global ideals. Before an evening session, the national flags that had colored the stage the first two days were replaced by a golden image of the world's undivided land masses. Apparently, the time had come to put pretense aside and face the goal: a borderless planet. Nation-states were out.

---

140. Os Guinness and David Wells, "Global Gospel . . ." http://conversation .lausanne.org/en/.

141. http://www.crossroad.to/text/articles/gorb10-95.html.

"Global governance . . . must result in the erosion of the spheres in the conduct of states and governments," explained plenary speaker Thabo Mbeki, South Africa's deputy president and Nelson Mandela's heir-apparent. The "birth of the global village" will "force everyone to develop new perspectives."[142]

The Commission on Global Governance released its recommendations in preparation for a World Conference on Global Governance, scheduled for 1998. Among those recommendations were specific proposals to expand the authority of the United Nations to provide the following:

▶ Global taxation

▶ A standing UN army

▶ An Economic Security Council

▶ UN authority over the global commons

▶ An end to the veto power of permanent members of the Security Council

▶ A new parliamentary body of "civil society" representatives (NGOs)

▶ A new "Petitions Council"

▶ A new Court of Criminal Justice (accomplished in July 1998 in Rome)

▶ Binding verdicts of the International Court of Justice

▶ Expanded authority for the Secretary General[143]

Also in 1995, the United Nations published a 420-page report, *Our Global Neighborhood*, that laid out these plans for "global governance" in further detail.[144]

Again in 1995, Arthur Schlesinger Jr., in *Foreign Affairs* (July/August 1995) wrote, "We are not going to achieve a new world order without paying for it in blood as well as in words and money." One way or another! Is that a prophecy?

A month later, Schlesinger wrote another remarkable article in *Foreign Affairs* comparing the beginning of the twentieth century with the end of that century. Little did he know that history would repeat what the awful twentieth had to learn:

> For historians, this euphoria [for a real New World Order] rang a bell of memory. Did not the same radiant hope accompany the transition from the nineteenth to the twentieth century? This most

---

142. http://www.crossroad.to/text/articles/gorb10-95.html.

143. http://www.sovereignty.net/p/gov/gganalysis.htm.

144. Ibid.

terrible hundred years in Western history started out in an atmosphere of optimism and high expectations. People of good will in 1900 believed in the inevitability of democracy, the invincibility of progress, the decency of human nature, and the coming reign of reason and peace. David Starr Jordan, the president of Stanford University, expressed the mood in his turn-of-the-century book *The Call of the Twentieth Century*. "The man of the Twentieth Century," Jordan predicted, "will be a hopeful man. He will love the world and the world will love him."[145]

In chorus came others repeating the refrain:

"In the next century, nations as we know it will be obsolete; all states will recognize a single, global authority. National sovereignty wasn't such a great idea after all"—Strobe Talbot, President Clinton's Deputy Secretary of State.[146]

Jim Garrison, president of the New Age Gorbachev Foundation, said:

"We are going to end up with world government. It's inevitable. . . . There's going to be Conflict, Coercion and Consensus. That's all part of what will be required as we give birth to the global civilization."[147]

Note too another line in the chorus, from David Rockefeller, September 23, 1994:

"This present window of opportunity, during which a truly peaceful and interdependent world order might be built, will not be open for too long. We are on the verge of a global transformation. All we need is the right major crisis and the nations will accept the New World Order."[148]

Remember that last line!

My point is, it might be taking somewhat longer to achieve the "new world" dream that key world leaders have been working on behind the scenes for decades. *But the trajectory has never been sharper than today.* One has to be blind and deaf not to detect its forward motion in politics, social programs, and financial enterprises, as well as in religious confederations never thought possible a generation ago.

The 2008 presidential contender John McCain put all this in front of us

---

145. Arthur Schlesinger Jr., "Has Democracy a Future?" *Foreign Affairs*, September/October 1995.

146. *Time*, July 20, 1992.

147. Dennis Cuddy, "Ruling Elite Working Towards World Govt." *The Daily Record*, October 17, 1995, 4.

148. http://www.mega.nu:8080/ampp/timeline.html. Emphasis added.

just a few years ago. Writing in the November/December 2007 issue of *Foreign Affairs*, Senator McCain proposed that "democratic nations should be linked in one common organization: a worldwide League of Democracies." He promised that "If I am elected president, during my first year in office I will call a summit of the world's democracies to seek the views of my counterparts and explore the steps necessary to realize this vision."

McCain's goals:

1. "Harnessing the political and moral advantages offered by united democratic action."

2. "Bringing concerted pressure to bear on tyrants."

3. "Defeating radical Islamists."

McCain emphasizes that steps two and three involve the options of using economic sanctions or necessary military force to achieve these goals. In a speech in Los Angeles he noted that there were "one hundred democratic nations around the world to advance our values and defend our shared interests."[149]

Makes one wonder even more!

Outgoing British Prime Minster Gordon Brown surveyed the speed of change:

> "Historians will look back and say this was no ordinary time but a defining moment—an unprecedented period of global change and a time when one chapter ended and another began."[150]

Mechanisms in Place

Take FEMA (Federal Emergency Management Agency), for instance. Not many Americans (or anybody else) know what FEMA really is legislated to do in a crisis (and we all know the current political maxim: *"Never let a crisis go to waste"*).

FEMA was given huge powers in 1979. It has the power, in case of "national emergency," to suspend laws, move entire populations, arrest and detain citizens without a warrant, and hold them without trial. It can seize property, food supplies, and transportation systems—and can suspend the Constitution.

Not only is it the most powerful entity in the United States, it was not even created under Constitutional law by the Congress. *It was a product of an executive order from President Carter.* An executive order becomes law simply by a signature of the U.S. president—it does not even have to be approved by the representatives or senators in the Congress.

---

149. See Gregory Hamilton, August 8, 2008, "Northwest Religious Liberty Association."

150. *The Sunday Times*, March 1, 2009.

A state of "national emergency" could be a terrorist attack, a natural disaster, or a stock market crash, for example. Here are just a few executive orders associated with FEMA that would suspend the Constitution and the Bill of Rights. These executive orders have been on record for nearly thirty years and could be enacted by the stroke of a presidential pen:

#10995: Right to seize all communications media in the United States.

#10997: Right to seize all electric power, fuels, and minerals, both public and private.

#10999: Right to seize all means of transportation, including personal vehicles of any kind, and assume total control of highways, seaports, and waterways.

#11000: Right to seize any and all American people and divide up families, in order to create workforces to be transferred to any place the government sees fit.

#11001: Right to seize all health, education, and welfare facilities, both public and private.

#11002: Right to force registration of all men, women, and children in the United States.

#11003: Right to seize all airspace, airports, and aircraft.

#11004: Right to seize all housing and finance authorities in order to establish "Relocation Designated Areas" and to force abandonment of areas classified as "unsafe."

#11005: Right to seize all railroads, inland waterways, and storage facilities, both public and private.

#11921: Authorizes plans to establish government control of wages and salaries, credit, and the flow of money in U.S. financial institutions.[151]

Couple all that with presumed obeisance to global governance, and you have a very scary scenario. Consider this appraisal:

The most shining example of America to the world has been its peaceful transition of government from one administration to another. Despite crises of great magnitude, the United States has maintained its freedom and liberty. This nation now stands on the threshold of rule by non-elected people asserting non-Constitutional powers. Even Congress cannot review a Martial Law action until six months after it has been declared. For the first time in American history, the reins of government would not be transferred from one elected element to another, but the Constitution, itself, can be suspended. The scenarios established to trigger FEMA into action are generally found in the society today, economic collapse, civil unrest, drug problems, terrorist attacks, and protests against American

---

151. http://www.theforbiddenknowledge.com/.../fema_executive_orders.htm.

intervention in a foreign country. All these premises exist; it could only be a matter of time in which one of these triggers the entire emergency necessary to bring FEMA into action, and then it may be too late, because under the FEMA plan, there is no contingency by which Constitutional power is restored.[152]

Never Waste a Crisis

"Rule 1: Never allow a serious crisis to go to waste," White House Chief of Staff Rahm Emanuel told *The New York Times* right after the election. "They are opportunities to do big things."[153] Over the same weekend, Secretary of State Hillary Rodham Clinton told members of the European Parliament: "Never waste a good crisis."[154] Then President Obama explained in his Saturday radio and Internet address that there is "great opportunity in the midst of" the "great crisis" befalling America.

Emanuel was echoing the Hegelian dialectic. The Hegelian dialectic is a framework for manipulating the masses into accepting a predetermined solution.

In short, the Hegelian dialectic is as follows:

First, create a problem of monumental proportions.

Second, stir up hysteria by every means possible.

Third, when people hysterically demand a solution—the solution offered will take away rights, cost considerable money, and put more power in the hands of the power-grabbing bureaucrats.[155]

To put into plain language when used to advance a partisan idea, it's fear-mongering. Franklin Roosevelt said that all we have to fear is fear itself. Later leaders among us today say all we have to fear is the *loss* of fear itself.

In other realms of life, exploiting a crisis for your own purposes is an outrage. If a business uses a hurricane warning, for example, to price-gouge on vital supplies, it is a crime.

Jonah Goldberg wrote:

> Imagine a child falls down a well. Now imagine I offer to lend the parents my ladder to save her, but only if they promise to paint my house. Would you applaud me for not letting a crisis go to waste? Or would you think I'm a jerk?[156]

---

152. Ibid.

153. *Wall Street Journal* Weekend interview, November 7, 2008.

154. Reuters, March 7, 2003, speech at the European Parliament.

155. http://www.intellectualconservative.com.

156. *Los Angeles Times*, March 10, 2009.

I linger on this emphasis (never wasting a crisis and the Hegelian dialectic) because that is where we are all going to end up, step by step, as we enter what we may call the last of the last days.

Hegel's laserlike principle, underwritten by the fascists and the communists in the twentieth century, is alive and well virtually anywhere today. It arises in most any serious discussion!

Note how William Shirer caught the Hegelian principle in his blockbuster book, *The Rise and Fall of the Third Reich:*

> The State "has the supreme right against the individual, whose supreme duty is to be a member of the State . . . for the right of the world spirit is above all special privileges."[157]

The lesson for us today: The Hegelian dialectic is the framework for guiding our thoughts and actions into conflicts that lead us to a predetermined solution—often almost silently. Dialogues and consensus-building are primary tools of most leaders, whether in federal government, local school boards, or in local church boards! Intimidation and even suggested terror are also useful weapons in the dialogue. The only hope for anyone is to cut the dialectic madness, or else one ends up in a place he/she did not envision before entering the dialogue or "discussion." Thanks to dramatic political lurches—and aided by the exponential magnification of the Internet and the seething blogosphere—no matter what the issue, the invisible dialectic aims to control both the conflict and the resolution of differences and leads everyone involved into a new cycle of conflicts, until everyone has conceded to Someone Else's desired end! In the world of governance, we see evidence of Hegel's principle at work as we fall into the trap of the Third Way agenda: world government is the synthesis! More later!

Global Monetary System

So much can be said about the mushroom cloud rising over the economic frazzle of 2008–2011, and we have not seen the end of it all. When the G20 leaders met in London in early April 2009, headlines proclaimed that the world economy went global overnight—world leaders admitted that it could be managed only by joint action. No more could a nation act in isolation.[158] The interconnectedness of national economies became most evident in the financial fever that sickened most all money markets. The amazing mobility of capital meant that there was only one way to cool the fever—a world monetary system.

The report was specific:

---

157. William Shirer, *The Rise and Fall of the Third Reich* (New York: Simon & Schuster, 1960), 144.

158. http://www.theaustralian.news.com.au/story (April 3, 2009).

Each [G20 leader] came to London hardened by stunted economic growth, and public anger about how lax economic regulation in the US has caused a crisis that has reverberated around the world and, according to the OECD (Organisation for Economic Co-operation and Development), will leave one in 10 people jobless within a year.[159]

On February 26, 2010, Dominique Strauss-Kahn, the head of the International Monetary Fund, suggested that the organization might one day be called on to provide countries with a global reserve currency that could serve as an alternative to the U.S. dollar. He said having other alternatives to the dollar "would limit the extent to which the international monetary system as a whole depends on the policies and conditions of a single, albeit dominant country."[160] His voice is just one of many suggesting a world currency to solve the current financial turmoil.

By November 6, 2010, the whole world stepped on a new conveyor belt that was going at mach speed: Ben Bernanke, U.S. Federal Reserve Bank chairman, announced that the bank would purchase $600 billion (spelled with a *B*) "to provide additional stimulus to help the economy recovery and to avoid potentially additional disinflation." All this, after bringing interest rates down to near zero and after "buying" $1.7 trillion (spelled with a *T*) in government and mortgage bonds during the financial crisis.[161]

Bernanke called this extraordinary decision "quantitative easing." Or, in other words, "fiat printing of money." This is nothing more than George Orwell's "doublespeak," wherein "language deliberately disguises, distorts, or reverses the meaning of words. Doublespeak may take the form of euphemisms (for example, 'downsizing' for layoffs), making the truth less unpleasant, without denying its nature. It may also be deployed as intentional ambiguity, or reversal of meaning (for example, naming a state of war 'peace'). In such cases, doublespeak disguises the nature of the truth, producing a communication bypass."[162]

Immediately, government leaders around the world were aghast—the backlash grew. The decision propelled gold above $1,400 an ounce. Germany, Brazil, China, and Japan reacted with alarm.

German Finance Minister Wolfgang Shäuble lashed out:

It doesn't add up when the Americans accuse the Chinese of currency manipulation and then, with the help of their central bank's printing presses, artificially lower the value of the dollar.[163]

---

159. Ibid.

160. Associated Press, Washington, February 26, 2010.

161. *The Wall Street Journal*, November 8, 2010.

162. "Double speak," *Wikipedia Free Encyclopedia*.

163. Op cit., *Journal*.

(The fear rests in the fact that printing more dollars tends to weaken the dollar by raising the value of the currency in other countries. Thus, though U.S. exports are more attractive, the exports of other nations are dampened. Trade wars are awful—one of the causes of the world depression in the early 1930s with the Smoot-Hawley Tariff Act: the U.S. placed heavy tariffs on incoming products, causing other countries to retaliate; farmers had no foreign markets, and manufacturers could not get needed imports.)

It's a giant game of chicken, and all the world knows it. It is undeniable that Beijing plays games with China's currency in order to bolster exports. To put it bluntly, China keeps its people artificially poor, their wages artificially low, and their savings diminished in value, in order to increase the profits flowing into the state enterprises run by Beijing's power elite. When one considers that China's economic strategy is predicated on creating needless poverty for its people, it all seems a lot less clever.[164]

I will leave this new economic bomb now, or I will never finish this book. Every one of us will be thinking and living differently by this time next year!

Worldwide Dis-Employment

The simple fact facing the world (throughout Europe and the United States, especially) is that any decrease in the employment rate in the United States (for example) will be a long time coming, if ever! The United States needs one hundred and thirty thousand new jobs a month, just to care for the influx of the young and the immigrants into the labor force—never mind the 4.3 million now unemployed for over a year! The pity is that "many of them will never work again."[165]

The other side of this sudden modern problem is that a large share of the potential workforce, now unemployed, keeps pressure on government spending for social programs (not just jobless benefits), such as food stamps and Medicaid. Consumer spending is sapped, malls are quiet, as are restaurants, car lots—and the trickle runs downhill.

However, when sovereign governments attempt to curtail long-enjoyed entitlements, the streets are filled with rioters, buildings are wrecked, transportation is shut down, and police response is tested. Think of Greece, France, and Britain in 2010.

Social Justice

Social justice is a concept that focuses on human rights and equality in the everyday lives of people, at every level of society. Many movements in many countries are working toward the realization of a world where all members of a society, regardless of background, have basic human rights

---

164. See Kevin Williamson, *National Review* Online, November 9, 2010.

165. *The Kiplinger Letter,* October 29, 2010.

and equal access to the benefits of their society.

The Green Party, for example, considers social and economic justice as one of its Four Pillars, defining this principle as the right and opportunity of all people "to benefit equally from the resources afforded us by society and the environment."[166]

Liberation Theology is a movement in Christian theology which construes the teachings of Jesus Christ in terms of liberation from unjust economic, political, or social conditions. It has been described by proponents as an interpretation of Christian faith through the eyes of the poor's suffering, struggle, and hope—and by detractors, as Christianity perverted by Marxism and communism.

I include this concern here for social justice, because it increasingly is a prominent factor in all matters involving the public fund. The central divide is whether the U.S. Constitution guarantees its citizens equality of "opportunity" or equality of "outcome."

For decades now, our educational system has been flying under a form of social justice wherein children on the playground must not play games where someone is the loser. Or in the classroom, no one should lose self-worth by being discriminated against with a poor grade.

Some religious leaders operate on the same principle: It's just not fair that some should go through life with less of this world's goods and pleasures.

For example, one of the issues considered "social injustice" concerns land and who owns it.

> Land . . . cannot be treated as an ordinary asset, controlled by individuals and subject to the pressures and inefficiencies of the market. Private land ownership is also a principal instrument of accumulation and concentrated wealth and therefore contributes to social injustice. . . . Public control of land use is therefore indispensable.[167]

A prolific writer, Cass Sunstein,[168] presently is the administrator (czar) of The White House Office of Information and Regulatory Affairs in the Obama Administration. One of his many books, *The Second Bill of*

---

166. Green Party of the United States, http://www.gp.org/tenkey.shtml.

167. U.N. Conference on Human Settlements, Vancouver, 1976.

168. Cass R. Sunstein, with Richard H. Thaler, authored *Nudge: Improving Decisions About Health, Wealth, and Happiness* (New Haven, CT: Yale University Press, 2008). An intensely interesting book, it made a strong case for "nudging" by the private sector or by government "to steer people's choices in directions that will improve their lives." Someone has said that dictatorships (see Germany in the 1930s) never start by force but by gentle nudges, until one's freedom to choose is behind them. The ultimate goal of the far right or the far left (Germany or Soviet Union) is to make the public as dependent as possible on the federal government.

Rights: FDR's Unfinished Revolution and Why We Need It More Than Ever (2004), fits into this discussion of social justice. Among those rights are a right to an education, a right to a home, a right to health care, and a right to protection against monopolies.

In the days ahead, the social justice principle will become a major voice in the economic decisions made by governments, nationally and internationally—and eventually, by a world government. You will hear more of the rights of the oppressed to challenge what they term, "the oppressor."

Freedom of the Airways

One of the remarkable innovations etched into those priceless documents, The Declaration of Independence and the Constitution of the United States, is the guarantee of freedom of speech for all. Breathtaking, when compared to other countries!

Government officials have whacked away at limiting this freedom ever since 1776, one way or another. But in the first week of December 2010, a new ploy is being floated by the Federal Communications Commission (FCC in the United States), including the control of interstate and international communications by radio, television, wire, satellite, and cable—and a proposal to sustain "traditional media" by requiring broadcasters to reflect ethnic diversity and a commitment to public affairs programming to keep their license.

Also, Michael Copps, one of the five FCC commissioners, threatened free speech and enterprise with what seems to many to be an outrageous proposal that's clearly aimed at conservative stations viewed as a threat to the administration's agenda. He said that to "help media help democracy," the FCC should conduct a "public value test" of every commercial broadcaster before renewing their license, and the process should occur every four years instead of the current eight, according to the plan.[169]

In other words, if a station doesn't pass the public value test, it goes on probation for a year and eventually loses its broadcasting rights, if it doesn't demonstrate "measurable progress" to serve the public interest. The so-called public value test features seven parts, including how well stations reflect ethnic diversity, a meaningful commitment to news and public affairs programming, and political advertising disclosure.

Who sets up the criteria, and who decides what is fair and in the public interest? You guessed it! Think of those groups that control either the executive or representative branches—votes will count more than Constitutional protections.

---

169. http://radiomagonline.com/fcc/fcc-copps-public-value-test-license-renewal-1203.

World Union of Protestant Churches

Much can be written about the many attempts within the last one hundred years to unify Protestant churches. The most well-known group is the World Council of Churches (WCC), composed of Orthodox, Anglican, and mainline Protestant traditions.

But in November 2007, a first-of-a kind global gathering of the broadest range of Christian traditions gathered in Limuru, near Nairobi, Kenya. The Global Christian Forum (GCF) consisted of about half Evangelicals and Pentecostals, joining the other half of participants from members of the World Council of Churches. Organizers claimed it was the most diverse group of church leaders ever assembled.

Evangelicals and Pentecostals had come into the planning, recognizing that this was indeed a "new table," where they were regarded as equal partners with others, so they made a major contribution to the shape of the forum. It represented a new approach from the ecumenical side, but also, many changes had been taking place on the evangelical and Pentecostal side, where sharing with others had become more acceptable and the old suspicion of social responsibility had been turned around into bold new initiatives in "transformational mission."

Hitherto, prominence had been given to questions of "Faith and Order," wherein the old ecumenism focused on structural unity and doctrinal agreement. Such issues would likely be divisive and the preserve of academic interests and ecclesiastical leadership. But in the grassroots, there is often found a very different dynamic of practical cooperation, expressed in active faith and committed, sacrificial service. Thus, in some ways, existing ecumenical initiatives seem to have run their course, having placed heavy time and resources pressures on their constituency.

All this underlines the felt need that is emerging, calling for the reconfiguration of ecumenism, as the modern age gives way to the postmodern. The GCF process represents this hope of a "transformed ecumenism," because it gives a different context in which to address the diversity that exists within the worldwide Christian family.

What this means is that the participants see "truth" as far more than some doctrinal statement (important as these are in themselves); instead, they see truth in terms of a holistic embracing of the emotional, spiritual, physical, and social aspects of life, as well as the intellectual, so that a proper place is given to the *affective* dimension in our relationship with God and with others. This will restore matters such as prayer and worship to center stage and so provide a means of enriching and balancing theological reflection; it will also put questions of church order into a "more healthy" perspective.[170]

170. http://www.globalchristianforum.org/nairobi; http://au.christiantoday
.com/article/transforming-ecumenism.

This reminds me of the following insight:

But there has been for years, in churches of the Protestant faith, a strong and growing sentiment in favor of a union based upon common points of doctrine. To secure such a union, the discussion of subjects upon which all were not agreed—however important they might be from a Bible standpoint—must necessarily be waived.[171]

Peace to All the World!

A rising chorus sung by scientists, politicians, and academia has been building for many years: *The only way for world peace is world governance. And for many, that road leads through religion.*

A prophet of sorts, H. G. Wells in 1928 voiced thoughts regarding the future of this planet:

The political world of the Open Conspiracy must weaken, efface, incorporate, and supersede existing governments. The Open Conspiracy is the natural inheritor of socialist and communist enthusiasms. . . . The character of the Open Conspiracy will not be plainly displayed. It will be a world religion.[172]

Lord Beaverbrook, an extraordinary Canadian/Britisher famous during the Second World War as Winston Churchill's go-to man for aircraft and war production, said, "World peace requires world order. World order requires world law. World law requires world government."[173]

Winston Churchill, searching through his remarkable war years, wrote:

The creation of an authoritative world order is the ultimate aim toward which we must strive. Unless some effective world Super-Government can be set up and brought quickly into action, the prospects for peace and human progress are dark and doubtful.[174]

Albert Einstein stated:

"Mankind's desire for peace can be realized only by the creation of a world government."[175]

---

171. *The Great Controversy*, 444.

172. *The Open Conspiracy: Blue Prints for a World Revolution* (London: C.A. Watts & Co., Ltd., 1928), chap. 5.

173. Ed Rowe, *New Age Globalism* (Herndon, VA: Virginia Growth Publishing, 1955), 62.

174. Winston Churchill, *Never Give In!* (New York: Hyperion Books, 2003), 443.

175. http://physics.augustana.edu/einstein.html.

Charles Malik, former president of the General Assembly of the United Nations and Ambassador to the United States from Lebanon, once said:

"The only hope for this western world is an alliance between the Roman Catholic church which is the most commonly, influential, controlling, unifying, element, in Europe and the Eastern Orthodox Church. . . . The only hope of the western world lies then in a united Europe under the control of the Pope."[176]

I cite these salient words said about half a century ago simply to emphasize that we are not dealing with some modern conspiracy theory. Those on the inside of the earth's worst hours saw no other real victory over evil—unless there is world peace through world governance. And for some, that peace would rest on a world religion.

When we speak of world governance, we mean that all nations would be united under one flag with one common currency, one common language, one world tax, and a world police force. As Robert Muller, former Assistant Secretary General of the United Nations, said, "We must move as quickly as possible to a one-world government; a one-world religion; under a one-world leader."[177]

The Report of the Secretary General of the General Assembly of the United Nations, in September 2001, included the "road map towards the implementation of the United Nations Millennium Declaration" that was signed by 147 heads of state and government and 189 member states in total.

In Section II, under the heading, "Peace, security and disarmament" the following outline included strengthening the rule of law and taking action against transnational crime: the international community, including the United Nations, will continue to assist states in ratifying treaties, harmonizing their domestic laws with international obligations, widening the jurisdiction of the International Court of Justice and promoting the rapid entry into force of the Rome Statute of the International Criminal Court.[178]

Moving directly into the religious world, on January 2, 2004, the Associated Press reported that Pope John Paul II rang in the New Year with a renewed call for peace in the Middle East and Africa and the creation of a new world order based on respect for the dignity of man and equality among nations.

For many pages in his classic review of Pope John Paul II, Malachi

---

176. Don Hudgens, *Let's Abolish War* (Denver, CO: BILR Corporation, 1986), 60.

177. Malachi Martin, *The Keys of This Blood* (New York: Simon & Schuster, 1990), 491.

178. http://www.arcticbeacon.com/articles/3-Jan-2008.html.

Martin surveyed with great detail the pope's interest in global governance and how it will be achieved. When Mikhail Gorbachev called John Paul II "the world's highest moral authority" on December 1, 1989, in the Vatican, he was simply acknowledging how all world leaders, East and West, see and treat the Pope.[179]

The pope made it clear that "men have no reliable hope of creating a geopolitical system unless it is on the basis of Roman Catholic Christianity: 'One can only regret the deliberate absence of all transcendent moral references,' he told everyone in his January 13, 1990, speech to the international diplomatic corps of Vatican Rome: 'Christ is the strength of Europe and the king of all nations,' he asserted."[180]

I find the opening paragraphs of Malachi Martin's super work on the thinking of Pope John Paul II to be remarkably prescient:

> Willing or not, ready or not, we are all involved in an all-out, no-holds-barred, three-way global competition. Most of us are not competitors, however. We are the stakes. For the competition is about who will establish the first one-world system of government that has ever existed in the society of nations. . . .

> The competition is all-out because, now that it has started, there is no way it can be reversed or called off. . . . As to the time factor involved, those of us who are under seventy will see at least the basic structures of the new world government installed. Those of us under forty will surely live under its legislative, executive and judiciary authority and control . . . not as something around a distant corner of time, but as something that is imminent. As a system that will be introduced and installed in our midst by this final decade of the second millennium.[181]

But the arm of global Rome did not die with the passing of Pope John Paul II. What was deeply in place then was only a platform for Pope Benedict XVI. (After all, it is well-known that Benedict XVI did much for the implementation of John Paul II's thought.)

On cue, on July 4, 2009, Benedict XVI issued his encyclical, *Caritas in Veritate* (Charity in Truth) and on July 7 presented it as a press conference, the day before the G8 (Group of Eight world leaders) summit at L'Aquila, Italy.[182]

Message: Humanity needs a higher moral authority.

---

179. Martin, op. cit., 492.

180. Ibid., 15, 16.

181. Reuters, July 7, 2009; *The Washington Post*, July 5, 2009; *USA Today*, July 13, 2009.

182. http://www.usasurvival.org/docs/Global_Religion.

The pope said that every economic decision has a moral consequence and called for "forms of redistribution of wealth" overseen by governments to help those most affected by crises.

Herein is much for which to congratulate the pope, for emphasizing the message of the book of James (which rebukes the rich of the world in the last days for oppressing and misusing the poor and for their unrestrained, unregulated capitalism). We all need to take our ethics of stewardship past our gifts of tithes and offerings.

But what becomes ominous is his advocacy of a "world political authority to manage the economy. . . . Such an authority would need to be regulated by law, . . . to seek to establish the common good" (Point 67). The "common good" could be expected to include a weekly worship day throughout the world—a thought already in the works.

But the pope is not a mere generalist. He emphasizes that this new "world political authority" would bring all nations into compliance for "the common good":

> Such an authority would need to be universally recognized and to be universal with the effective power to ensure security for all, regard for justice, and respect for rights. Obviously it would have to have the authority to ensure compliance with its decision from all parties (Point 67).[183]

Through it all, I am reminded of how quickly people will give up their freedoms for the illusion of security and the false hope of prosperity through government control.

More later about the call for a world leader who comes with all the promises and solutions to all the great global problems. *The Wall Street Journal* had it right: "Pope Benedict XVI issued a rare papal critique of the global economic crisis, calling for a 'true world political authority.' "[184]

---

183. Ibid.
184. June 8, 2009.

CHAPTER SIX

THEME:

Jesus will return when the whole world will "marvel" and be "of one mind" regarding a universal religious leader.

The Astonishing Appeal of the Pope

And all the world marveled" (Revelation 13:3, NKJV; "wondered," KJV)—they "are of one mind" (Revelation 17:13).

I write this chapter with these ominous, graphic predictions in the book of Revelation hovering over my computer. Each paragraph simply unfolds how these words in the book of Revelation are being fulfilled in our lifetime.

In the previous chapter we looked at the amazing and growing chorus singing the need for and expectation of a "new world order" or "global governance." In this chapter we will look at that same dramatic focus from another camera angle.

This parallel movement found enormous traction in the rise of Pope John Paul II, beginning even before he became the 263rd successor to Peter the Apostle, as our Catholic friends would say it. In the rise of Cardinal Joseph Ratzinger to become Pope Benedict XVI, the same forward thrust of the papacy, begun with Pope John Paul II, continued with flank speed.[185]

In 1976, the Polish archbishop from Krakow, Karol Wojtyla, speaking before a New York City audience, said:

---

185. The fastest speed of which a ship is capable. The term is used exclusively aboard warships to describe an emergency speed.

"We are now standing in the face of the greatest historical confrontation humanity has gone through . . . a test of 2,000 years of culture and Christian civilization, with all of its consequences for human dignity, individual rights, and the rights of nations."

But, he continued, "Wide circles of American society and wide circles of the Christian community do not realize this fully."[186]

Of course, the soon-to-be pope was speaking of the three major global powers—the Soviet Union, under Mikhail Gorbachev; the United States, led by Ronald Reagan; and the most deeply experienced major power, the papacy.[187] Each in their time had the same geopolitical aims; each had a grand design for world governance "that will replace the decaying nation system."[188]

After a few short years, the grand design in the mind of Gorbachev faded, leaving only two world powers to lead the inexorable flow of "the new world order." In this flow, we can see the beginning of the fulfillment of the predictions in Revelation 13–18; now we see more clearly the end game that will usher in the framework for the fulfilling of Revelation 17:13, when the nations of earth, with "one mind," will give their power and authority to the power represented by the "beast." The global power recognized by all as the United States and the global power recognized by all as the papacy will join in common interests, with "one mind."

From the beginning of his pontificate in October 1978, Pope John Paul II astonished the world with his decision to become a decisive factor in determining the New World Order. He did it without press agents or a clever propaganda machine—he did it himself. In his first 12 years, he made 45 papal trips to 91 countries, giving a total of 1,559 speeches in 32 languages, being heard in the flesh or on audio-video hookups by more than 3.5 billion people.[189]

But even more astonishing, Pope John Paul II never went as a casual tourist or a distinguished visitor. Hardly! He was formally received by the host government in a category far above a Billy Graham or Dalai Lama or any other religious leader. To his Vatican home, 120 diplomatic missions were sent by their governments. Every comment on his thoughts

---

186. Malachi Martin, *The Keys of This Blood* (New York: Simon & Schuster, 1990), 16.

187. Ibid., 17. Martin observed that the "final contender in the competition for the new world over is not a single individual leader or a single institution or territory. It is a group of men who are united as one in power, mind and will for the purpose of achieving a single common goal: to be victorious in the competition for the new global hegemony."

188. Ibid., 19.

189. Ibid., 490.

and acts was front-page news. And no government complained or tried to argue with him. No one gave him the right to speak as the authority on all things religious, political, and moral—he simply assumed it.

Always cementing these international relationships, yet, he was always waiting. For what? He had been waiting . . .

. . . for an event that will fission human history, splitting the immediate past from the oncoming future. It will be an event on public view in the skies, in the oceans, and on the continental landmasses of this planet. It will particularly involve our human sun, which every day lights up and shines upon the valleys, the mountains and the plains of this earth for our eyes. But on the day of this event, it will not appear merely as the master star of our so-called solar system. Rather, it will be seen as the circumambient glory of the Woman whom the apostle describes as "clothed with the sun" and giving birth to "a child who will rule the nations with a scepter of iron."[190]

Truly, human vision uniting with biblical forecast!

One of the driving forces in Pope John Paul II's life was that he took the Fatima[191] message personally. He believed that he was designated as God's servant in the divine plan and providence, that he had an unpleasant message and, perhaps, a thankless job. He strongly felt that he had to warn the world of his conviction that human catastrophe on a worldwide scale was impending. However, he knew this would not come without a warning, but that only those with renewed hearts would "recognize it for what it is and make preparations for the tribulations that will follow."[192]

Let's take a quick overview of Pope John Paul II's record since 1978, until he died in 2005:

---

190. Ibid., 639

191. On October 13, 1917, three peasant girls claimed they saw and heard Mary, our Lord's mother, who gave them three messages. The first two messages were soon revealed, but the third was not to be opened until 1960. The first put the church, as well as society in general, on notice that they were heading toward the eternal punishment of hell. The second is understood as a prophecy of World War II and that Russia would spread evil throughout the world and many would suffer and die. The third message, written by the surviving child who became a Carmelite nun in Coimbra, Portugal, was opened by John XXIII, who felt it had no relevancy to his pontificate, so it was returned to its hiding place in the Pope's quarters until Pope John Paul II made it available. The message referred to physical and spiritual chastisement of the nations of the world, including Roman Catholics—all of which may be mitigated by prayers to "Mother Mary."—Ibid., 627–633.

192. Ibid., 637.

▶ June 7, 1982. President Ronald Reagan and Pope John Paul II talked for fifty minutes in the Vatican Library, later called "one of the great secret alliances of all time." Focus of the conversation? The collapse of the Soviet Union and the encouragement of reform movements in Hungary, Czechoslovakia, and the pope's beloved Poland.[193]

▶ 1984. On September 22, 1983, Senator Dan Quayle appealed to the U.S. Senate: "Under the courageous leadership of Pope John Paul II, the Vatican State has assumed its rightful place in the world as an international voice. It is only right that this country show its respect for the Vatican by diplomatically recognizing it as a world state."[194] In the following year, President Reagan appointed the first ambassador to the Vatican (not a personal representative), thereby recognizing for the first time the political significance of the central government of the Roman Catholic Church.[195]

▶ December 1, 1989. Vatican Summit—President Gorbachev and the pope represented two contrasting visions of a "new world order." When Gorbachev addressed John Paul II as "the world's highest moral authority," he recognized that he was not dealing with a "straw man."[196] Gorbachev, several years later, said, "I have carried on an intensive correspondence with Pope John Paul II since we met at the Vatican in December 1989. And I think ours will be an ongoing dialogue. . . . I am certain that the actions undertaken by John Paul II will play an enormous political role now that profound changes have occurred in European history."[197]

▶ 1989. The impending collapse of the Soviet Union was due primarily to the "great secret alliance"; and "the rush to freedom in Eastern Europe is a sweet victory for John Paul II."[198] "While Gorbachev's hands-off policies were the immediate cause of the chain reaction of liberty

---

193. *Time*, February 24, 1992, 28.

194. Pope John Paul II "insists that men have no reliable hope of creating a viable geopolitical system unless it is on the basis of Roman Catholic Christianity."—Martin, op. cit., 492.

195. Thomas P. Melady, *The Ambassador's Story—The United States and the Vatican in World Affairs* (Huntington, IN: Our Sunday Visitor, Inc., 1994), 50.

196. Ibid., 491.

197. *South Bend Tribune*, March 9, 1992, cited in Dwight K. Nelson, *Countdown to the Showdown* (Fallbrook, CA: Hart Research Center, 1992), 40, 41.

198. *Life*, December 1989.

that has swept over Eastern Europe in the past few months, John Paul deserves much of the longer-range credit."[199]

▶ May 1, 1991. Pope John Paul II's *Centesimus Annus* (The Hundredth Year: On the Hundredth Anniversary of *Rerum Novarum*). A remarkable *restatement* of Pope Leo XIII's overview of the rights of workers worldwide and how various government forms deny these rights. Ironically, both popes argue for religious liberty for all, yet call for government recognition of Sunday as the workers' day of rest and worship.[200]

▶ February 24, 1992. Cover story of *Time* magazine: "Holy Alliance— How Reagan and the Pope conspired to assist Poland's Solidarity movement and hasten the demise of Communism: An Investigative Report." Carl Bernstein reported, "Step by reluctant step, the Soviets and the communist government of Poland bowed to the moral, economic, and political presence imposed by the Pope and the President."[201]

▶ Summer, 1993, Colorado Youth Festival. After the pope's visit to Colorado, the Vatican sensed a new opportunity to forge with the United States a plan to exert a "moral authority in world affairs."[202]

▶ January 9, 1994. Israel and the Vatican sign a "fundamental agreement" after forty-five years of troubled relationships. Israeli diplomats say that "the agreement acknowledges the inherent stake of the Catholic Church in the Holy Land; the church is not a guest . . . but part and parcel of the reality of Israel."[203]

▶ March 29, 1994. "Evangelicals and Catholics Together: The Christian Mission in the 3rd Millennium"—a meeting and document that many say reversed five hundred years of church history. To imply that both sides preach the same Christ, understand authority and the "church" the same way, or hold the same understanding of "justification by grace through faith" is a test of credulity, but no matter: Both sides "contend together" to uphold "sanctity of life, family values, parental choice in education, moral standards in society, and democratic institutions worldwide." Further, "We affirm that a common set of core values is found in the teachings of religions, and that these form the basis of a global ethic . . . and which are the conditions for a

199. *Time*, December 4, 1989.
200. http://www.ewtn.com/library/ENCYC/JP2HUNDR.HTM.
201. *Time*, February 24, 1992, 24–35.
202. Alan Cowell in *The New York Times*, August 18, 1993.
203. *National Catholic Register*, January 9 and 16, 1994.

sustainable world order." New phrases such as the church being responsible "for the right ordering of civil society" are more than interesting. Further, they agree that "it is neither theologically legitimate nor a prudent use of resources" to proselytize among active members of another Christian community.[204] As many say, "an historic moment."[205] Indeed!

▸ October 16, 1994. Israel's first ambassador to the Vatican said his meeting with the pope opened a "new epoch of cooperation." The pope expressed his long-standing request for "international guarantees" to protect the "sacred character of Jerusalem," a city sacred to Christians, Muslims, and Jews.[206]

▸ November 10, 1994. In his apostolic letter, *"Tertio Millennio Adventiente"* ("The Coming Third Millennium"), the pope built on the new era opened up by Vatican II—the "profound renewal" that opened up the Catholic Church to other Christians; the focus of each year from 1995 to the Grand Jubilee year of 2000; symbolic journeys to Bethlehem, Jerusalem, and Mount Sinai "as a means of furthering dialogue with Jews and the followers of Islam; and to arranging similar meetings elsewhere with the leaders of the great world religions." The years between 1994 and 2000 were busy indeed, as the pope fulfilled the plans laid out in this letter.[207]

▸ November 13, 1994. In his column, "Why Catholics Are Our Allies," Charles Colson (carrying through the agenda developing for decades) wrote, "Believers on the front lines, battling issues such as abortion, pornography, and threats to religious liberty, find themselves sharing foxholes with conservatives across denominational lines—forging what theologian Timothy George calls 'an ecumenism of the trenches.' . . . The great divides within Christendom no longer fall along denominational lines but between conservatives and liberals *within* denominations. . . . Let's be certain that we are firing our polemical rifles against the enemy, not against those fighting in the trenches alongside

204. Full text of the document in Clifford Goldstein, *One Nation Under God?* (Boise, ID: Pacific Press® Publishing Association, 1996), 143–160. See "Catholics and Evangelicals in the Trenches," *Christianity Today,* May 16, 1994; J. I. Packer, "Why I Signed It," ibid., December 12, 1994.

205. John White, former president of the National Association of Evangelicals, *USA Today,* March 30, 1994. On March 29, 1994, *The Oregonian* summarized an Associated Press story with subtitle "Catholic and evangelical leaders vow to join in a common bond to work toward shared values."

206. *National Catholic Register,* October 16, 1994.

207. *National Catholic Register,* December 11, 1994.

us in defense of the Truth." [208]

▶ January 2, 1995. *Time*—"John Paul II, Man of the Year." "People who see him—and countless millions have—do not forget him. His appearances generate electricity unmatched by anyone else on earth. . . . When he talks, it is not only to his flock of nearly a billion; he expects the world to listen. . . . In a year when so many people lamented the decline in moral values or made excuses for bad behavior, Pope John Paul II forcefully set forth his vision of the good life and urged the world to follow it. . . . John Paul's impact on the world has already been enormous, ranging from the global to the personal. . . . With increased urgency . . . John Paul presented himself, the defender of Roman Catholic doctrine, as a moral compass for believers and nonbelievers alike. . . . Billy Graham said, 'He's been the strong conscience of the whole Christian world.' " [209]

▶ January 21, 1995. In Colombo, Sri Lanka, "Pope John Paul II ended an exhausting Asian tour with a call for the world's great religions to unite on behalf of shared moral values." [210]

▶ May 30, 1995. The papal encyclical *"Ut Unum Sin"* ("That They May Be One"), laid out, unambiguously, a powerful strategy for church unity; on one front, to develop a non-confrontational relationship with Islam; on the other, to achieve unity throughout the Christian world. This document committed the Roman Catholic Church to full communion with the Eastern Orthodox Church, stressing that unity is more important than jurisdiction. And to the Protestant churches, he reminded them that the "Petrine ministry" belongs to all Christians, whether they recognize it or not. [211]

▶ October 7, 1995. When Pope John Paul II presided at a Mass in New

---

208. *Christianity Today*, November 14, 1994. One of the books I read in my early ministry was Paul Blanchard's *American Freedom and Catholic Power* (Boston: The Beacon Press, 1949). In this breathtaking book, written long before others were writing with such precision, he revealed the strategy of how the Catholic Church would eventually dominate the politics of the United States. How would they do this? The church would turn the eyes of conservative Protestant America toward common values such as birth control, abortion, family values, and control of education. In that same year, America saw a very effective advertising campaign sponsored by the Knights of Columbus to remove misconceptions about Rome.—*EndTime Issues*, September 1999.

209. *Time* magazine, December 26, 1994 / January 2, 1995, 53, 54.

210. *The Orlando Sentinel*, January 22, 1995.

211. http://www.vatican.va/holy_father/John_Paul_II/encyclicals/document. Richard John Neuhaus, *The Wall Street Journal*, July 6, 1995.

York's Central Park, an estimated 125,000 people turned out to see not only the leader of the world's largest Christian church but also an ecumenical procession of Protestant, Orthodox, and other non–Catholic religious leaders, including "political power broker Pat Robertson at the head of the line." After the Mass and an intimate visit with the pope, Robertson "insisted that a new day is dawning in the relationship between conservative Protestants and traditional Roman Catholics."[212]

▸ July 7, 1998. *"Dies Domini"* ("Lord's Day"). From the first sentence, the pope focused on "the Lord's Day—as Sunday was called from Apostolic times." The entire document is amazing in subtle mal-exegesis, but very persuasive to the surface reader. Outlined in 87 sections, note the following: "62. It is the duty of Christians therefore to remember that, although the practices of the Jewish Sabbath are gone, surpassed as they are by the 'fulfillment' which Sunday brings, the underlying reasons for keeping 'the Lord's Day' holy—inscribed solemnly in the Ten Commandments—remain valid, though they need to be reinterpreted in the light of the theology and spirituality of Sunday. . . . 66. . . . My predecessor Pope Leo XIII in his Encyclical *Rerum Novarum* spoke of Sunday rest as a worker's right which the State must guarantee. . . . 67. . . . Therefore, also in the particular circumstances of our own time, Christians will naturally strive to ensure that civil legislations respect their duty to keep Sunday holy."[213]

▸ October 27, 28, 1998. Archbishop Lean–Louis Tauran said that Jerusalem "has long been at the center of the Holy See's concerns and one of its top priorities for international action. . . . The Holy See believes in the importance of extending representation at the negotiating table in order to be sure that no aspect of the problem is overlooked."[214]

▸ October 30, 1998. A nine-page document signed by Cardinal Ratzinger (Pope Benedict XVI, since 2005) emphasized that popes alone can determine the limits of those at the negotiating table (see above). Publicly, Ratzinger said, "It is clear that only the pope . . . as successor of Peter, has the authority and the competence to speak the last word on the means of exercising the pastoral ministry of the universal truth." "The papacy," he said, "is not an office of the presidency . . . and cannot be conceived of as a type of political monarchy."[215]

212. Joseph L. Conn, "Papal Blessing?" *Church and State*, November, 1995.

213. http://www.vatican.va/holly_father/john_paul_IIapostolic_letters/ enframe28_en.htm.

214. http://www.vatican.va.

215. Associated Press, October 10, 1998, 1:12 P.M.

▶ May 12, 1999. The Anglican-Roman Catholic International Commission (eighteen Anglican and Roman Catholic members), continuing a dialogue that began in 1981, published an agreed statement with amazing convergences, such as, "62. An experience of universal primacy of this kind would confirm two particular conclusions we have reached: (1) that Anglicans be open to and desire a recovery and re-reception under certain clear conditions of the exercise of universal primacy by the Bishop of Rome; and (2) that Roman Catholics be open to and desire a re-reception of the exercise of primacy by the Bishop of Rome and the offering of such a ministry to the whole Church of God."[216]

▶ September 1, 1999; March 8, 12, 23, 2000. Pope apologizes for "its past mistakes . . . and to ask pardon for the historical offenses of its sons [sic]. . . . The wounds of the past, for which both sides share the guilt, continue to be a scandal for the world." Auxiliary Archbishop Rino Fisichella of Rome said of the March 12 meeting in St. Peter's: "Pope John Paul II wanted to give a complete global vision, making references to circumstances of the past, but without focusing on details out of respect for history. . . . The Church is not the one who has sinned, the sinners are Christians, and they have done so against the Church, the bride of Christ."[217]

▶ October 31, 1999. In the spring of 2000, my wife and I visited Augsburg, Germany, with one purpose—to visit the Reformation Church in which the Confession of the Princes was presented to Charles V

---

216. http://www.ewtn.corn/liberty/theology/arcicgh1. John Wilkins, editor of *The Tablet*, commented: "This 'Gift of Authority' now joins the other documents developed by this conference as an agenda in waiting. The commission's work is like a deposit in a bank. Its value will be evident when the time comes for it to be withdrawn for us." http://www.natcath.com/NCR_Online archives. Dr. George Carey, Archbishop of Canterbury said, "In a world torn apart by violence and division, Christians need urgently to be able to speak with a common voice, confident of the authority of the gospel of peace."—Oliver Poole, "Churches Agree Pope Has Overall Authority," BBC News, May 13. http://www.antipas.org/magazine/articles, churches_agree_people.

217. ZENIT,—*Rome*, March 12, 13, 2000. "John Paul has one foot in the dimension of history (where mess, error, violence, fanaticism, and stupidity flourish merrily) and the other in the dimension of eternity (where he must insist the holiness and infallibility of the church as the mystical body of Christ remain intact). It is awkward: How does infallibility own up to its fallibilities and yet remain infallible? The Pope's solution: by being vague about the actual sins and by attributing them, in any case, to men and women who are Catholics and not to the Catholic Church itself."—Lance Morrow, "Is It Enough to Be Sorry?" *Time*, March 27, 2000.

in 1530. D'Aubigné wrote that "this was destined to be the greatest day of the Reformation, and one of the most glorious in the history of Christianity and of mankind. . . . The Confession of Augsburg will ever remain one of the masterpieces of the human mind enlightened by the Spirit of God."[218] But on October 31, 1999, in that very church, 482 years to the day after Martin Luther had nailed those ninety-five theses to the door of the village church in Wittenberg, the Lutheran World Federation (not including all branches of the Lutheran Church, such as the Missouri Synod) signed with the Roman Catholics the Joint Declaration on the Doctrine of Justification, after thirty years of consultation. Goose pimples, up and down my spine!

What is so amazing is that four hundred years before, Protestants and Catholics were in profound disagreement over the doctrine of justification, leading to vicious, deadly consequences. Just one more example of how diminished the clarity of truth is today and how much "relationship" and "unity" have emerged as the most important issues for so many leading voices in modern Christianity.[219] All these thoughts blew through my mind as I sat solemnly in those same pews, where stalwart princes once put their lives on the line and where, 482 years later, "princes of the church" voted in the fog of their lost precision of thought.

▶ November 7, 1999. In New Delhi, India, Pope John Paul II, recognizing Catholicism's minority status in India, said that "no state, no group has the right to control either directly or indirectly a person's religious convictions . . . or the respectful appeal of a particular religion to people's free conscience."[220]

▶ July 27, 2000. Congressional Gold Medal (U.S.A.): "To authorize a gold medal to be awarded on behalf of the Congress to Pope John Paul II in recognition of his many and enduring contributions to peace and religious understanding, and for other purposes. . . . The Congress finds that Pope John Paul II . . . is recognized in the United States and abroad as a preeminent moral authority; has dedicated his Pontificate to the freedom and dignity of every individual human being and tirelessly traveled to the far reaches of the globe as an exemplar of faith; has brought hope to millions of people all over the world oppressed by poverty, hunger, illness, and despair; transcending temporal politics,

---

218. J. H. Merle D'Aubigné, *History of the Reformation of the Sixteenth Century* (New York: Robert Carter and Brothers, 1875), bk. 14, chap. 7, 563, 566.

219. *Christianity Today*, October 25, 1999; http://www.tcsn.net/fbchurch/fb/cdecia.htm.

220. Associated Press, November 8, 1999.

has used his moral authority to hasten the fall of godless totalitarian regimes, symbolized in the collapse of the Berlin wall; has promoted the inner peace of man as well as peace among mankind through his faith-inspired defense of justice; and has thrown open the doors of the Catholic Church, reconciling differences within Christendom as well as reaching out to the world's great religions."[221]

▶ June 5, 2000. President Putin asks Pope John Paul II for "help in gaining Russia's political and military integration in Europe." Putin called his stop "a very significant visit."[222]

▶ September 5, 2000. *Dominus Jesus:* A thirty-six-page update from the Congregation for the Doctrine of the Faith, it *rejects* in unambiguous terms the notion that "one religion is as good as another," that the Catholic Church is "complementary" to other religions, and that Protestants, for example, are "Churches in the proper sense."[223]

▶ October 2000. Queen Elizabeth II, head of the church and state of England, visited Pope John Paul II and was "pleased to note the important progress that has been made in overcoming historic differences between Anglicans and Roman Catholics—as exemplified in particular by the meeting of Anglicans and Roman Catholics in Canada this year. I trust that we shall continue to advance along the path which leads to Christian unity."[224]

▶ January 6, 2001. The pope's Apostolic Letter, "At the Beginning of the New Millennium," among other directives, emphasized the importance of Sunday as "a special day of faith, the day of the Risen Lord and of the gift of the Spirit, the true weekly Easter. . . . We do not know what the new millennium has in store for us, but we are certain that it is safe in the hands of Christ, the 'King of kings and Lord of lords' (Rev. 19:16); and precisely by celebrating his Passover not just once a year but every Sunday, the Church will continue to show to every generation 'the true fulcrum of history, to which the mystery of the world's origin and its final destiny leads.' "[225]

▶ January 31, 2001. President George W. Bush told twenty-five Catholic leaders that his interest was to "draw on Catholic wisdom and

---

221. http://www.feds.com/basic_svc/public_law/106-175.htm.

222. CNN.com. June 5, 2000.

223. Catholic World News—Vatican Updates—09/05/2000; *Christianity Today,* September 11, 2000.

224. http://www.britain.it/royalvisit/3e.hdtm.

225. http://www.vatican.va/holy_father/John_Paul_it/apost_letters/ documents.

experience . . . . I think you are seeing a historic and ground-breaking moment in the participation of Catholics in public life." Archbishop Caput, present for the dialogue, said Catholic social teaching is based on two pillars: dignity of the individual and commitment to the common good. Bush has often referred to the "common good" as an important administrative goal.[226]

▶ March 22, 2001. Washington, D.C.'s Pope John Paul II Cultural Center opened; first it was proposed for Krakow, Warsaw, or Rome, but the pope chose Washington, D.C., which he described as "the crossroads of the world."[227] "Cardinal Maida said there was no illusion that putting the center in Washington would precipitate an immediate change in the thinking of presidents, Supreme Court Justices, Members of Congress or other officials. . . . But as we tell the story better, people will be affected by osmosis."[228]

▶ May 2001. The pope, the first Catholic leader to enter the Umayyad Mosque in the Syrian capital of Damascus, participated in an organized prayer service. For Muslims, it is the oldest stone mosque in the world, while for Christians, it is the alleged place where John the Baptist was buried. The pope led in Christian prayers, while his Muslim counterpart, Sheikh Ahmed Kataro, led in Muslim prayers. By this dramatic act of worshiping in a mosque, the pope underlined his commitment to work toward a rapprochement with the Muslims.

▶ September 2001. The pope, in Almaty, Kazakhstan, twelve days after the horrors of September 11, renewed his commitment to work toward a new partnership with Muslims, in his message to the predominantly Muslim nation of Kazakhstan. The pope declared, " 'There is one God.' The Apostle proclaims before all else the absolute oneness of God. This is a truth which Christians inherited from the children of Israel and which they share with Muslims: it is faith in the one God, 'Lord of heaven and earth' (Luke 10:21), almighty and merciful. In the name of this one God, I turn to the people of deep and ancient religious traditions, the people of Kazakhstan." [229]

The pope then appealed to both Muslims and Christians to work together to build a "civilization of love": "This 'logic of love' is what he

226. "Bush Meets With Catholics on Faith-based Initiatives," *National Catholic Register,* February 11–17, 2001.
227. Pat McCloskey, "Washington's New Pope John Paul II Cultural Center," *St. Anthony Messenger,* April 2001.
228. *The National Catholic Register,* October 26–November 1, 1997.
229. http://www.vatican.va/holy_father/john_paul_ii/homilies/2001/ documents/hf_jpii_hom_20010923_kazakhstan_astana_en.html.

[Jesus] holds out to us, asking us to live it above all through generosity to those in need. It is a logic that can bring together Christians and Muslims, and commit them to work together for the 'civilization of love.' It is a logic which overcomes all the cunning of this world and allows us to make true friends who will welcome us 'into the eternal dwelling-places' (Luke 16:9), into the 'homeland' of heaven."

▶ January 24, 2002. In Assisi, Italy, the pope and more than one hundred religious leaders from around the world, including Orthodox patriarchs, Jewish rabbis, grand muftis, sheikhs and other Muslim representatives, Buddhists and Shinto monks, Hindu leaders, Zoroastrians (whose adherents are mostly in India and Iran), leaders of traditional African religions, Protestant leaders, and twenty-five Roman Catholic cardinals and approximately thirty bishops shared in a day pursuing "authentic peace." Ending the day, the pope lit a symbolic lamp of peace with the words: "Violence never again! War never again! Terrorism never again! In God's name, may all religions bring upon earth justice and peace, forgiveness, life and love."[230]

▶ October 16, 2003. In celebrating Pope John Paul II's twenty-five years as leader of the Roman Catholic Church, Tracy Wilkinson of the *Los Angeles Times* wrote, "This planet now is a very different place [compared to October 16, 1978], and John Paul II . . . has had a hand in shaping events to a degree unrivaled by any other religious figure in modern history. His election on Oct. 16, 1978 'was itself a breaker of precedents,' the Jesuit magazine *America* said in an editorial this month, 'and ever since his election John Paul II's pontificate has been setting records that none of his predecessors could have imagined.' "[231]

▶ April 2, 2005. Pope John Paul II died, after holding "the chair of St. Peter" for twenty-six years. He had appeared on the cover of *Time* magazine more than any other person, ever—sixteen times. President George W. Bush and his wife, Laura, made the following statement (in part): "Laura and I join people across the earth in mourning the passing of Pope John Paul II. The Catholic Church has lost its shepherd, the world has lost a champion of human freedom, and a good and faithful servant of God has been called home."

President Bush then issued an executive order that the flag of the United States, "as a mark of respect for His Holiness, Pope John Paul II," shall be flown at half-mast on all federal government buildings throughout the United States and its territories until sunset of his interment. This order

230. *Christian Science Monitor,* January 24, 2002; "Pope Hosts Ecumenical Assembly for Peace at Assisi," *Inq7.net*, January 24, 2002.

231. *The Sacramento Bee,* October 16, 2003.

included all United States embassies and other facilities abroad, as well as all naval vessels.

At the pope's funeral, three U.S. presidents knelt for about five minutes in front of a pope's casket, heads bowed. More than one hundred official delegations also attended, including four kings, five queens, and more than seventy prime ministers. More than seven hundred thousand people rubbed shoulders in St. Peter's during the three-hour ceremony. On the streets of Rome, an estimated four million pilgrims watched the funeral on large screens. Around the world, it was estimated that more than two billion people watched the funeral in stadiums, churches, and private homes. This was the largest funeral in the history of the world! And analysts say that it was the largest gathering of world leaders ever!

This remarkable gathering was a rare display of religious plurality and diversity, including red-capped Catholic cardinals, black-clad Orthodox priests, Arab head scarves, Jewish skull caps, Central Asian lambskin hats, and black veils worn by some women.

And now Pope Benedict XVI, Pope John Paul's most trusted companion, will continue with even sharper voice the strongest statements regarding the importance of Sunday throughout the world. Largely understood is that the new pope was most probably the writer, or at least the key resource, for much of the heavy literary productions of Pope John Paul II.[232]

In his Christmas message to the world, December 25, 2005, Pope Benedict XVI called for a new world order. He said, "The life-giving power of his [Christ's] light is an incentive for building a *new world order* based on just, ethical and economic relationships."[233]

The drum roll didn't miss a beat!

The new pontiff argues a concept that Hindus, Buddhists, Muslims, and Christians will have difficulty rejecting: The Catholic church is primarily concerned with "ethical and economic relationships"—those universal moral values based in the nature of man—and the church will control the meaning of "universal" and "moral." This meaning is wrapped up in how the church defines "natural law." Finding agreement first in "natural law" (which seems easy today), it is only a half step to Sunday as a day of rest for all in the world—in the interest of the "inalienable rights" of all mankind.

---

232. Pope Benedict XVI, handpicked by the previous pope in many ways, was "God's Rottweiler," "The Grand Inquisitor," "Cardinal 'No,'" "John Paul's Doctrinal Enforcer," "The Panzer Kardinal."—*The Australian*, April 21. *Time*, April 18, added, "Vatican Rasputin." On May 2, 2005, *Time* quoted the *London Mirror*, "Papa Ratzi."

233. ZENIT, December 25, 2005. http://www.zenit.org/article-14918?l=english.

Speaking early in his term to a group of Polish bishops, Pope Benedict XVI built his case and then said, "It is very important, especially where a pluralistic society prevails, that there be a correct notion of the relationship between the political community and the Church and a clear distinction between the tasks which Christians undertake, individually or as a group, on their own responsibility as citizens guided by the dictates of a Christian conscience, and the activities which, in union with their pastors, they carry out in the name of the Church."[234] Fascinating comment, especially when six Catholic judges (of the total nine justices) are now on the Supreme Court of the United States!

In other words, when the pope exercises his moral authority, no objective standard outside the church will be allowed, from this point forward, to determine what is right and wrong. Catholic politicians, the pope argues, "must take action against any form of injustice and tyranny, against domination by an individual or a political party and any intolerance."[235]

A *Time* writer observed:

> In the Catholic triad of how we know truth—an eternal dialogue between papal authority, scriptural guidance and the experience of the faithful—Benedict XVI has tilted the balance decisively back toward his own unanswerable truth. . . . For Benedict, if your conscience tells you something is wrong that differs from his teaching, it is a false conscience, a sign not of personal integrity but of sin.[236]

When the church determines "the nature of the injustice, the tyranny, and the intolerance, no persons or group of persons will be able to assert the claims of the Bible, for instance, as a defense against the claims of the Church." Thus, in the United States, "no appeal to a Constitution" will be powerful enough to hold back the encroachments of the church. Every person in the world will be at the mercy of Rome. There will be no earthly power to stop her.[237]

The Ecumenical Pope

Pope Benedict XVI announced in his first sermon (April 20, 2005) that he has a primary commitment to work without sparing energies for the reconstitution of the full and visible unity of all the followers of Christ. In his first official address, Benedict declared:

"I will work with all my power to arrange the full and visible unity

---

234. ZENIT, December 18, 2005. Cited in Marcus Sheffield, http://www .adventcry.org/archive/2005/12-25-2005.html.

235. Ibid.

236. *Time*, October 9, 2006, 40, 41.

237. Marcus Sheffield, op. cit.

of all those who follow Christ. I know that good will is not enough. Concrete measures must be undertaken. All I can do I will do to forward the fundamental basis of ecumenism. I will exert every effort that might be helpful to achieve an agreement with the leaders of other churches. I speak to all those who follow other religions or who are searching for an answer to the questions of life and have not found them yet."[238]

Later that day, he sent a letter to the chief rabbi of Rome, promising "to continue the dialogue and strengthen the collaboration" with the Jews. At his April 24 "inauguration Mass," Protestant heretics and Orthodox schematics had places of honor next to (nominally) Catholic bishops.[239]

Many were surprised at the Vatican announcement to resume talks with the Anglican Church. The talks were suspended in 2003 after the Episcopal Church in the United States (a part of the world Anglican Church) allowed the consecration of an openly gay bishop. John Paul II warned that this would create difficulties. But obviously, Pope Benedict XVI was willing to put such differences aside in the interest of unification of the two churches.

His talks with the Archbishop of Canterbury at the Lambeth Palace, London, on September 17, 2010, surely strengthened the linkage. The pope said in his remarks:

"For us Christians this opens up the possibility of exploring, together with members of other religious traditions, ways of bearing witness to the transcendent dimension of the human person and the universal call to holiness, leading to the practice of virtue in our personal and social lives. Ecumenical cooperation in this task remains essential, and will surely bear fruit in promoting peace and harmony in a world that so often seems at risk of fragmentation."[240]

Many theologians, Catholic as well as others, believe the shifts under Pope Benedict XVI aren't simply a small matter of rules, clarifications, or a tidying up of doctrine—the meaning of the kingdom of heaven, for example. The emphasis after Vatican II was on experiencing the kingdom of God on earth and not simply in the afterlife. This focus used such concepts as "becoming," "change," and "social justice."[241]

238. http://www.thinkinganglicans.org.uk/archives/001120.html. (I note that this sermon has been translated several ways.)

239. "Benedict XVI's Ecumenical One-World Church," *Traditionalmass.org.* April 24, 2005.

240. *Catholic Exchange,* April 18, 2010.

241. *The Christian Science Monitor,* July 18, 2007.

In a larger sense, Pope Benedict XVI is rolling back these concepts, separating them, emphasizing that Christ's kingdom can't be experienced here. He wants everyone to focus on uniting the world, as we all prepare for heaven after death.

A prominent Protestant spokesman, Timothy George, noted Benedict XVI's passion for the unity of all Christians and why the issue has never been more important (in the pope's own words):

"We saw that the confessional controversies we had previously engaged in were small indeed in the face of the challenge we now confronted, together, to bear witness to our common faith in the living God and in Christ, the incarnate Word."[242]

In other words, the issue today is not to confront each other theologically but to join with each other in combating social concerns such as pornography, disease, abortion, crime, sexual deviation, etc. The success of the Vatican in softening the anti-Catholic teachings and prophetic interpretations of Protestant churches can be seen in the evangelical acceptance of Roman Catholicism as a legitimate Christian religion. Noting again Timothy George, he said that "Roman Catholicism is not a cult, and the pope is not Antichrist."[243] Apparently, Protestants are not protesting anymore against the fundamental heresies embedded in Roman Catholicism.[244]

After saying all this, we must recognize a certain core truth that is firmly embedded in Pope Benedict XVI's mind. On September 5, 2000, then Cardinal Ratzinger, Prefect of the Congregation for the Doctrine of the Faith, released a document, *Dominus Iesus* ("Lord Jesus"), that he composed.[245] Why did he do so?

In this Vatican Declaration, salvation is to be found in and through the unique, universal Roman Catholic Church! In essence, Vatican conservatives like Ratzinger (at that time) believed Vatican II had gone too far: Earlier terminology calling non-Catholic churches "sister churches" was really meant to be understood as children of the "mother" of all other churches. In other words, all other religions are not equally valid ways of salvation. Protestant churches are not to be called "churches" but "ecclesial communities." Right! Rome never changes![246]

---

242. *Christianity Today*, June 2008, 49–52.

243. Ibid.

244. Samuele Bacchiocchi, "Benedict XVI: The Man and His Mission," June 26, 2005.

245. http://www.vatican.va/.../rc_con_cfaith_doc_20000806_dominus-iesus_en.html.

246. "Rome never changes. She claims infallibility. It is Protestantism that will change. The adoption of liberal ideas on its part will bring it where it can clasp the hand of Catholicism." Ellen G. White, *Last Day Events*, 130.

However, one must be discerning when quoting the popes! Watch their language closely. Pope Benedict XVI, addressing a group of foreign ambassadors on May 18, 2006, said:

"Peace is rooted in respect for religious freedom. . . . It is important that throughout the world all people can adhere to the religion of their choice and practice it freely and without fear, because no one can base his existence only on the search for material well-being."[247]

Think that through!

Further, Pope Benedict appeals to many Bible-oriented Protestants: he will not become prey to a modern "dictatorship of relativism which does not recognize anything as for certain and which has as its highest goal one's own ego and one's own desires."[248] Thus, he will find a new respect and eventual allegiance from Protestants who applaud this leadership in putting the searchlight on the emptiness of "relativism."

Revival of Sunday Observance

One of the pope's strategies to combat "moral relativism" is to revive liturgical practices, especially the Sunday Eucharistic celebration.

At a mass in Vienna, September 9, 2007, Pope Benedict XVI said, "Without Sunday [worship] we cannot live!" "Give the soul its Sunday, give Sunday its soul," he chanted before a rain-soaked crowd of 40,000. He further stated that Sunday had its origin "as the day of the dawning of creation—the church's weekly feast of creation."[249]

World Respect

On April 13, 2008, before the arrival of Pope Benedict XVI at Andrews Air Force Base in Washington, D.C., President Bush was interviewed by a reporter for the Eternal World Television Network (EWTN), a Catholic television network. His remarks seemed prophetic.

The reporter wrote, "The president explained the reasons he would meet Pope Benedict's airplane upon its arrival at Andrews, saying that this unprecedented greeting was due to the particular significance of the pope.

"One, he speaks for millions," said Bush. "Two, he doesn't come as a politician; he comes as a man of faith; and three, I so subscribe to his notion that there's right and wrong in life, that moral relativism undermines the capacity to have hopeful and free societies. I want to honor his convictions as well."

---

247. http://www.catholicnews.com/data/stories/cns/0602889.htm.

248. http://www.ewtn.com/pope/words/conclave.

249. TheTrumpet.com, September 17, 2007.

President Bush said that Pope Benedict's words provided support for politicians in difficult situations.

Then the interviewer asked President Bush what he saw when he looked into the eyes of the pope and the president replied, "God."

On Sunday, October 17, 2010, Kevin Rudd, Australia's Foreign Minister, officially opened the first permanent Chancery of the Australian Embassy to the Holy See (Vatican State). Rudd said:

"It's a good day for our relationship with the Holy See. It is a day which we should celebrate. . . . It reflects first and foremost our mark of respect and high regard to the role of the Catholic Church in Australia."[250]

Rehabilitating Martin Luther!

More than interesting are the reports that Pope Benedict XVI is to rehabilitate Martin Luther, arguing that he did not intend to split Christianity but only to purge the church of corrupt practices. According to Vatican insiders, the pope will argue that Luther, who was excommunicated and condemned for heresy, was not a heretic.

Cardinal Walter Kasper, the head of the Pontifical Council for Promoting Christian Unity, said the move would help to promote ecumenical dialogue between Catholics and Protestants. It is also designed to counteract the impact of July's [2008] papal statement describing the Protestant and Orthodox faiths as defective and "not proper Churches."

Cardinal Kasper said, "We have much to learn from Luther, beginning with the importance he attached to the word of God." It was time for a "more positive" view of Luther, whose reforms had aroused papal ire at the time but could now be seen as having "anticipated aspects of reform which the Church has adopted over time."

Luther challenged the authority of the papacy by holding the Bible as the sole source of religious authority, making it accessible to ordinary people by translating it into the vernacular. Some theologians argue that Luther did not intend to confront the papacy "in a doctrinaire way" but only to raise legitimate questions—a view Pope Benedict XVI apparently shares.[251]

Surely, a new wind is blowing!

These following, prescient words take on new solemnity today—as if they were written yesterday:

This is the religion which Protestants are beginning to look upon

250. http://news.theage.com.au/breaking-news-world/rudd-opens-aust-em-bassy-to-holy-see-20101017-16o10.html.

251. *The Sunday Times*, March 6, 2008.

with so much favor, and which will eventually be united with Protestantism. This union will not, however, be effected by a change in Catholicism, for Rome never changes. She claims infallibility. It is Protestantism that will change. The adoption of liberal ideas on its part will bring it where it can clasp the hand of Catholicism. . . . The professed Protestant world will form a confederacy with the man of sin, and the church and the world will be in corrupt harmony.[252]

"And all the world marveled" (Revelation 13:3, NKJV; "wondered," KJV)—they "are of one mind" (Revelation 17:13).

---

252. Ellen G. White, *Last Day Events*, 130.

CHAPTER SEVEN

THEME:
> Jesus will return when the United States has enabled the formation of a universal unity, not only of doctrine, but also of practice.

United States—the Great Enabler

We have been reviewing the almost breathtaking role that the United States has played in world affairs—economically and militarily. It took on this role, not because it wanted to, but because of its remarkable assets, best wrapped up in its signal message of freedom.

But all this global influence is not a big surprise! What if everyone realized that the unsurpassed development of the United States in the New World, beginning in the seventeenth century, was foreseen in the Bible?

For more than 155 years, Adventist scholars have understood that the study of Revelation 13:11–17 focused on the development and last-day significance of the United States of America.

Of course, more than a century ago, such a line of thought, to most, seemed preposterous. But it launched a concept and worldview that has become more relevant today than ever. That the fledgling United States, then barely seventy-five years old, would become a world superpower—well, nothing could have seemed more unimaginable!

John N. Andrews was the first in a long line to spell out the future of the United States. Following his review of history and of how major world powers had been predicted in the book of Daniel, Andrews noted that the world empires were "ever tending westward" and that, following this trend, "we still look westward for the rise of the power described in this prophecy [Revelation 13:11–17]."[253]

Young Andrews did his homework, reflecting his thoughts in his magazine article: "In the west an opposing and still more wonderful American empire is E M E R G I N G." In many pages of his 1851 article, Andrews noted the biblical features of this young country that he saw symbolized by the beast with lamblike horns. For him, these two horns denoted the "civil and religious power of this nation—its Republican civil power, and its Protestant ecclesiastical power."

Later, he continued, "It is of itself a wonder, a system of government which has not its like elsewhere. . . . The two-horned beast is from the time of its rise a power contemporary with the first beast [papacy], and not the first beast in another form."

Andrews went on to connect the coming showdown between seventh-day Sabbath keepers and those enforcing the "the mark of the beast" through the powers of the two-horned beast, the United States.

Far-Fetched and Delusional?

This is heady stuff! For those living in the 1850s, this kind of thinking indeed seemed far-fetched and delusional. Think about it—the population of this young country was less than twenty-four million. California, our thirty-first state, was admitted to the Union only the year before Andrews penned his article. In 1850, a one hundred-acre wheat field remained the largest any one man could farm. That year, the first Singer sewing machine was patented. Kerosene and the safety elevator had not yet been invented; a railroad from the East had not yet reached Chicago, and oil had not yet been discovered. Compulsory school attendance was not yet law. And to think that this mostly agricultural expanse would become a world superpower defied credibility!

Why was Andrews so positive about declaring the United States to be the "two-horned" beast of Revelation 13? Obviously, not because of what he read in the newspapers! Young John was reading his Bible! He might also have had access to historical records that had linked the papacy with the first beast of Revelation 13 for several centuries[254] and the United States with the "two-horned" beast.[255]

Now we can understand the validity of another prescient comment written in 1888 regarding the role of the United States, as time moved on and as the end time galloped into the present:

---

253. *Review and Herald*, May 1851.

254. See LeRoy E. Froom, *The Prophetic Faith of Our Fathers* (Washington, D.C.: Review and Herald® Publishing Association, 1948), vol. 4, 1091.

255. Ibid., 1099.

Since the middle of the nineteenth century, students of prophecy in the United States have presented this testimony to the world. In the events now taking place is seen a rapid advance toward the fulfillment of the prediction. With Protestant teachers there is the same claim of divine authority for Sundaykeeping, and the same lack of scriptural evidence, as with the papal leaders who fabricated miracles to supply the place of a command from God. The assertion that God's judgments are visited upon men for their violation of the Sunday-sabbath, will be repeated; already it is beginning to be urged. And a movement to enforce Sunday observance is fast gaining ground.[256]

Solemn Days Ahead

But with prophetic insight, Ellen White saw more—ominously more:

When Protestantism shall stretch her hand across the gulf to grasp the hand of the Roman power, when she shall reach over the abyss to clasp hands with spiritualism, when, under the influence of this threefold union, our country shall repudiate every principle of its Constitution as a Protestant and republican government, and shall make provision for the propagation of papal falsehoods and delusions, then we may know that the time has come for the marvelous working of Satan and that the end is near.[257]

When the leading churches of the United States, uniting upon such points of doctrine as are held by them in common, shall influence the state to enforce their decrees and to sustain their institutions, then Protestant America will have formed an image of the Roman hierarchy, and the infliction of civil penalties upon dissenters will inevitably result.[258]

The Protestants of the United States will be foremost in stretching their hands across the gulf to grasp the hand of spiritualism; they will reach over the abyss to clasp hands with the Roman power; and under the influence of this threefold union, this country will follow in the steps of Rome in trampling on the rights of conscience.[259]

The beast with two horns is also to say "to them that dwell on the earth, that they should make an image to the beast"; and, furthermore, it is to command all, "both small and great, rich and poor, free

256. Ellen G. White, *The Great Controversy,* 579 (1911).
257. Ellen G. White, *Testimonies for the Church,* vol. 5, 451 (1885).
258. White, *The Great Controversy,* 445.
259. Ibid., 588.

and bond" to receive the mark of the beast (Revelation 13:11–16). It has been shown that the United States is the power represented by the beast with lamblike horns, and that this prophecy will be fulfilled when the United States shall enforce Sunday observance, which Rome claims as the special acknowledgment of her supremacy.[260]

Political corruption is destroying love of justice and regard for truth; and even in free America, rulers and legislators, in order to secure public favor, will yield to the popular demand for a law enforcing Sunday observance. Liberty of conscience, which has cost so great a sacrifice, will no longer be respected. In the soon-coming conflict we shall see exemplified the prophet's words: "The dragon was wroth with the woman, and went to make war with the remnant of her seed, which keep the commandments of God, and have the testimony of Jesus Christ" (Revelation 12:17).[261]

A time is coming when the law of God is, in a special sense, to be made void in our land. The rulers of our nation will, by legislative enactments, enforce the Sunday law, and thus God's people be brought into great peril. When our nation, in its legislative councils, shall enact laws to bind the consciences of men in regard to their religious privileges, enforcing Sunday observance, and bringing oppressive power to bear against those who keep the seventh-day Sabbath, the law of God will, to all intents and purposes, be made void in our land; and "national apostasy" will be followed by national ruin.[262]

The people of the United States have been a favored people; but when they restrict religious liberty, surrender Protestantism, and give countenance to popery, the measure of their guilt will be full, and national apostasy will be registered in the books of heaven. The result of this apostasy will be national ruin.[263]

As America, the land of religious liberty, shall unite with the papacy in forcing the conscience and compelling men to honor the false sabbath, the people of every country on the globe will be led to follow her example.[264]

"The less we make direct charges against authorities and powers, the greater work we shall be able to accomplish, both America and in foreign countries. Foreign nations will follow the example of the United States.

260. White, *The Great Controversy*, 578, 579.

261. Ibid., 592.

262. Ellen G. White, *Review and Herald*, December 18, 1888.

263. White, *Review and Herald*, May 2, 1893.

264. White, *Testimonies*, vol. 6, 18.

Though she leads out, yet the same crisis will come upon our people in all parts of the world."[265] It is our work to magnify and exalt the law of God.

Where Is This All Heading?

What does all this mean? In a quick overview, we note several events that will happen in rapid succession:

Protestants of the United States will reach across the gulf to grasp some form of spiritualism[266] and over the abyss to clasp hands with the papacy; under this threefold union, this country will follow in the steps of Rome in trampling on the rights of conscience—all in the interest of the "common good."

Leading churches of the United States will unite upon doctrines and/ or shared values in influencing the government to enforce their decrees and to sustain their institutions; thus Protestant America will form an image of the papacy.

Revelation 13 will be fulfilled when the United States enforces Sunday observance, which Rome claims as the acknowledgment of her supremacy.[267]

Political corruption will destroy love of justice and regard for truth in free America; rulers and legislators, in order to secure public favor, will yield to the popular demand for enforcing Sunday observance. Liberty of conscience will no longer be respected.

Countries all over the earth will follow the example of the United States in exalting the religious leadership of the papacy and in enacting worldwide Sunday laws.

National apostasy is to be followed by national ruin.

Does any of this sound like someone's delusional conspiracy theory? What do we see in our daily newspapers and in round-the-clock TV news?

265. Ibid., 395.

266. See chapters 8 and 9 in this book for possible fulfillments.

267. "Sunday is a Catholic institution and its claim to observance can be defended only on Catholic principles. . . . From beginning to end of Scripture there is not a single passage that warrants the transfer of weekly public worship from the last day of the week to the first." *Catholic Press,* Sydney, Australia, August 1900. "Sunday is our mark of authority. . . . The church is above the Bible, and this transference of sabbath observance is proof of that fact." *The Catholic Record,* London, Ontario, September 1, 1923. " 'Question: Which is the Sabbath day?' 'Answer: Saturday is the Sabbath.' 'Question: Why do we observe Sunday instead of Saturday?' 'Answer: We observe Sunday instead of Saturday because the Catholic Church in the Council of Laodicea (A.D. 336) transferred the solemnity from Saturday to Sunday.' " Peter Geiermann, *The Convert's Catechism of Catholic Doctrine,* 50. http://www.jeremiahproject.com/ prophecy/ecumenism-ect.html.

Is there now anything far-fetched in Ellen White's description of the end time in the United States? Is there anything in her description of the United States in the last days that sounds like a mere projection of what she observed in the nineteenth century? Does her emphasis on truth—that it should be honored, cherished, and protected—sound passé and outmoded in our liberal/conservative, religiously extreme/politically correct, and tolerant/intolerant twenty-first century?

The Uniting of Protestants and Catholics on "Common" Doctrines

In a previous chapter, we noted that in March 1994, forty prominent religious leaders formulated a document called "Evangelicals and Catholics Together: The Christian Mission in the 3rd Millennium."[268] This document surely surprised many on both sides of the Christian world. Some said it reversed five hundred years of Protestant church history, while others were equally troubled that it presented an incorrect picture of Protestantism today.[269]

Would Martin Luther or any of the other Reformers have said, "Evangelicals and Catholics are brothers and sisters in Christ"?

The forty leaders affirmed that Evangelicals and Catholics should together contend against abortion and pornography and share the common values of honesty, law observance, work, caring, and chastity, mutual respect between the sexes, parenthood, and family. And yes, they contended that "Christians individually and the church corporately also have a responsibility for the right ordering of civil society."

This "right ordering of civil society" fails to distinguish between legislating morality in the area of human freedom and laws that govern how one worships the God of morality. It seems to me that "religious" legislation in the end time will come under the guise of laws that will address social crises—a smooth way to segue into "rational" reasons to unite for the "common good."[270]

---

268. http://www.highbeam.com/doc/1P2-4221532.html.

269. http://www.gty.org/Resources/.../A149.

270. By executive order on December 12, 2002, President Bush launched his Faith-Based Initiative, a program that promotes federal funding of faith-based organizations. Although funding has been available to religious social service agencies for many years, this executive order permits federal giving directly to churches. Gerald Grimaud, former Pennsylvania assistant Attorney General and currently in private practice in Tunkhannock, Pennsylvania, wrote: "With the breakdown of the wall of separation, both church and state will pay a great price, as will the individual. Yes, church social programs and the needy will benefit in the short run. However, with state funding comes government intrusion into church programs, forms, applications, questions, monitoring,

Further, as these two religious forces—Evangelicals and Roman Catholics—unite in "common cause," pursuing the "common good," they will prod legislative assemblies to "enforce their decrees and to sustain their institutions," in essence, a repeat of papal history, which for centuries used the state to sustain and enforce its religious programs. This repeat of history is therefore called "an image of the Roman hierarchy"—a mirror reflection of centuries of church-state union and its appalling consequences.

The result of this civil enforcement of religious decrees will be the "infliction of civil penalties upon dissenters."[271]

A national crisis of any kind would precipitate this "document of common values" into a clarion call for these common values to rise up in unprecedented national unity—a unity framed in legislation.

Political Corruption Leads to Popular Demands

Ellen White forecast that "political corruption" would destroy "love of justice" and eventually lead to "the popular demand" for the enforcement of a Sunday law.[272] For most people this prediction has seemed absurd—nothing like this could happen in a country that reveres the First Amendment to its Constitution! *It all depends on definitions.*

For the Supreme Court today to affirm a national Sunday law as a special religious day seems highly unlikely. But the same Court could easily act on precedent and support the contention that Sunday is the most likely day in the week to promote neighborhood and national unity on "common values."

For years, the Supreme Court has used its *Lemon* test to determine church-state relationships. The test opines that a law must have a secular purpose and not advance or hinder the interests of any religion.

But the Supreme Court is not above reversing itself, depending on shifts toward the right or left with replacements. The facts are obvious that religious freedom in the United States is wonderful theory, but the applications of that theory depend on the subjective presuppositions of a vacillating court.

For instance, our constitutional protections were eclipsed for a while after the Japanese attack on Pearl Harbor, December 7, 1941. The incarceration of approximately one hundred and twenty thousand Americans of Japanese heritage, young and old, proved that in times of national crisis, such protections were nonexistent—all in response to public opinion.

---

supervising, auditing, managing, and even prosecutions. And over time, sadly, the mission of church programs will be neutered."—*Liberty,* March/April 2003.

271. Ellen G. White, *The Great Controversy,* 445.

272. Ibid., 592.

When the Supreme Court upheld Congress and the executive arm, Judge Robert Jackson, in dissent, wrote that the ruling was a "subtle blow to liberty. . . . The principle then lies like a loaded weapon ready for the hand of any authority that can bring forward a plausible claim of an urgent need."[273]

Omnipotence of the Majority

Alexis de Tocqueville, in his peerless analysis of American life and government, wrote: "If ever the free institutions of America are destroyed, that event may be attributed to the omnipotence of the majority, which may at some future time urge the minorities to desperation."[274]

The day is coming, sooner than most anyone can imagine, when the majority will suddenly look at this country as many foreign countries do today. At a time when our government is trying to sell the American Way of Life worldwide, many countries are doing their best to keep us out. Why? Compared to their cultures, we look decadent and forbidding—they see our crime statistics, our flaunting of sexual excess and perversion, our alcohol problems, and the extravagant portrayal of all this decadence in our entertainment media.

Any day now, the "majority" will decide that the "American Way" of today must return to the "American Way" of a century ago. Revulsion against decadence will become a national issue. The convergence of natural and economic disasters will inflame the general public with a common cry: "Something has to be done!"

The unifying issue that the "majority" will agree on will likely be a national day of rest. Perhaps led by the Evangelicals and Catholics who already have joined hands, "the majority" will demand that our legislators, using the language of "urgent need," force some kind of national unity. In response to the biblical pronouncement that "righteousness exalteth the nation," a national Sunday law would be a visible witness that the United States is pulling its moral house together.

Common Community Day

We are not dealing with future "maybes." In the Netherlands, on December 5, 2002, the *Nederlands Dagblads* reported that two opposing political parties voted to make Sunday a "Community Day," but, the report said:

> Their ideas about such a day differ like night and day. The Christian Union asks for the closing of shops on Sundays and strives to make Sunday a day of rest for everyone. By contrast, the Labor Party

273. Korematsu v. United States, 1943.
274. Alexis de Tocqueville, *Democracy in America* (New York, NY: Signet Classic, 2001), 120.

allows people to do whatever they like on Sundays. . . . This law, however, will cut the weekend by 50 percent, from the two days to only one day which will be Sunday, the only official day of rest.

I can assure you that more countries will soon follow—a coming Sunday law in the United States is as real as the sun shining tomorrow morning.

We don't have to look far to see the groundwork already laid for a national Sunday law in the United States. In 1961 a majority ruling of the U. S. Supreme Court in *McGowan v. Maryland* upheld the constitutionality of Sunday laws, even though they only happened "to coincide or harmonize" with a religion! Talk about legal fiction! The Court was telling Americans that if the majority were to enjoy the benefits of a uniform day of rest, that benefit would outweigh any burden that such a law would impose on a minority group.

Of course, most anyone could see through that reasoning, *even as the dissenting judges did.* The case would not have come to the Supreme Court if religious underpinnings were not in place! *But the majority ruled.* This 1961 ruling has cast a dark shadow forward; soon, thunderclouds will roll.

United States: Superpower

Revelation 13:12–14 outlines an ominous scenario: the United States has the power and influence to lead other nations into "worshiping" the papacy as the spiritual leader of the world. In the midst of spectacular economic distress or terrible natural disasters, the United States will dramatically coerce those who "dwell on the earth" to link with the papacy, the linchpin in establishing world peace.

Some might ask, does the United States really have that much world influence, and does it really want it?

Incredible as it might have sounded in the nineteenth century and for most of the twentieth, the United States, in a few short years, has been vaulted by circumstances into the position of being the only superpower on planet Earth. No other world power in history—not the Persian or Roman or Spanish or British empires—has ever been the "sole" superpower.

Today, the United States has few close competitors. America, for example, outspends the next twenty countries combined on its military—a force that the rest of the world expects us to employ as the world's first response to troubles anywhere. But far beyond its military might is America's leadership in technology and humanitarian relief.

With world leadership slipping into increasingly common reference to the New World Order or global governance (as we saw in a previous chapter), the thought that only America could make it happen is a no-brainer.

But what is so incongruous, so difficult, to put together, is that the United States—though admittedly the most powerful political nation on earth—is also the foremost example of a nation established on the principles of freedom, both political and religious! The world had never before seen a nation so resolutely wrap itself within a phenomenal Declaration of Independence and unparalleled Constitution, such as the first thirteen colonies did in 1776 and 1787–1789. And then further, in 1791, it produced the unprecedented Bill of Rights as the first Ten Amendments to the Constitution. Then, without parallel, the new nation extended its leadership without conquering another nation and, though fighting to liberate other countries, asked nothing in return except some land to bury its dead.

Both of these unique documents rested on simple principles that were nobly set forth in the Declaration of Independence—"truths to be self-evident, that all men are created equal, and that they are endowed by their Creator with certain unalienable [natural, incapable of being surrendered] rights, among which are life, liberty, and the pursuit of happiness." The document was signed by fifty-six heroic men under their own personal commitment: "With a firm reliance on the Protection of Divine Providence, we mutually pledge to each other our Lives, our Fortunes and our sacred Honor."

Could Those Dire Predictions Really Happen?

So how will Satan's lies and deceptions set up the United States to be the world leader in uniting all nations under a religious authority that has universal clout and enough muscle to enforce economic hardship and persecution on those they hate? How will satanic lies become so believable that "the world worshiped the beast" (Revelation 13:4)?[275]

A Brief Reality Check

In chapter 6, we reviewed Pope John Paul II's masterful world strategy. One of his primary goals was to unite the world's religions, seen especially in his 1994 apostolic letter *"Tertio Millennio Adventiente"* ("The Coming Third Millennium"). This goal was more directly detailed in his 1995 encyclical *"Ut Unum Sin"* ("That They May Be One"). And then, among other events in 2000, the U.S. Congress authorized a Congressional Gold Medal to be presented to Pope John Paul II as a recognition of his "preeminent moral authority." The presentation stated that the pope, in "tran-

---

275. See chapter 10 for a larger examination of evil's four-step strategy that will unfold in its fiercest display in the last of the last days.

scending temporal politics, has used his moral authority to hasten the fall of godless totalitarian regimes . . . has promoted the inner peace of man as well as peace among mankind through his faith-inspired defense of justice, and has thrown open the doors of the Catholic Church, reconciling differences within Christendom as well as reaching out to the world's great religions."[276]

Proceeding with his global peace plan, Pope John Paul II gathered more than one hundred international religious leaders in Assisi, Italy, in 2002, pursuing "authentic peace."[277]

Pope John Paul II made a point of wooing Mecca to Rome. His emphasis that all Christians and Muslims worship the same God and that their mutual responsibility is to build a "civilization of love" is a "logic of love" that will bring all Christians and Muslims together in world peace.

All this is destined to bear fruit. The day is coming when something like the following might happen: Walking across the Hudson River and into the United Nations building, some religious figure (perhaps even a representation of the Virgin Mary) will galvanize world leaders buried under the weight of dozens of world conflicts. From that powerful rostrum, world delegates will hear peace plans to solve Ireland's neverending hostility between Irish Catholics and Protestants; proposals that will meld Israelis and Palestinians and do the same for racial divisions in all countries; Muslims and their neighbors the world over will suddenly see a workable plan for peace. The delegates stand in unison, recognizing that this dynamic religious leader has laid out the most sensible solutions for all their problems. They can only wonder why these solutions weren't thought of before! So reasonable, so believable!

The papacy, working through political and religious leaders, will soon have its way, breaking down all kinds of traditional international barriers as it receives the adulation of the whole world—an adulation led by the United States. Remember this: "All the world marveled and followed the beast. So they worshipped the dragon [Satan] . . . who gave authority to the beast; and they [the world] worshipped the beast, saying, 'Who is like the beast?' "

Further, the two-horned beast "exercises all the authority of the first beast and causes the earth and those who dwell in it to worship the first beast, whose deadly wound was healed . . . and he deceives those who dwell on the earth . . . telling those who dwell on the earth to make an image to the beast" (Revelation 12:9; 13:3, 4, 11–14).

Almost in contrapuntal fugue relationship, religious leaders in the United States are unfolding the predictions of Revelation 13. Such leaders

276. http://wahiduddin.net/decalogue.htm.

277. http://www.kazakhstan.org.sg/content/intro.php?act=menu&c_id=4.

throughout the nation focused on "Ten Commandments Day," Sunday, May 7, 2006.[278] Tens of thousands of congregations across the United States heard their pastor emphasize the importance and authority of God's law. Hard to imagine! Strange as it may seem, Protestant and Jewish stalwarts are increasingly united in support of the Ten Commandments' relevancy— a posture that is 180 degrees from most of their rhetoric for more than a century. Unfortunately, however, they are not yielding to the obvious intent of the fourth commandment.

What is their driving purpose? They point to a host of disturbing trends and court actions that they believe have undermined faith and morals:

> Recent court rulings have threatened the very fabric and foundation of our culture and faith. The Ten Commandments and all other references to God, which have served as the moral foundation and anchor of our great country, are systematically being removed from public places. Public displays of the Ten Commandments and other symbols of our faith have been a powerful visual testimony to the fact that the United States of America is "one nation under God." Their removal from public places shows that those with a secular humanist agenda are intent on destroying the moral heritage of our nation. The Ten Commandment Commission was founded to counter the secular agenda and help restore the Ten Commandments and Judeo-Christian values to their rightful place in our society.[279]

In his book *The New World Order*, Pat Robertson wrote:

> The utopians have talked of world order. Without saying so explicitly, the Ten Commandments set the only order that will bring world peace—with devotion to and respect of God at the center, strong family bonds and respect next, and the sanctity of people, property, family, reputation, and peace of mind next.[280]

In respect to the fourth commandment, the Sabbath, Robertson opined:

> The next obligation that a citizen of God's world order owes is to himself. "Remember the Sabbath day, to keep it holy," is a command for the personal benefit of each citizen. Our minds, spirits, and bodies demand a regular time of rest. Perhaps God's greatest gift to mankind's earthly existence is the ability to be free from work one day a week.[281]

---

278. http://www.wake-up.com/daystar/ds2006/Apr.htm.

279. Web site for the Ten Commandment Commission: http://tencommandmentsday.com.

280. Pat Robertson, *The New World Order* (Dallas: Word Publishing, 1991), 233.

281. Ibid., 236.

Pat Robertson is only one voice among many who are calling for the necessity and urgency of Sunday sacredness. From labor union leaders, official denominational resolutions, magazine columnists, and the papacy itself, the crescendo is developing. Note Pope John Paul II's (July 7, 1998) apostolic letter *"Dies Domini"* ("The Lord's Day").[282]

Worldwide Polarization Against Sabbath Keepers

What seems most incredible at the moment is the prediction that there will be a *worldwide* polarization against Sabbath keepers. The universal authority of the "beast" power of Revelation 13 will, with great craft, use the panic being caused throughout the world by natural disasters, interlocking economic distress, and unsettled ethnic/religious conflicts to accomplish its long-sought goals. The prestige and power of the United States will become the model of how to unify the majority around the world in calling for God to calm the world's storms as surely as Jesus calmed the raging Sea of Galilee.

It almost takes one's breath away: When "America, the land of religious liberty, shall unite with the papacy in forcing the conscience and compelling men to honor the false sabbath, the people of every country

---

282. See chapter 6 for more elaboration of this apostolic letter: "62. It is the duty of Christians therefore to remember that, although the practices of the Jewish Sabbath are gone, surpassed as they are by the 'fulfillment' which Sunday brings, the underlying reasons for keeping 'the Lord's Day' holy—inscribed solemnly in the Ten Commandments—remain valid, though they need to be reinterpreted in the light of the theology and spirituality of Sunday. . . . 64. For several centuries, Christians observed Sunday simply as a day of worship, without being able to give it the specific meaning of Sabbath rest. Only in the fourth century did the civil law of the Roman Empire recognize the weekly recurrence, determining that on 'the day of the sun' the judges, the people of the cities and the various trade corporations would not work. . . . 65. By contrast, the link between the Lord's Day and the day of rest in civil society has a meaning and importance, which go beyond the distinctly Christian point of view. The alternation between work and rest, built into human nature, is willed by God himself, as appears in the creation story in the Book of Genesis. . . . In this matter, my predecessor Pope Leo XIII in his Encyclical *Rerum Novarum* speaks of Sunday rest as a worker's right which the State must guarantee. In our own historical context there remains the obligations to ensure that everyone can enjoy the freedom, rest and relaxation which human dignity requires, together with the associated religious, family, cultural and interpersonal needs which are difficult to meet if there is no guarantee of at least one day of the week on which people can *both* rest and celebrate. . . . 67. . . . Therefore, also in the particular circumstances of our own time, Christians will naturally strive to ensure that civil legislation respects their duty to keep Sunday holy."—*"Dies Domini,"* July 7, 1998.

on the globe will be led to follow her example."[283] "The Sabbath question is to be the issue in the great final conflict in which all the world will act a part."[284] A "new world order," indeed!

All of these predictions regarding the impact of a politico-religio virus (such as the international enforcement of Sunday laws)—that begins like a pimple in the United States but one day will spread rapidly through the bloodstream of world communities—are no longer only a bad dream. Most dialogue on almost any TV talk show or weekly magazine refers to the worldwide influence and power of the United States. When the United States selects the foreign countries that will receive billions of dollars annually on the basis of what's best for America, when terrible earthquakes and famines call forth massive U.S. humanitarian relief anywhere in the world, when the nations of the world expect the U.S. military to resolve civil wars overseas, no one any more doubts the clout of American opinion and action.

Since September 11, 2001, the ability of the United States to remain a benign banker to the world morphed into the realization that something must be done to guarantee peace, prosperity, and the spread of human rights on every continent. Such goals, in order to survive, "will require the expenditure of American will and might." Condoleezza Rice, National Security Adviser to President George W. Bush, when asked if the United States is "overly ambitious," replied:

> "Was it overly ambitious of the United States to believe that democracy could be fostered in Japan and that peace could finally be brought between Germany and France? It succeeded because it proceeded from values that Americans understand. Truman and his team understood that America could not afford to leave a vacuum in the world."[285]

Last Act in the Drama

A significant time factor kicks in at this point—the actual enforcement of Sunday laws worldwide becomes universal.

The substitution of the false for the true is the last act in the drama. When this substitution becomes universal God will reveal himself. When the laws of men are exalted above the laws of God, when the

---

283. White, *Last Day Events*, 135.
284. Ibid.
285. Jay Tolson, "The New American Empire?" *U.S. News & World Report*, January 13, 2003.

powers of this earth try to force men to keep the first day of the week, know that the time has come for God to work.[286]

Obviously, this may be almost too much to contemplate at this time. Adventists are known the world over as law-abiding people. In addition, they are also known for their unambiguous defense of America's liberties, even willing to die for them when their president calls for their services in time of war.

But because of world panic and the crafty manipulation of legislators and jurists, "the whole world is to be stirred with enmity against Seventh-day Adventists."[287] And the following *pseudo-logic* will prevail:

> The whole world keeps Sunday, they say, and why should not this people, who are so few in number, do according to the laws of the land?[288]

> The judges will refuse to listen to the reasons of those who are loyal to the commandments of God because they know the arguments in favor of the fourth commandment are unanswerable. They will say, "We have a law, and by our law he ought to die." God's law is nothing to them. "Our law" with them is supreme. Those who respect this human law will be favored, but those who will not bow to the idol sabbath have no favors shown them.[289]

Adventists in many levels of government and in the academic and business world will discover that their friends of "wealth, genius, [and] education, will combine to cover them with contempt. Persecuting rulers, ministers, and church members will conspire against them. With voice and pen, by boasts, threats, and ridicule, they will seek to overthrow their faith . . . [they] shall be treated as traitors . . . denounced as enemies of law and order, as breaking down the moral restraints of society, causing anarchy and corruption. . . . Their conscientious scruples will be pronounced obstinacy, stubbornness, and contempt of authority."[290]

Word Games

Of course, governments must balance liberty of the individual with security of the individual. The problem is that word games are often played, such as "anti-terrorism" or "child protection" and "common values."

---

286. White, *Last Day Events*, 135.

287. Ibid., 136.

288. Ibid.

289. Ibid., 145, 146.

290. Ibid., 146.

Such words can easily attack the constitutional rights of the targeted "enemy."

Well-intentioned prosecutors and courts can easily mask and override fundamental rights in the name of security, imposing such things as preventive detention; denial of a detainee's right to counsel; denial of the right to prepare a defense; denial of the right to interview and call witnesses; or denial of the right to trial and due process before sentencing. Thus basic rights for which tens of thousands of American service men have fought and died will be denied in the name of national security.

If ever there was a time for mental and moral clarity in the Adventist Church, it is now! It is now time for Adventist lawyers and judges to speak out in defense of the God-given right of individual freedom, when it comes to conscience and core beliefs. It is now time for church leadership, including pastors and administrators, to think boldly regarding their responsibility to lead their church into careful thinking—before the storm breaks!

Emotional identification with euphemistic slogans snared Germany under Hitler, including many Adventist leaders.

A Powerful Heads-Up

We are not talking in general terms, or in the complacency that it will not happen "in *my* day." Nor should we think that the potential confusion would come from some group other than one's own! We should all contemplate in great seriousness the following prediction—a prediction as certain as the coming of Jesus:

As the storm approaches, a large class who have professed faith in the third angel's message, but have not been sanctified through obedience to the truth, abandon their position and join the ranks of the opposition. By uniting with the world and partaking of its spirit, they have come to view matters in nearly the same light; and when the test is brought, they are prepared to choose the easy, popular side. Men of talent and pleasing address, who once rejoiced in the truth, employ their powers to deceive and mislead souls. They become the most bitter enemies of their former brethren. When Sabbathkeepers are brought before the courts to answer for their faith, these apostates are the most efficient agents of Satan to misrepresent and accuse them, and by false reports and insinuations to stir up the rulers against them.[291]

---

291. White, *The Great Controversy*, 608.

If this preview of things to come is not a powerful heads-up, then I don't know what can get our attention. From another direction: Being a Saturday keeper is far different than being a Sabbath keeper!

In her chapter entitled "The Impending Conflict,"[292] Ellen White provided the background for the amazing shift from post-modernism (wherein objective moral authority is abandoned and personal feeling/opinion are the norms) to the time when "reasons" are given for the enforcement of laws that deny others the right of religious liberty. (Have we not seen examples of these things during the last forty years?):

And as the claims of the fourth commandment are urged upon the people, it is found that the observance of the seventh-day Sabbath is enjoined; and as the only way to free themselves from a duty which they are unwilling to perform, popular teachers declare that the law of God is no longer binding. Thus they cast away the law and the Sabbath together. As the work of Sabbath reform extends, this rejection of the divine law to avoid the claims of the fourth commandment will become well-nigh universal. The teachings of religious leaders have opened the door to infidelity, to Spiritualism, and to contempt for God's holy law, and upon these leaders rests a fearful responsibility for the iniquity that exists in the Christian world.

Yet this very class put forth the claim that the fast-spreading corruption is largely attributable to the desecration of the so-called "Christian Sabbath," and that the enforcement of Sunday observance would greatly improve the morals of society.[293]

After her predictions of end-time disasters of all kinds and that "these visitations are to become more and more frequent and disastrous," she wrote:

And then the great deceiver will persuade men that those who serve God are causing these evils. The class that have provoked the displeasure of Heaven will charge all their troubles upon those whose obedience to God's commandments is a perpetual reproof to transgressors. It will be declared that men are offending God by the violation of the Sunday-sabbath, that this sin has brought calamities which will not cease until Sunday observance shall be strictly enforced, and that those who present the claims of the fourth commandment, thus destroying reverence for Sunday, are troublers of the people, preventing their restoration to divine favor and temporal prosperity.[294]

---

292. Ibid., 582–592.
293. Ibid., 587.
294. Ibid., 590.

Even more explicit, Mrs. White previewed how those proclaiming the legitimacy of the seventh day of the week as the biblical Sabbath will be declared "lawbreakers":[295]

Those who honor the Bible Sabbath will be denounced as enemies of law and order, as breaking down the moral restraints of society, causing anarchy and corruption, and calling down the judgments of God upon the earth. Their conscientious scruples will be pronounced obstinacy, stubbornness, and contempt of authority. . . . Ministers who deny the obligation of the divine law will present from the pulpit the duty of yielding obedience to the civil authorities as ordained of God. In legislative halls and courts of justice, commandment-keepers will be misrepresented and condemned. A false coloring will be given to their words; the worst construction will be put upon their motives.[296]

But all is not dismal. So much good news remains ahead. Captains of industry, business leaders, politicians, and jurists will suddenly see the truth about what is happening. Many attorneys and judges will see the validity of the arguments made by Sabbath keepers—and the sense of fairness and personal obligation in the face of truth will prevail and will cause them to stand with the accused and trust the Lord of the universe:

Some who are numbered among merchants and princes will take their position to obey the truth. God's eye has been upon such as they have acted according to the light they have had, maintaining their integrity.[297]

But so long as Jesus remains man's intercessor in the sanctuary above, the restraining influence of the Holy Spirit is felt by rulers and people. It still controls to some extent the laws of the land. Were it not for these laws, the condition of the world would be much worse than it now is. While many of our rulers are active agents of Satan, God also has His agents among the leading men of the nation. The enemy moves upon his servants to propose measures that would greatly impede the work of God; but statesmen who fear the Lord are influenced by holy angels to oppose such propositions with unanswerable arguments. Thus a few men will hold in check a powerful current of evil. The opposition of the enemies of truth will be restrained that the third angel's message may do its work. When the final warning shall be given, it will arrest the attention of these

---

295. Ibid., 591.
296. Ibid., 592.
297. White, *Selected Messages*, bk. 3, 421.

leading men through whom the Lord is now working, and some of them will accept it, and will stand with the people of God through the time of trouble.[298]

Such unambiguous forecasts were once only a nineteenth-century outline of the future in the United States and the rest of the world. Here, in the beginning of the twenty-first century, we are living in the enormous and spectacular unfolding of these predicted insights.

Protestant spokesmen declare that God's law is no longer binding and that the seventh-day Sabbath was a Jewish custom—thus removing the religious argument for the authority of the fourth commandment of the Decalogue.

At the same time, others will declare that calamities are the result of God's displeasure on those who are "violating" the Sunday "sabbath."

The rise of end-time corruption becomes one of the reasons for supporting Sunday sacredness and regaining temporal prosperity. Joining the "corruption" argument will be the colossal increase and severity of natural disasters—further "reasons" for national action to show God our collective repentance.

When supporters of the seventh-day Sabbath continue their defense of religious liberty and the biblical Sabbath, they will be "denounced as enemies of law and order"—an amazing, illogical charge.

In the halls of justice, supporters of the biblical Sabbath will be "misrepresented and condemned." "A false coloring" will be given to their defense of freedom and biblical authority.

Also in those halls of justice and corporate board rooms, men and women of character will recognize truth when they see it, perhaps for the first time. And they will join those representing the God of heaven and the integrity of His government.

No one today can accurately imagine how all this will play out. We can only guess at the specific national crises that will generate a call for national unity. But the purpose is clear: the majority will vote for common values, in the hope that God can bring peace to the nation—Sunday legislation is the pawn.

All the while, this surge for national unity leading to Sunday enforcement will bring out the worst in people who prefer legislation rather than dialogue over the issues that divide.

The various crises will feed on each other, whether they are economic, terrorism, rampant disease, or natural disasters. All this only spells "national ruin" and the prelude to the seven last plagues. Probation will close.

---

298. White, *The Great Controversy*, 610.

The neural pathways of faithful loyalists who regard the command-ments of God as their hedge and joy are settled into the truth so that they will never, ever, say no to God. The neural pathways of those who have rejected the wooing of the Holy Spirit are also settled into a pattern of self-will and self-gratification. They too will never change—habit pat-terns are set forever.[299]

What should we conclude in this review of United States in prophecy?

That which might have seemed far-fetched in the middle of the nine-teenth century is front-page news today. Although the world influence of the papacy and the United States was many years in the future, bibli-cal scholars such as John N. Andrews painted an amazing scenario of the future, on the basis of biblical study alone. Ellen White emphatically enlarged this biblical picture in ways that no one on earth could have imagined in her day—but how precisely her predictions have now be-come daily reality!

Adventists don't get their prophetic understanding from reading to-day's news. Never have, and never will. They let the newsmakers validate their prophetic road map, not write it. In other words, we don't re-create our view of last-day events in every new generation. We "have the pro-phetic word made more sure" (2 Peter 1:19).

Adventists in the nineteenth century may have had to use their imagi-nations. Adventists today only have to use their eyes and ears. Nightfall does not come at once. At twilight, everything remains seemingly un-changed. But at twilight we should sense the coolness of the air, lest we suddenly become lost in the darkness.[300]

God never leaves His people without "present truth" (2 Peter 1:12). Why did God give this picture of the future to Ellen White? Because He has never left His people without "present truth." John the revelator wrote that in the end time, the papacy's "deadly wound was healed" (Revelation 13:13). That time has come! And today's reality is much beyond anyone's anticipation of it, even forty years ago! It surely is "present truth" today.

Ellen White offers end-time people clear, believable counsel:

> In order to endure the trial before them, they must understand the will of God as revealed in his Word; they can honor him only as

---

299. "Just as soon as the people of God are sealed in their foreheads—it is not any seal or mark that can be seen but a settling into the truth, both intel-lectually and spiritually, so they cannot be moved—just as soon as God's people are sealed and prepared for the shaking, it will come. Indeed, it has begun already." White, *Last Day Events*, 219, 220.

300. Thoughts that I remember Supreme Court Justice William O. Douglas saying, although I can't remember the words exactly. The truth he is emphasizing will be never more needed than in the days ahead.

they have a right conception of his character, government, and purposes, and act in accordance with them. None but those who have fortified the mind with the truths of the Bible will stand through the last great conflict.[301]

Our response to God's graciousness and the counsel of His last-day messenger is to keep walking into the light until the Light Bearer returns. Everyone in the world has enough light to make moral decisions, even though it might be seen only through a crack in the door.

No other people have a clearer map for the road ahead. No other people have been given the responsibility of sharing the truth about the future with others. How will we ever face up to reality, when we realize that we knew something about the future that we could have made clearer to our children, to our neighbors, to men and women everywhere—but we neglected this privilege and duty?

The only peaceful, reassuring way to face the last of the last days is to keep trusting God's Word—which alone can give us the road map—and the courage to walk into the setting sun.

---

301. White, *The Great Controversy*, p. 593.

CHAPTER EIGHT

THEME:
> Jesus will return after a great portion of this world has been fogged in with a counterfeit spirituality.

The Tsunami of the New Spirituality–Emerging Church Movement

Sometimes we can look at a Bible text or hear it quoted for years, until we might as well be reading the telephone directory.

One of those texts may be Paul's warning regarding earth's last days:

> That in the last days perilous times will come: for men will be lovers of themselves, . . . having a form of godliness but denying its power. . . . For the time will come when they will not endure sound doctrine, but according to their own desires, because they have itching ears, they will heap up for themselves teachers; and they will turn their ears away from the truth, and be turned aside to fables (2 Timothy 3:1, 2, 5; 4:3, 4).

Paul is giving us a heads-up! The old veteran is not talking about what will be going on in Buddhism, Hinduism, or Islamism. He is warning the Christian church that in the end time, the gospel that turned the world upside down in the first century (Acts 17:6) would become so watered down that the secret of its power would be muted.

In the last days, Christians will seek teachers and preachers who will focus on their "felt" needs, rather than their "real" needs. They will want our Lord's name but not His character. They would prefer to "feel" their religion rather than build reasons for their faith that was once delivered to first-century loyalists (Jude 3).

In no other biblical study that I am aware of is the warning more accurate: The error that hits us is never 100 percent wrong or evil! That is not the way "deception" works. "A form of godliness" is always pleasing. In fact, some of the most powerful speeches that swing the masses, some of the most acclaimed best sellers, week after week, are often 90 percent true! We are enthralled with the force of the good, while the bad slips in so easily. In other words, all New Spirituality/Innovation/Emergent Church/Spiritual Formation materials and speakers have appealing messages—the real issues are those left unsaid that should be said, and what is being said so eloquently is often contrary to clear biblical principles.

Let's take a look at what has been happening in Evangelical Protestantism during the past twenty years. One of the most remarkable developments is the emergence of new types of worship services and the burst of mega-churches throughout the United States. A tsunami of books such as *The Purpose Driven Life*[302] and *Your Best Life Now*[303] are heralded around the world for their practical spiritual counsel, heavily buttressed with biblical texts. So what's the problem?

But something deeper is going on. The skew in the second half of the twentieth century is not a shift from the historical defense of the Bible's accuracy to modern liberalism, as it was in the first half of the last century. The shift now is from a traditional, biblical base to a more psychological, sociological base, heated by the philosophies of pragmatism and New Spirituality. Of course, the Bible is used, yet often it is not only misquoted and mistranslated, but it becomes a grab bag to support whatever concept the user chooses to promote. That is the new twist.

For more than a century, liberal Protestants jettisoned the Bible as a reliable spiritual authority. Today's Evangelicals, once the guardians of the authority of Scripture, do not deny the Bible itself, but rather, by its use, give the appearance that the Bible is no longer that important on certain core points. That creates a new and short step then to other sources of thinking that seem more relevant, more personal, more satisfying.

History shows us that when those looking for authentic spirituality do not find it in places where the authority of the Bible is supposedly upheld, they will seek elsewhere for some kind of personal assurance. But few of

302. Rick Warren, *The Purpose Driven Life* (Grand Rapids, MI: Zondervan, 2002).

303. Joel Osteen, *Your Best Life Now* (New York: Time Warner Book Group, 2004).

those seekers return to their traditional church services, because they have felt burned over with dry, irrelevant sermons, boring liturgies, and repetitive traditions. Such seekers, and they are many in *all* churches, still look for something that seems more personally satisfying, without changing the language and feel of Christianity. And that is exactly what is happening. Many pastors, realizing this spiritual desert, search for new spiritual experiences that will validate their ministries and please their congregations.

Newsweek (August 29, 2005) featured a cover story called "In Search of the Spiritual." The subtitle was, "Move over, politics. Americans are looking for personal, ecstatic experiences of God, and, according to our poll, they don't much care what the neighbors are doing."

This New Spirituality emphasis has captured the attention and commitment of a great number of younger people, especially. New Spirituality promises contact with God in ways not experienced in other, more conventional Christian paths.

Distinguish Between Spiritualism and Spirituality

We must distinguish between age-old Spiritualism and rampant New Spirituality. Spiritualism is the open appeal to find Dead Family Members, Reality, God, Cosmic Consciousness—whatever—through *direct* contact with the "other" world. It could be through channeling, Ouija boards, séances, certain kinds of extra-sensory perception, etc.

New Spirituality, at this point in time, doesn't go in that direction, although it has much in common with Spiritualism. Both concepts or movements do, however, believe in either the immortal soul or the subjective ability to find God or reality within themselves through any number of modalities. Neither believes in the final authority of Scripture.

Modern Mood in the Twenty-First Century

Pollster George Gallup stated, in his book *The New American Spirituality,* that spirituality is very much alive, but it is without biblical foundation:

> Contemporary spirituality can resemble a grab bag of random experiences that does little more than promise to make our eyes mist up or our heart warm. We need perspective to separate the junk food from the wholesome, the faddish from the truly transforming.[304]

The problem, as Gallup sees it, is the massive level of biblical illiteracy

---

304. George Gallup, *The New American Spirituality* (Colorado Springs: Victor, 2000), 15.

among Christians generally throughout the world. "Half," he says, "of those describing themselves as Christians are unable to name who delivered the Sermon on the Mount. Many Americans cannot name the reason for celebrating Easter or what the Ten Commandments are. People think the name of Noah's wife was Joan, as in Joan of Ark."[305]

Then Gallup describes the "great disconnect"—the wide gulf between what Americans in general and Christians in particular *claim to believe* and how they *actually live.* So he concluded that this "cluster of moral and theological shortcomings seemingly throws into question the transforming power of religious beliefs," leading Gallup to state: "Just because Americans claim they are more spiritual does not make them so."[306] And then he asks the burning question: "Is the church really rediscovering its spiritual moorings, or just engaging in retreat from seemingly insoluble problems?"[307]

Filling the Vacuum

Whether the typical church is doing its job or not may be a no-brainer. Most people are spiritually hungry, and they will find some spiritual guru who promises to satisfy their innate spiritual search. Itching ears will find teachers to satisfy their desires (2 Timothy 4:3).

That is why the tsunami of New Spirituality is sweeping over the American church, especially. It comes in many forms. Many, if not most, of the mega-churches, as expressed in their web networks and books they endorse, are riding this wave, though they might not foresee pending disasters or huge disappointments.

In 2007, Willow Creek Community Church's (South Barrington, Illinois) mesmerizing balloon burst, at least for Pastor Bill Hybels. He was brave and honest enough to sponsor a four-year self-evaluation of their highly acclaimed program, as to what it had really been doing for thirty years. The report was entitled—*Reveal: Where Are You?*

Hybels said: *"It rocked my world"*— the findings were *"earth-shaking," "ground breaking,"* and *"mind blowing."* Willow Creek now realized that their seeker-friendly programs were "a mistake."[308] Lesson learned: For Willow Creek, "growing" a congregation goes beyond "attracting" people to church—they needed to restructure their church program to grow their members, BUT—Willow Creek is now on the path into becoming another Emerging Church! What will the hundreds of copycats in many denominations now say to their congregations?

---

305. Ibid., 30.

306. Ibid., 32, 29.

307. Ibid.

308. http://www.ministers-best-friend.com/Willow-Creek-Church-Repents .html.

Rick Warren's Saddleback Church (Lake Forest, California) has been flirting with an Emerging Church/Innovation/New Spirituality approach since 2004, as I outlined in *Truth Matters* in 2006.[309] But it has progressed to far more than mere flirting in the last five years! If I were updating that book today, I would add at least four more chapters! Amazing what a few years of following an incomplete "Purpose" will do, even to a gifted man! Nobody today wonders whether Warren has plunged into New Spirituality.

Note how Rick Warren uses Eugene Peterson's *The Message* (modern paraphrase): In translating the words of our Lord's Prayer, "in earth as it is in heaven," Peterson does something very interesting—it became "as above, so below." These words are a well-understood mystical occult phrase that goes back to Hermes Trismegistus, supposed contemporary of Abraham—teaching that the fundamental truth of the universe is: spirit and truth, invisible and visible, form a unity to which we are intimately linked (Google this phrase if you don't believe me)! This phrase has been used often over the years to express thoughts common to New Spirituality.[310]

Again, Warren quotes Ephesians 4:6 (New Century Version): "He rules everything and is everywhere and is in everything." Here again he chooses a biblical translation/paraphrase that does not rightly interpret the apostle Paul. Paul was speaking *to Ephesian believers*—"in you all," that is, the "faithful in Christ Jesus." The New Age/New Spirituality teaches that God is "in" everyone and "in" everything.

Indeed, Warren is well known by the company he keeps—people he endorses and/or speaks with side-by-side: Ken Blanchard—*The One Minute Manager;* Bernie Siegel—*Love, Medicine and Miracles;* John Marks Templeton—New Age–based Foundation; Leonard Sweet—Methodist, Dean of Theology, Drew University—*Quantum Spirituality*—for starters.

Here is a sample of Sweet's thinking:

> Quantum spirituality bonds us to all creation as well as to other members of the human family. . . . This entails a radical doctrine of embodiment of God in the very substance of creation. . . . But a spirituality that is not in some way entheistic (whether pan- or trans-) that does not extend to the spirit-matter or the cosmos, is not Christian.[311]

But I hasten to make my appreciation known: Promoters of New

---

309. Herbert E. Douglass, *Truth Matters* (Nampa, ID: Pacific Press® Publishing Association, 2006).

310. http://radiantwoman.wordpress.com.

311. Leonard Sweet, *Quantum Spirituality: A Postmodern Apologetic* (Dayton, OH: Whaleprints for Spirit/Venture Ministries, Inc., 1991, 1994), 125.

Spirituality generally are gracious, charming, and in a way, very believable! They believe what they say; they believe that what they have experienced should be shared with the world. And much of what they say is indeed appealing—the sale of their books proves it! However, New Spirituality's focus and emphasis are light years away from biblical teaching!

John MacArthur, well-known pastor and author in southern California, summed up this tsunami drift:

> The evangelical consensus has shifted decidedly in the past two decades. Our collective message is now short on doctrine and long on experience. Thinking is deemed less important than feeling. . . . The love of sound doctrine that has always been a distinguishing characteristic of evangelicalism. Add a dose of mysticism to this mix and you have the recipe for unmitigated spiritual disaster.[312]

The Age of Aquarius

As we have discovered in the past forty years, the term "New Age" is synonymous with "The Age of Aquarius." The central teaching of both philosophies is that we are supposed to understand, one way or another, that God is within each person and "can be found therein." The New Age movement that seemed so radical in the '60s and '70s did not really die out. Rather, it integrated into society seemingly everywhere—medicine, business, education, science, and finally, even the last frontier—the Evangelical church. Though the banner is no longer "New Age," its key elements have morphed to a great degree into this now-pervasive New Spirituality.[313]

I don't have the space fully to explain New Age thought, but I can alert you as to how and through whom New Age concepts are creeping into the pulpits and seminaries of *all* churches everywhere. Usually, new movements or changes within Christianity come with great leaders proclaiming new ways to look at the "gospel," such as Luther (Lutherans) and later, John Wesley (Methodists). But the New Age sneaks in like a cancer. Beginning unnoticed, it gradually eats away and finally takes over the whole body, unless it is recognized for what it is and summarily treated.

For many evangelical churches, New Age concepts were first rejected and then welcomed. An amazing biblical fog has been wrapped around the old New-Age notions, with only few voices recognizing the hidden cancer. Ears have been tickled. Most do not realize that they are now full of theological cancer but live on in bliss with their New Age anesthetic.

---

312. John MacArthur, *Reckless Faith* (Wheaton, IL: Crossway Books, 1994), 154, 155.

313. One of the most lucid books on how New Spirituality is changing the face of Christianity is Ray Yungen's *A Time of Departing* (Silverton, OR: Lighthouse Trails Publishing Company, 2002).

New Spirituality Feeders

Author of one of the best sellers of all time, *The Road Less Traveled,*[314] Scott Peck's various books occupy a substantial share of bookstore space under "Self-help." When the book was first published, I was an instant admirer. (In fact, his *People of the Lie* is still the best book I have ever read on analyzing evil.) But when I reached his question—"What does God want from us?" and then his answer, "It is for the individual to become totally, wholly God"[315]—I knew something troubling was happening, although at that time, I was unaware of his New Age journey.

Among similar citations, Peck wrote in his book *A World Waiting to Be Born*:

> This process of emptying the mind is of such importance it will continue to be a significant theme. . . . It may help to remember, therefore, that the purpose of emptying the mind is not ultimately to have nothing there; rather it is to make room in the mind for something new, something unexpected, to come in. What is the something new? It is the voice of God.[316]

Further, Jesus was "an example of the Western mystic [who] integrated himself with God," and Jesus' message to us was: "cease clinging to our lesser selves [and find] our greater true selves." Contemplative prayer[317] "is a lifestyle dedicated to maximum awareness."[318]

Michael D'Antonio, secular journalist, in his book *Heaven on Earth*, wrote that he saw Peck as "becoming the Billy Graham of the New Age . . . a major New Age leader."[319]

Thomas Merton

Thomas Merton (1915–1968) has probably influenced New Spirituality more than any other person in the twentieth century. And he's

---

314 Scott Peck, *The Road Less Traveled* (New York: Simon & Schuster, 1985).

315. Scott Peck, *People of the Lie* (New York: Simon & Schuster, 1978), 283.

316. Scott Peck, *A World Waiting to Be Born* (New York: Bantam Books, 1997), 88, 89.

317. Contemplative prayer is not biblical prayer, no matter how spiritual it sounds. Rather, it is a turning off of our minds—putting them into neutral, in order to experience "the silence." Throwing our minds out of gear, trusting God to fill it, not only has no biblical warrant, but is an open door to spiritual deception. Paul said, "I shall pray with the spirit, and I shall pray with the mind" (1 Corinthians 14:15, RSV).

318. Scott Peck, *A World Waiting to Be Born* (New York: Bantam Books, 1997), 83.

319. Michael D'Antonio, *Heaven on Earth* (New York: Crown Publishing, 1992), 342, 352.

probably the most quoted by promoters of the New Spirituality/Innovation/Emergent Church movement. Roman Catholics highly praise Merton's works. One of his classic works sets forth Merton's core belief:

> It is a glorious destiny to be a member of the human race . . . now I realize what we all are. . . . If only they [people] could all see themselves as they really are. . . . I suppose the big problem would be that we would fall down and worship each other. . . . At the center of our being is a point of nothingness which is untouched by sin and by illusions, a point of pure truth. . . . It is in everybody. This little point . . . is the pure glory of God in us.[320]

Henri Nouwen

A Dutch Catholic priest (1932–1996), Henri Nouwen authored forty books on the spiritual life. A *Christian Century* magazine survey conducted in 2003 indicated that Nouwen's work was a first choice for both Catholic and mainline Protestant clergy.

Nouwen is praised for his warm, comforting appeal and impressive piety. But he walked firmly on the path of New Spirituality. Note his endorsement of the mantra,[321] a common thread in New Spirituality: "The quiet repetition of a single word can help us to descend with the mind into the heart. . . . This way of simple prayer . . . opens us to God's active presence."[322]

Or in *Bread for the Journey:* "Prayer is 'soul work' because our souls are those sacred centers where all is one. . . . It is in the heart of God that we can come to the full realization of the unity of all that is."[323]

Nouwen and Merton believed that their priestly experiences with silence were something that Protestants should understand—they should get the blessing of silence, shorthand for contemplative prayer.

Thomas Keating and Basil Pennington

Keating and Pennington, two Catholic monks, have written a number of popular books on contemplative prayer, such as *Centered Living, The*

---

320. Thomas Merton, *Reflections of a Guilty Bystander* (Garden City, New York: Doubleday, 1966), 140ff.

321. *Mantra,* as used in Eastern religions and New Spirituality thought, means a repeated word or phrase. The basic process is to focus and maintain concentration **without thinking** about what one is thinking about. Conscious thinking is gradually tuned out, until an altered state of consciousness is achieved.

322. Henri Nouwen, *The Way of the Heart* (San Francisco: Harper, 1981), 81.

323. Henri Nouwen, *Bread for the Journey* (San Francisco: Harper, 1997), readings for January 15, November 16.

Way of Centering Prayer, and *Open Mind, Open Heart.* In *Finding Grace at the Center,* they wrote:

> We should not hesitate to take the fruit of the age-old wisdom of the East and "capture" it for Christ. Indeed, those of us who are in ministry should make the necessary effort to acquaint ourselves with as many of these Eastern techniques as possible. . . . Many Christians who take their prayer life seriously have been greatly helped by Yoga, Zen, TM, and similar practices, especially where they have been initiated by reliable teachers and have a solidly developed Christian faith to find inner force and meaning to the resulting experiences.[324]

Pennington wrote, "The soul of the human family is the Holy Spirit."[325]

Gerald May

Gerald May, psychiatrist, is known for his leadership in the Christian twelve-step field and for being a cofounder and teacher in the Shalem Prayer Institute in Washington, D.C.[326] The Institute is a powerful leader in contemplative prayer. Admittedly strongly influenced by Eastern religions, he wrote in *Addiction and Grace* (acclaimed as a classic in addiction recovery) that "our core . . . one's center . . . is where we realize our essential unity with one another and with all God's creation." He then states how this is achieved: "I am not speaking here of meditation that involves guided imagery or scriptural reflections, but of a more contemplative practice in which one just sits still and stays awake with God."[327]

In his *The Awakened Heart* he made it even clearer that he is clearly in the mystical panentheistic[328] camp, when he talks about "cosmic presence," as revealed in "the Hindu greetings of *jai bhagwan* and *namaste* that reverence the divinity that both resides within and embraces us all."[329]

---

324. Thomas Keating and Basil Pennington, *Finding Grace at the Center* (Petersham, MA: St. Bede's Publishing, 1978), 5, 6.

325. Basil Pennington, *Centered Living, The Way of Centering Prayer* (New York: Doubleday, 1986), 104.

326. An attracton for some Adventist leaders.

327. Gerald May, *Addiction and Grace* (San Francisco: Harper, 1988), 102, 166.

328. Panentheism combines the classic theism (a personal God) with pantheism (God is impersonal, pervading all creation). Panentheism is the foundational worldview of those engaged in mystical, contemplative prayer—God's presence in all things. That is why so many New Spirituality leaders talk about "all is one."

329. Gerald May, *The Awakened Heart* (San Francisco: Harper, 1991), 179.

John Main

John Main, a Benedictine monk (1926–1982), seems to be quoted by most everyone in New Spirituality. He popularized contemplative prayer as the "way of the mantra" first taught to him by a Hindu monk.[330] In 1977, he and Laurence Freeman founded a monastery in Montreal, Quebec, dedicated to a revival of ancient prayer modalities, chief of which is repeating a mantra. *Ma-ra-na-tha*—an Aramaic word that means "Come, Lord Jesus," is often chosen for their mantras. Today, Ottawa, Ontario, has become the Canadian capital for Christian meditation, with practitioners in at least 114 countries. Australia alone has three hundred groups throughout the country.[331]

Evangelical Hybrids

One of the most well known leaders of the New Spirituality Movement, Richard Foster, the founder of Renovaré, is committed to working for the renewal of the Church of Jesus Christ in all her multifaceted expressions. Renovaré holds regional and local conferences, bringing together Christians across denominational lines for renewal. Foster's best known books include *Celebration of Discipline* (hailed by *Christianity Today* as one of the ten best books of the twentieth century[332]), *Streams of Living Water, Freedom of Simplicity,* and *The Challenge of the Disciplined Life.*

Of course, Foster has much that is devotionally helpful. But it doesn't take long to realize that Foster advocates a prayer movement that indeed can be proven to have strong links to Eastern mysticism.[333] Contemplative prayer, saturated with the influences of New Age, Eastern mysticism, universalism, and pantheism, is now infiltrating Christianity big time. In addition to his own writings, Foster has a great proclivity to quote or endorse others who are closely linked to Buddhism, such as the Catholic mystic Thomas Merton, whom he quotes thirteen times in *Celebration of Discipline.* Merton wrote, "I think I couldn't understand Christian teaching the way I do if it were not in the light of Buddhism."[334]

In the back of *Celebration of Discipline,* Foster listed Tilden Edward's

---

330. "Lives of the Heart and Soul," *Maclean's* magazine, September 17, 1987, 42.

331. http://en.wikipedia.org/wiki/John_Main.

332. *Christianity Today,* April 24, 2000.

333. "Every distraction of the body, mind, and spirit must be put into a kind of suspended animation before this deep work of God upon the soul can occur." *Celebration of Discipline* (San Francisco: Harper, 1978 edition), 13.

334. Frank X. Tuon, *The Dawn of the Mystical Age* (New York: Crossroad Publishing Co., 1997), 127.

book *Spiritual Friend* as an "excellent book on spirituality." Edward's position is well known: "This mystical stream [contemplative prayer] is the Western bridge to Far Eastern spirituality."[335]

I mention Thomas Merton and Tilden Edward only as examples of many other indisputable Christian mystics, such as Dallas Willard, Calvin Miller, Madame Guyon, and John of the Cross, each of whom Foster quotes often—and all heavily indebted to Eastern mysticism, especially Buddhism. The fascinating as well as alarming factor here is that Foster and others wrap their particular goals and methodologies with biblical words so that average readers feel they are truly being blessed. In fact, many Evangelicals would be disturbed by the charge that Foster is promoting a pseudo-Christian mysticism.[336]

Most people only read the froth of Foster and don't think twice about what he says regarding visualization, one of the modalities of finding "reality" within: "You can actually encounter the living Christ in the event. It can be more than an exercise of the imagination, it can be a genuine confrontation. . . . Jesus Christ will actually come to you."[337]

Further, he writes: "In your imagination allow your spiritual body, shining with light, to rise out of your physical body . . . up through the clouds into the stratosphere . . . deeper and deeper into outer space until there is nothing except the warm presence of the eternal Creator."

Then he goes on to say that this is more than imagination, but reality created with the mind.[338]

Brennan Manning

Brennan Manning is a delightful ex-Catholic priest who wrote *The Ragamuffin Gospel,* an emotionally gripping focus on God's forgiving nature and His love for the unworthy—but he works with a limited gospel. He, like Foster, has struck a responsive chord among Evangelicals who buy into his pleasing, passionate graciousness.

In his *Signature of Jesus,* Manning characterizes a contemplative spiritualist as one who "looks upon human nature as fallen but *redeemed,* flawed

---

335. Tilden Edward, *Spiritual Friend,* (New York: Paulist Press, 1980), 18.

336. In *Christianity Today,* October 2005, Richard J. Foster and Dallas Willard were interviewed in "The Making of the Christian." If one read only this article, he or she would have no idea what kind of philosophies and methodologies for which these two gracious men are known. It shows again that most anybody can be received with open arms if they continue to use conventional Christian terms in promoting their core messages that do not begin with the authority of the Bible.

337. Richard Foster, *Celebration of Discipline* (San Francisco: Harper, 1988), 26.

338. Ibid., 27.

but in essence good."[339] He wrote: "The first step in faith is to stop thinking about God at the time of prayer."[340] The second step is "without moving your lips, repeat the sacred word [or phrase] inwardly, slowly, and often." If distractions come, "simply return to listening to your sacred word."[341] He also encourages his readers to "celebrate the darkness" because "the ego has to break; and this breaking is like entering into a great darkness."[342]

Manning strongly supports Basil Pennington's book on *Centering Prayer*, saying that Pennington's methods provide "a way of praying that leads to a deep living relationship with God."[343]

Other Best-selling New Spirituality Authors

Leonard Sweet's[344] *Soul Tsunami* is filled with positive quotes and material from New Agers and globalists such as James Redfield, author of *The Celestine Prophecy*, Sarah Ban Breathnach, Annie Dillard, Wayne Dyer, and countless other well-known mystics and/or New Agers.

Sweet has been the bugle call for the Emergents: "God is birthing the greatest spiritual awakening in the history of the church. God is calling you to midwife that birth. Are you going to show up?"[345]

This passage from Sweet's *Quantum Spirituality* is common to New Spirituality: "If I find Christ, I will find my true self and if I find my true self, I will find Christ."[346]

Authentic Christians should pause and ask three questions:

1. Should Christians run from basic biblical principles (as they understandably flee from dry sermons and stale church programs) to cutting-

---

339. Brennan Manning, *Signature of Jesus* (Colorado Springs, CO: NavPress, 2002), 125.

340. Ibid., 212.

341. Ibid., 218.

342. Ibid., 145.

343. Brennan Manning, *The Ragamuffin Gospel* (Sisters, OR: Multnomah Press, 1990), back cover.

344. Endorsement on the cover of Sweet's book *Soul Tsunami* (Grand Rapids: Zondervan, 1999): "*Soul Tsunami* shows us why these are the greatest days for evangelism since the first century." Sweet is well known for his focus on unity—a worldwide oneness reflected in the growing union between the East and the West. In Sweet's *Quantum Spirituality*, we read: "Energy-fire experiences take us into ourselves only that we might reach outside of ourselves. Metanoia is a de-centering experience of connectedness and community." "The power of small groups is in their ability to develop the discipline to get people 'in-phase' with the Christ consciousness and connected with one another." 147.

345. Ibid., 34.

346. Ibid., 125.

edge, exotic New Spirituality, just because it couches its language in Christian terms, promising a fresh devotional life?

2. Should Christians allow the "instant gratification" appeal that permeates modern living to fog their spiritual connection with the God of the Bible—a very personal Father, Son, and Holy Spirit? Lasting friendships with other people take time to nurture, to learn all one can about the other. New Spirituality promises a new kind of "instant" gratification in the mantras of contemplative prayers.

3. Should Christians fall for "whatever works"—a phenomenal shift of the last century, not only in politics or science, but also in the religious world?

The Christian world once believed, generally, that truth is determined by what God has said and not on what seems to work "for me." The test of truth should not be, "Will it make me feel good about myself?" New Spirituality promises a self-actualized self-fulfillment and a union with God that is nowhere recommended in the Bible.

Bible "Endorsements"?

For example: Psalm 46:10 is frequently used to promote "listening" or contemplative prayers: "Be still and know that I am God." The DVD entitled *Be Still* bears the inscription of Psalm 46:10 on its case.[347]

But as one would do for any text, let's read the whole Psalm. David is surely not emptying his mind from thought or words of any kind. Notice how the Psalm begins: "God is our refuge and strength, a very present help in trouble." Or verse eight: "Come, behold the works of the Lord." Ignoring context is dangerous!

Christian Colleges and Seminaries

For those of us who were familiar with these colleges and seminaries a few decades ago, all this is mind-boggling. This list includes: Assemblies of God Theological Seminary, Biola University, Canadian Mennonite University, George Fox University Seminary, Mars Hill Graduate School, Simpson University, Trinity Western University, Wheaton College Graduate School, etc. For example, Assemblies of God Theological

---

347. April 2006, Fox Home Entertainment released the *Be Still* DVD, featuring Richard Foster, Dallas Willard, Calvin Miller, and Beth Miller—all with one main message: You cannot know God if you do not practice the art of going into the silence. That silence is not normal prayer, talking to a personal God, but a special state of mind induced through contemplative prayer that helps "believers" to avoid the addiction to use words. It seems that Beth Miller, a well-known Evangelical, was misled in not recognizing the intent of the other speakers on the DVD, and she issued a statement that said she does not promote mystical type/Eastern meditation (Emmaus, PA: Rodale Press, 2001), ix.

Seminary program is led by Earl Creps, whose syllabi include materials from Henri Nouwen, Brian McLaren, Ken Blanchard, Dan Kimball, Sally Morgenthaler, and Leonard Sweet. Some of these seminaries, Adventists know well.

To be familiar with the reader's denominational seminary, check out courses, or even master's and doctoral programs, that feature "spiritual formation," "innovation," and similar terms. Of course, almost any church since the apostle Paul puts great emphasis on "spiritual formation," as another term for "growth in grace" or for "sanctification." But the present-day curriculum using this term and the typical reading list of books by authors listed above is light years away from the biblical instruction.

"Insider" Terms Used by Contemplatives

Like most experts in any field, "contemplatives" also enjoy some special knowledge that others don't have; they use "inside" language, which is clear to the initiated but means little to "outsiders." For instance, you can track this "inside" language by noting any of the following:

Spiritual Formation, Spiritual Disciplines, Beyond Words, Being in the Present Moment, Slow Prayer, Awareness of Being, Mantra, Inner Light, Divine Center, Practicing the Presence, Dark Night of the Soul, Centering Prayer, Centering, Ignation Contemplation, Innovation, Spiritual Direction, Divine Mystery, A Thin Place, Ancient Prayer Practices, Yoga, Palms Up-Palms Down, Lectio Divina, The Jesus Prayer, Jesus Candles, Breath Prayers, Prayer Stations, Labyrinths and Enneagrams.[348]

An Intriguing Book

One of the most intriguing books published shortly after September 11, 2001, is *From the Ashes—A Spiritual Response to the Attack on America*.[349] In the introduction, Steven Waldman wrote: "At times like this, we can all benefit from hearing a wide variety of voices. That is why we at Beliefnet, the leading multifaith Web site on religion and spirituality, teamed up with Rodale, Inc. to collect the most eloquent and wise voices across the faith spectrum."[350]

---

348. The Enneagram (or Enneagon) is a nine-pointed diametric figure which is used in a number of teaching systems. The figure is believed to indicate the dynamic ways that certain aspects of things and processes are connected and change.

349. Beliefnet, ed., *From the Ashes—A Spiritual Response to the Attack on America* (Emmaus, PA: Rodale Books, 2001), 19–21.

350. Ibid., ix.

One of those "eloquent and wise voices" is Neale Donald Walsch, who wrote:

The Bible, which is only one of humanity's many sources of spiritual teaching, carries this message throughout, in both the Old Testament and the New. (Have we not all one father? Has not one God created us? Why then are we faithless to one another, profaning the covenant of our fathers?—Malachi 2:10 . . . so we, though many, are one body in Christ, and individually members one of another,— Romans 12:5 . . . Because there is one bread, we who are many are one body—1 Corinthians 10:17).

This is a message the human race has largely ignored. . . .

We must change ourselves. We must change the beliefs upon which our behaviors are based. We must create a different reality, build a new society. And we must do so not with political truths or with economic trusts, and not with cultural truths or even the remembered truths of our ancestors—for the sins of the fathers are being visited upon the sons. We must do with new spiritual truths. We must preach a new gospel, its healing message summarized in two sentences:

"We are all one. Ours is not a better way, ours is merely another way."

This fifteen-word message, delivered from every lectern and pulpit, from every rostrum and platform, could change everything overnight.[351]

One of the Alliance's co-founders and member of its board of directors, Marianne Williamson, presented these New Spirituality ideas on *The Oprah Winfrey Show* shortly after September 11. She outlined a peace plan based on New Age principles that would be an "alternative to Armageddon." And she announced that Walsch would soon be presenting his 5-Step Peace Plan.

Explosion of Peace Plans

What shall we make of all this and much more? Since September 11, 2001, this planet has seen an enormous explosion of peace plans, some devoted to the "gospel" of the New Spirituality/Emergent Church movement—that their "gospel" is the only way to a true and lasting world peace. And these plans are not mere wishes.

Let's be unequivocally clear: All of us seek peace. All of us want poverty, ignorance, and disease to be banished from this planet. Our challenge comes down to one question: What is the gospel message that permeates these various humanitarian-uplift plans?

---

351. Ibid., 19–21.

Modern peace plans are magnificently organized and enchantingly deceptive. What better way could be devised to set up the world with a unified voice that would heap ridicule on any group that would try to expose their errors? Never before has the whole world been so wired and connected as today—Web-based computer systems, global cell-phone networks, greater international air travel, GPS systems, etc. A united voice, "one mind," could speak, and immediately the whole world would see and hear![352]

One of the most widely known "peace plans" began with a home-run announcement in Angel Stadium, Anaheim, California, on April 16, 2005, before thirty thousand people, by Rick Warren, author of the best-selling book *The Purpose Driven Life* and founding pastor of Saddleback Church in Lake Forest, California.

Warren unveiled the church's commitment to a new reformation in Christianity and a vision for a worldwide spiritual awakening in the twenty-first century through the PEACE Plan that he believes will mobilize one billion foot soldiers from the Christian church on missions by the year 2020. He said that "people suffer each day from problems so big no government can solve them. The only thing big enough to solve the problems of spiritual emptiness, selfish leadership, poverty, disease, and ignorance is the network of millions of churches all around the world."[353]

He emphasized that "the Scripture shows us that Jesus shared the Good News, trained leaders, helped the poor, cared for the sick, and taught the children. Our P.E.A.C.E. Plan will just do the five things Jesus did while he was here on earth."[354]

Warren explained that P.E.A.C.E. is an acronym that stands for "Plant churches, Equip servant leaders, Assist the poor, Care for the sick, and Educate the next generation."[355]

Since that time his church program has airlifted thousands of people and supplies to various villages in Africa.

Labyrinth

Another remarkable signal of New Spirituality is the "labyrinth"[356]

---

352 See chapter 5: "The Almost Invisible Arms of Globalization."

353. http://www.crossroad.to/charts/millennium-goals-peace.htm; http://www.rickwarren.com/about/thepeaceplan.

354. http://www.rickwarren.com/about/thepeaceplan.

355. Ibid.

356. The labyrinth is a path usually designed with intricate passageways and blind alleys. The most famous labyrinth of ancient times was the Cretan lair of the mythological Minotaur. Turf labyrinths still exist in England, Germany, and Scandinavia and were linked to fertility rituals. The Roman Catholic Church adopted the practice, and Christians made their

that is being featured at many Evangelical conferences, especially where younger members are being attracted. Often called "A-maze-ing Prayer," the labyrinth feature seems to fill the hunger of those turned off by well-choreographed worship services, every minute filled with music, videos, and preaching. Walking the "labyrinth" offers a private, unhurried, mystery-filled, meditative experience.

It seems that hungry experience-seekers are like moths drawn to the flame, ever seeking to know "god" through some kind of spiritual experience. Something seems to click in this pursuit. If you were handed a Ouija board and told that it has been totally redeemed by your spiritual leader and that it would bring you into a greater experience of God, would you take the occult device, looking for the promised higher spiritual experience? The labyrinth shares a main goal with the Ouija board—that of communicating with the occult.

In Deuteronomy 12:1–4 and in Exodus 34:10–17, we are admonished not to use anything connected to pagan ritual. We need to carefully trace "spiritual disciplines" to their origins and associations before becoming sucked in. There is one source of true spirituality—all other suggestions and enticements come from demonic sources.

At the National Pastor's Conference in San Diego, March 9–13, 2004 (which seemed to lead the way), the labyrinth path was formed by black lines on a thirty-five-foot-square piece of canvas laid on the floor. Participants were given a CD player with headphones to guide the journey through the eleven stations on the passageway. They were told not to rush but to slow down, breathe deeply, and fully focus on God.[357]

Later in 2004, Graceland, at Santa Cruz, California, featured the labyrinth as part of its annual art event and sold "The Prayer Path" kit that transformed a room into a medieval prayer sanctuary. Leaders who promote these labyrinths rejoice that meditative prayer "resonates with hearts of emerging generations."

---

pilgrimages to cathedrals in Chartres, Rheims, or Amiens, where they completed their spiritual journeys in the cathedral labyrinths. The patterns of the labyrinth are similar to Buddhist mandalas and the Japanese Zen practice of *kinhim* ("walking meditation"). Jean Houston, in the early 1990s, introduced the Christian world again to the practice of seeking enlightenment through walking the labyrinth when she linked up with Lauren Artress, spiritual leader of Grace Cathedral in San Francisco—to bring people back to their center and allow them to experience "Spirit" for themselves. See http://www.gracecathedral.org/labyrinth. Jean Houston is listed on the Internet as one of the top-ten New Age speakers in North America. Many participants at Gorbachev's State of the World forum in 1997 also walked the labyrinth at Grace Cathedral.

357. http://www.inplainsite.org/html/the_labyrinth.html

Publishers

When I noticed that Zondervan Publishing Company, a leading New Spirituality publisher, sponsored the National Pastor's Convention in February 22–25, 2006, I wondered who else publishes New Spirituality materials. To my surprise, I discovered that InterVarsity Press, NavPress (Navigators), Multnomah Books, Integrity, Thomas Nelson, Bethany House, Harold Shaw, and Harper SF all publish these materials. If I listed all the books now available, most readers would be equally shocked—they are the up-front best sellers, wherever Christian books are sold!

In our next chapter, we will focus on how to recognize New Spirituality/Emergence authors and speakers.

CHAPTER NINE

THEME:

The last-day spiritual tsunami will have unprecedented appeal in uniting all peoples in all lands.

Identifying the New Spirituality

Continuing from chapter 8, let's summarize: Remember that error often comes wrapped in pleasing truth, perhaps even 90 percent truth. Then again, lots of error comes mixed with only 20 percent truth or even less!

What are the chief distinguishing characteristics of the New Spirituality/Innovation/Emerging Church/Spiritual Formation movement? Obviously, not every promoter of New Spirituality emphasizes each of these characteristics—but it is easy to identify its promoters. Below is a summary of the primary marks of New Spirituality as covered in chapter 8— each characteristic could be an entire book!

- ‣ Functional denial of the authority of Scripture
- ‣ Feelings eclipse reason in seeking truth
- ‣ Contemplative, repetitive prayers
- ‣ Visualizations to discover inner power and guidance
- ‣ Abundant reference to practices and teachings of mysticism and known mystics.

▸ Ancient "disciplines" are to be recovered and celebrated

▸ Unmediated link to the absolute—"god" is within everyone

▸ All paths lead to God

▸ Finding one's core—one finds this within: the great mystery called "god."

Emergent Church Movement

An interesting feature of many in the "Innovation/Emergent Church" movement is that they are exhibiting a reaction against many church-based programs. They find common ground among those who are do-ing their spiritual searching in local Starbucks stores, cafés, store-front buildings, and other leisure centers. In other words, they are repotting Christianity into new cultural and intellectual ground.

Some groups emphasize being simple followers of Jesus, avoiding the congregational milieu, and meeting in homes. They tend to be suspicious of church hierarchy and doctrinal formulations; they talk of "emerging authority." They are less concerned about safeguarding boundaries; they use words such as "liquid" churches. And they are far more open to a wider sphere of activity than just evangelism (which is a word not really in their vocabulary).

One of the key "inside" terms is "cross over to the other side," or varia-tions of these words. Brian McLaren emphasizes this concept in his book *The Church on the Other Side*.[358] Many followers use these terms to depict a radical break with historical evangelical thought and practice. McLaren goes beyond promoting a change in pastoral methods to deal with the "postmodern world." He challenges ministers to rethink their message and not just their methods.[359]

Postmoderns now insist that truth is no longer found in the objective teachings of the Bible but in whatever the individual or community ac-cepts—truth is whatever is arrived at through consensus. In other words, contradiction with historical Christianity is not only acceptable, it is wel-

---

358. Brian McLaren, *The Church on the Other Side* (Grand Rapids, MI: Zondervan, 2001).

359. Os Guinness said it well: "What happens . . . is drastic. Truths or cus-toms that do not fit in with the modern assumption are put up in the creedal attic to collect dust. They are of no more use. The modification or removal of offending assumptions is permanent. What begins as a question of tactics escalates to a question of truth; apparently, the mod-ern assumptions are authoritative. Is the traditional idea unfashionable, superfluous, or just plain wrong? No matter. It doesn't fit in, so it has to go." *Prophetic Untimeliness: A Challenge to the Idol or Relevance* (Grand Rapids, MI: Baker Book House, 2003), 58.

comed. However one says it, "crossing over to the other side" means, for many, an up-front denial of the biblical gospel. It makes one wonder what Jude would say today: "I found it necessary to write to you exhorting you to contend earnestly for the faith which was once for all delivered to the saints" (verse 3).

The Emergent Jewish Movement

Emergent Christian and Jewish leaders met in a first-ever meeting on January 16 and 17, 2006, at the Brandeis-Bardin Institute in Simi Valley, California, to think together in developing congregations that pushed beyond the traditional categories of "left" and "right."

Prominent Emergent Christian theologian Brian McLaren (Author of *A New Kind of Christian*) met with Synagogue 3000's (S3K) leadership three times later to discuss shared concerns, particularly surrounding attempts by younger Christians and Jews to express their spiritual commitments through social justice. "We have so much common ground on so many levels," he notes.

According to Emergent–U.S. National Coordinator Tony Jones, this meeting has historic possibilities.

"As emerging Christian leaders have been pushing through the polarities of left and right in an effort to find a new, third way, we've been desperate to find partners for that quest," Jones said. "It's with great joy and promise that we partner with the leaders of S3K to talk about the future and God's Kingdom."[360]

The Emergent Church movement is not a fad; it will find common ground across all denominational lines, especially among the young who search for new ways to express themselves in spiritual pursuits.

Additional Marks of Emergent Church Movements

▶ Bible no longer the ultimate authority for many well-known leaders

▶ Bible dumbed-down, with emphasis on images and sensual experiences

▶ More emphasis on "what's in it for me" in the "here and now"

▶ More emphasis on kingdom of God on earth rather than on Christ returning

▶ Many bridges established that lead to unity with the Roman Catholic Church

▶ Christianity needs to be re-invented to provide "meaning" for this generation

360. http://tribela.typepad.com/tribe_los_angeles/emergent_church.

▶ Trend toward ecumenical unity for world peace; many ways to God

Counterfeiting the Everlasting Gospel

What does New Spirituality have to do with "counterfeits" in the end time? A thoughtful writer wrote:

Satan can present a counterfeit so closely resembling the truth that it deceives those who are willing to be deceived, who desire to shun the self-denial and sacrifice demanded by the truth; but it is impossible for him to hold under his power one soul who honestly desires, at whatever cost, to know the truth.[361]

Ellen White nailed this counterfeit gospel as she observed it developing in her day with its new cloak:

There is a spurious experience prevailing everywhere. Many are continually saying, "All that we have to do is to believe in Christ." They claim that faith is all we need. In its fullest sense, this is true; but they do not take it in the fullest sense.

To believe in Jesus is to take him as our redeemer and our pattern. If we abide in him and he abides in us, we are partakers of his divine nature, and are doers of his word. The love of Jesus in the heart will lead to obedience to all his commandments. But the love that goes no farther than the lips, is a delusion; it will not save any soul.

Many reject the truths of the Bible, while they profess great love for Jesus; but the apostle John declares, "He that saith, I know him, and keepeth not his commandments, is a liar, and the truth is not in him." While Jesus has done all in the way of merit, we ourselves have something to do in the way of complying with the conditions. "If ye love me," said our Saviour, "keep my commandments."[362]

A counterfeit gospel will become a worldwide movement capturing the attention and praise of the media. It will be a limited gospel, a gospel of convenience that will satisfy modern "felt" needs. The consequence of the counterfeit limited gospel so prevalent today, especially in the seeker-friendly churches, as well in the Emergent Movement in all churches, is a church full of people enjoying the *grace of forgiveness* but with no clear grasp of the *grace of power* that will indeed make them into overcomers. One of the chief reasons for this limited understanding of the grace of power (Hebrews 4:16) is their cloudy understanding of why the commandments of God are essential to their salvation.

Larry Crabb, one of the best-known Christian counselors in

---

361. Ellen G. White, *The Great Controversy*, 528.
362. White, *Historical Sketches of the Foreign Missions*, 188, 189.

America, is spiritual director for the fifty-five-thousand-member American Association of Christian Counselors. His books are many. He predicted: "The spiritual climate is ripe. Jesus seekers across the world are being prepared to abandon the old way of the written code for the new way of the spirit."

Tony Campolo, in his book *Speaking My Mind,* said that "mysticism (contemplative prayer) provides some hope for common ground between Christianity and Islam." A world united under the cloak of spiritualism and New Spirituality is exactly what the biblical picture of the end times predicts.[363]

---

363. One example of many New Spirituality leaders is Alice Bailey. Note this excerpt from "The Externalization of the Hierarchy," Section II, The General World Picture: "The intelligent youth of all countries are rapidly repudiating orthodox theology, state ecclesiasticism and the control of the church. They are neither interested in man-made interpretations of truth nor in past quarrels between the major world religions. At the same time, they are profoundly interested in the spiritual values and are earnestly seeking verification of their deep seated unvoiced recognitions. They look to no bible or system of so-called inspired spiritual knowledge and revelation, but their eyes are on the undefined larger whole in which they seek to merge and lose themselves, such as the state, an ideology, or humanity itself. In this expression of the spirit of self-abnegation may be seen the appearance of the deepest truth of all religion and the justification of the Christian message. Christ, in His high place, cares not whether men accept the theological interpretations of scholars and churchmen, but He does care whether the keynote of His life of sacrifice and service is reproduced among men; it is immaterial to Him whether the emphasis laid upon the detail and the veracity of the Gospel story is recognized and accepted, for He is more interested that the search for truth and for subjective spiritual experience should persist; He knows that within each human heart is found that which responds instinctively to God, and that the hope of ultimate glory lies hid in the Christ-consciousness.

"Therefore, in the new world order, spirituality will supersede theology; living experience will take the place of theological acceptances. The spiritual realities will emerge with increasing clarity and the form aspect will recede into the background; dynamic, expressive truth will be the keynote of the new world religion.... When the racial problem has disappeared through the recognition of the one Life, when the economic problem has been solved by the nations working cooperatively together, when the problem of right government within each nation has been determined by the free will of their respective peoples, and the spirit of true religion is unobstructed by ancient forms and interpretations, then we shall see a world in process of right experience, right human relations and a spiritual moving forward to reality." http://laluni.hellowyou.ws/netnews/bk/esternalisation/extel1087.html.

Satan's Strategy During God's Last Appeal

But what will be Satan's strategy during this time when God's Spirit and power will be especially evident? Ellen White continued:

The enemy of souls desires to hinder this work; and *before the time for such a movement shall come, he will endeavor to prevent it by introducing a counterfeit.* In those churches which he can bring under his deceptive power he will make it appear that God's special blessing is poured out; there will be manifest what is thought to be great religious interest. Multitudes will exult that God is working marvelously for them, when the work is that of another spirit. Under a religious guise, Satan will seek to extend his influence over the Christian world.

In many of the revivals which have occurred during the last half century, the same influences have been at work, to a greater or less degree, that will be manifest in the *more extensive movements of the future.* There is an *emotional excitement,* a *mingling of the true with the false,* that is well adapted to mislead.[364]

What are the basic components of Satan's *"counterfeit"* that will mislead people into thinking "that God's special blessing" is present in their meetings? (Here is how we can identify the main elements in the New Spirituality/Innovation/Emergent Church/Spiritual Formation movement, *remembering that not all will embrace all these points in each one's emphasis!*)

"Emotional excitement, a mingling of the true with the false, that is well adapted to mislead."[365]

"Neglect the testimony of the Bible. . . soul-testing truths which require self-denial and renunciation of the world."[366]

"A wrong conception of the character, the perpetuity, and the obligation of the divine law . . . has resulted in lowering the standard of piety in the church."[367]

"Many religious teachers assert that Christ by His death abolished the law, and men are henceforth free from its requirements."[368]

"The hope of salvation is accepted without a radical change of heart or reformation of life."[369]

364. White, *The Great Controversy,* 464; emphasis supplied.
365. Ibid.
366. Ibid.
367. Ibid., 465.
368. Ibid., 468.
369. Ibid.

"Erroneous theories of sanctification, also, springing from neglect or rejection of the divine law, have a prominent place in the religious movements of the day."[370]

"There can be no self-exaltation, no boastful claim to freedom from sin, on the part of those who walk in the shadow of Calvary's cross. . . . Those who live nearest to Jesus discern most clearly the frailty and sinfulness of humanity, and their only hope is in the merit of a crucified and risen Saviour."[371]

"The desire for an easy religion, that requires no striving, no self-denial, no divorce from the follies of the world, has made the doctrine of faith, and faith only, popular doctrine."[372]

"The position that it is of no consequence what men believe is one of Satan's most successful deceptions."[373]

"In order to sustain erroneous doctrines or unchristian practices, some will seize upon passages of Scripture separated from the context, perhaps quoting half of a single verse as proving their point, when the remaining portion would show the meaning to be quite opposite."[374]

The belief "that Satan has no existence as a personal being."[375]

"It is a masterpiece of Satan's deceptions to keep the minds of men searching and conjecturing in regard to that which God has not made known, and which He does not intend that we shall understand."[376]

"The theory of eternal torment is one of the false doctrines."[377]

"A large class to whom the doctrine of eternal torment is revolting, are driven to the opposite error. . . . holding that the soul is naturally immortal, they see no alternative but to conclude that all mankind will finally be saved. . . . Thus, the sinner can live in selfish pleasure, disregarding the requirements of God, and yet expect to be finally received into His favor."[378]

---

370. Ibid., 469.
371. Ibid., 471.
372. Ibid., 472.
373. Ibid., 520.
374. Ibid., 521.
375. Ibid., 524.
376. Ibid., 523.
377. Ibid., 536.
378. Ibid., 537.

"Satan can present a counterfeit so closely resembling the truth that it deceives those who are willing to be deceived, who desire to shun the self-denial and sacrifice demanded by the truth."[379]

"The Bible is interpreted in a matter that is pleasing to the unrenewed heart, while its solemn and vital truths are made of no effect. Love is dwelt upon as the chief attribute of God, but it is degraded to a weak sentimentalism, making little distinction between good and evil. God's justice, His denunciations of sin, the requirements of His holy law, are all kept out of sight."[380]

"Thousands deify nature, while they deny the God of nature."[381]

"The line of distinction between professed Christians and the ungodly is now hardly distinguishable. Church members love what the world loves and are ready to join with them, and Satan determines to unite them in one body and thus strengthen his cause by sweeping all into the ranks of spiritualism."[382]

"So closely will the counterfeit resemble the true that it will be impossible to distinguish between them except by the Holy Scriptures."[383]

"Many claim that it matters not what one believes, if his life is only right. But the life is molded by the faith. If light and truth is within our reach, and we neglect to improve the privilege of hearing and seeing it, we virtually reject it; we are choosing darkness rather than light."[384]

I repeat—not everyone falling under the fog of last-day counterfeits will believe or be affected by all the earmarks of counterfeits as listed above. That fact alone gives us caution as we hear concepts promoted that are advocated by the emerging leaders in the New Spirituality/Innovation/Emergent Church/Spiritual Formation movement. But they all have common threads that Ellen White identified with such amazing prophetic predictions.

Summary

In the last twenty-five years, we have been watching a spiritual

---

379. Ibid., 528.
380. Ibid., 558.
381. Ibid., 583.
382. Ibid., 588.
383. Ibid., 593.
384. Ibid., 597.

tsunami sweeping over North America. Called New Spirituality/Emergent Church/Spiritual Formation, much of this amorphous movement crosses denominational lines. It includes those who have bolted their former denominational ties as they seek meaning in life through personal, subjective feeling. General bookstores, as well as Christian markets, are awash with best sellers that promote finding Reality through contemplative prayer, walking labyrinths, and imaging the fulfillment of promises made by prosperity preachers.

Turned off by conventional churches that have lost their spiritual pulse, these seekers also have turned off the Bible as a source of divine revelation. But these "turned-off" ones are not leaving the circle of Christianity in order to follow the occult world—they are helping the occult world remodel the Christian Church, without realizing it. When clear Bible texts are made to say that "God is in everything and everything is in God," we should recognize the subtle deception that is flooding even Christian bookstores.

Never has a generation of young and old, of rich and poor, thrown itself with such abandon into the winds of subjectivism, hoping to satisfy its desires for spiritual warmth without self-denial. The world on all continents is being led to conform to a universal spirituality that proclaims the oneness of all—a brotherhood of "believers" who live in tolerance toward one another's religious beliefs because the Reality they worship is deeper than divisive doctrine. Or so they think! This global, unifying spirituality positions the world to welcome, perhaps the Mother Mary, the Great Peacemaker. Or the great impersonator himself—Satan himself, when he imitates the return of Jesus.

Last-day appeals of "Can't we all be brothers and sisters?" will be more than intimidating, they will be coercive, leading to the day when men and women who "don't go along" will not be able to "buy or sell." In fact, they will be condemned "to be killed" for their defense of truth (Revelation 13:15, 17).

Yes, these are the days Paul predicted: "For the time will come when they will not endure sound doctrine, but according to their own desires, because they have itching ears, they will heap up for themselves teachers; and they will turn their ears away from the truth, and be turned aside to fables" (2 Timothy 4:3, 4).

And Jesus Himself warned: "Many will come in My name, saying, 'I am the Christ,' and will deceive many" (Matthew 24:5).

"For false christs and false prophets will rise and show great signs and miracles to deceive, if possible, even the elect. See, I have told you beforehand" (Matthew 24:24, 25).

Are we there yet?

CHAPTER TEN

THEME:

Jesus will return when Satan has reached maximum ferocity against God's loyalists.

Evil—the One Thing Satan Created!

A nd the dragon [the devil and Satan, vs. 9] was enraged with the woman [church], and he went to make war with the rest of her offspring, who keep the commandments of God and have the testimony of Jesus Christ" (Revelation 12:17).

"And then the lawless one will be revealed, whom the Lord will consume with the breath of His mouth and destroy with the brightness of His coming. The coming of the lawless one is according to the working of Satan, with all power, signs, and lying wonders, and with all unrighteous deception among those who perish, because they did not receive the love of the truth, that they might be saved" (2 Thessalonians 2:8–10).

In the great controversy between Christ and Satan, Satan caused the controversy, not God. God did not create evil—He created freedom. Evil is the dark side of freedom; when anyone says no to God, it is a law that evil and its consequences are the sure result.

Lucifer (the "light bearer"), was created "full of wisdom and perfect in beauty"—"the seal of perfection" (Ezekiel 28:12, 13). Mentally, physically, emotionally, socially, spiritually—he had it all!

The first of all created intelligences, he was the "anointed cherub who covers" (Ezekiel 28:14). He was "anointed" for a special purpose; he was God's minister of cosmic communications—the "bearer of God's light of truth"—the angel closest to the Godhead. Nothing was hidden from his gaze except private councils between God the Father and God the Son.

Think about it! Lucifer was eminently qualified to accurately represent the truth about God to all created intelligences who would eventually inhabit the universe. Did he not walk "up and down in the midst of the stones of fire" (Ezekiel 28:14)? Was he not privy to more truth about God's character and government than any other created being? Was he not highly exalted by God Himself?

He was that first link between the Creator and His creation. As God's light/truth bearer, his highest responsibility was say what is right about God. Whenever a question would arise, Lucifer had the qualifications and the job description to represent God's position fully and correctly.

Could any created being ever have a more important, fulfilling responsibility?

The divine record says: "You were perfect in your ways . . . till iniquity was found in you" (Ezekiel 28:15). How can anyone understand this proto–iniquity? Isaiah noted that Lucifer "said in his *heart*" (Isaiah 14:13; emphasis added) that he desired a still higher position, still more power! Of whom was he jealous? Over whom did he aspire to climb? Only One being stood between Lucifer and God the Father, and that was God the Son, through whom God created all things. Lucifer did not understand God the Son. He began to doubt God's statements that this Christ, this Anointed One, had been eternally co-equal with God the Father. Lucifer began to think God the Son was a created being who had been elevated to God-status. If the Son had been elevated from being a created being to being co-equal with God, why couldn't Lucifer also be so elevated? Who was holding Lucifer back from being so honored? Why was Lucifer not allowed to create if the Son was allowed to create? Lucifer went from distrusting God, to being jealous of Christ, to feelings of resentment and being discriminated against. Pride prevailed over reason. Lucifer allowed his pride and ambition to erode the divine bonding of trust and love.

> Little by little Lucifer came to indulge the desire for self-exaltation. . . . Though all his glory was from God, this mighty angel came to regard it as pertaining to himself. Not content with his position, though honored above the heavenly host, he ventured to covet homage due alone to the Creator.[385]

Apparently, Lucifer grew weary of telling what was good and right about God—he wanted some of that honor! He became less satisfied with his peerless privileges and wanted to be more than the executive vice

---

385. White, *Patriarchs and Prophets*, 35.

president of the universe! However it happened, and as preposterous as it now seems, he began to lay plans to also "sit on the mount of congregation on the farthest sides of the north" and be recognized "like the Most High."

Power Leads to Control and the Twilight of Freedom

So for the first time in the universe of free intelligences, the craving for "power," the "desire for self-exaltation," emerged. How such feelings and thoughts could possibly arise in one so close to God is beyond human understanding. Paul called it "the mystery of iniquity" (2 Thessalonians 2:7). Though it is unfathomable, this fateful desire for self-exaltation and power sows seeds of coercion and control—somebody, somewhere, will lose freedom.

Whenever the passion for power emerges in history or in our own hearts, we hear Satan's words: "I will ascend . . . I will exalt . . . I will be like the Most High" (Isaiah 14:13, 14). The religion of power (it becomes the passion of all lives that are not committed to the power of God) is the antithesis of genuine Christianity. The desire for power not only permeates secular philosophies, it unfortunately pervades much of what we call Christian aspirations and service. To be considered "somebody," to have a name that sets one apart or above another (the right title!), to be recognized as important (as symbolized by the corner office or the designated parking place), becomes the primary, overriding passion in life, rising even above one's commitment to responsibility and integrity.[386]

Fueling Satan's lust for power were mysterious feelings we now call jealousy, envy, and, inevitably, hatred. This prototype scenario is played out daily in those who have never been converted to Christ's way of looking at power and His example of how to use it.

Ezekiel wrote that Lucifer's iniquity, his disappearing rectitude, was also rooted in vanity—"Your heart was lifted up because of your beauty; you corrupted your wisdom for the sake of your splendor" (Ezekiel 28:17). Vanity is the other side of jealousy.

Slowly, imperceptibly, jealousy became envy, and Lucifer began to rationalize (justify) his strange feelings. Then his feelings became words—sly, devious, deceptive words. Lucifer, the brightest of all creation, was slowly, imperceptibly becoming Satan, the beginning of entropy[387] in a perfect universe.

---

386. See author's *God At Risk* (Roseville, CA: Amazing Facts, 2004), "Appendix C: The Heart of Power," 414–424.

387. "Entropy . . . the steady degradation or disorganization of a system or society."—*Webster's Ninth Collegiate Dictionary.*

Jesus said that Lucifer became "the devil . . . a murderer from the beginning . . . no truth in him . . . a liar, and the father of it" (John 8:44). John wrote: "He who sins is of the devil, for the devil has sinned from the beginning" (1 John 3:8). Hard to believe that Satan wanted to "be like the Most High" (Isaiah 14:14); actually, he wanted to murder God and take His place as ruler of the universe. (How else could he take God's place?) He later proved this by murdering Jesus!

John was told about this awful war that developed "in heaven" and how it affected planet Earth:

> Michael and his angels fought against the dragon; and the dragon and his angels fought, but they did not prevail, nor was a place found for them in heaven any longer. So the great dragon was cast out, that serpent of old, called the Devil and Satan, who deceives the whole world; he was cast to the earth, and his angels were cast out with him (Revelation 12:7–9).

God created a perfect planet; everything was "very good" when the first human couple was created (Genesis 1:31). But we have lived through nearly six thousand years of what has happened since Satan was "cast to the earth."

Evil is a bitter plant. Its consequences travel through the genetic stream. The history of this planet can be easily written as a chronicle of wars, bloodshed, suffering, and misery. Any way you figure it, "the wages of sin [evil] is death" (Romans 6:23).

But planet Earth now is in its last days—and it's never been this late before! We live in the days when the great controversy on this planet has reached its tipping point—Satan knows that he has a "short time" (Revelation 12:12). He is now enraged, furious, with God's loyalists, pulling out all the stops on his organ of fury and hate (Revelation 12:13).

What are Satan's chief weapons? He has had thousands of years of practice and experience, beginning before this earth was populated. We have his track record. He brought great grief to the heavenly family before he was "cast down" to this earth. He has been sharpening his skills ever since.

Satan's Four Integrated Skills

Satan is skilled in . . .

▶ the use of consistent, destructive lies (*pretense*)

▶ blaming others for the damage he is doing (*scapegoating*)

▶ clouding the issues; changing the meaning of words; substitution of opinion for absolute truths (*confusion*)

▶ the use of power to control or destroy others (*coercion*)[388]

Anyone infected with self-centeredness (as Lucifer-turned-Satan was) soon develops intolerance to criticism, a bottomless hate for the reprover (whether God or man), an intellectual deviousness that glorifies the means rather than the end, and a ghastly use of power to coerce others.

All the while, pretenders on evil's pathway learn ways to act *as if* they are respectable, trustworthy, deeply concerned about the feelings of others, and, yes, even the champions of individual rights and "freedom." But they are "pretenders."

The culmination of all this evil (and all that Satan represents) is to "hurt and destroy" (see Isaiah 65:25). That is exactly the framework in which events in the last acts of the great controversy prior to our Lord's second advent will take place: "He was granted power to give breath to the image of the beast, that the image of the beast should both speak and cause as many as would not worship the image of the beast to be killed" (Revelation 13:15).

No Theological Theory

I am not speaking of a theological theory. Nor is evil confined to other-worldly, unseen deviltry. Satan's character has been incarnated many times throughout human history. Consider Josef Stalin. On November 7, 1937 (Revolutionary Day), after the military parade in Red Square, at the feast in Marshal Kliment Voroshilov's home, Stalin gave a toast that was remarkably honest and chilling—and everyone there knew exactly what he was saying, for they all had lived through a ghastly bloodletting in which tens of thousands of Russian military leaders had been murdered:

> "I would like to say a few words, perhaps not festive ones. The Russian tsars did a great deal that was bad. They robbed and enslaved the people. They waged wars and seized territories in the interests of landowners. But they did one thing that was good—they amassed an enormous state. . . . We have united the state in such a way that if any part were isolated from the common-socialist state,

388. These four integrated skills move in sequence, pretense to coercion. Pretenders always appear as up-front supporters, covering up their real motives. Otherwise, it would not be deceit or deceptive. When the issues become more public, the pretender continues his deception by blaming someone else for the "mess." When the "mess" involves more people, and "sides" are being formed, the pretender continues his deceptions by confusing the issue, formulating new definitions for traditional words, always appearing to be supporting what he is destroying. When the pretender has enough followers, he uses deception again by appealing to the majority to silence the minority, one way or another.

it would not only inflict harm on the latter but would be unable to exist independently and would inevitably fall under foreign subjugation. Therefore, whoever attempts to destroy that unity of the socialist state . . . is an enemy, a sworn enemy of the state and of the peoples of the USSR. And we will destroy each and every such enemy, even if he is an Old Bolshevik; we will destroy all his kin, his family. We will mercilessly destroy anyone who, by his deeds or his thoughts—yes, his thoughts—threatens the unity of this socialist state. To the complete destruction of all enemies, themselves and their kin!"

Approving exclamations followed: "To the great Stalin!"[389]

Recognizing Satan's Strategy in the Last Generation

How will Satan use *pretense*—the use of consistent, destructive lies—in attempting to destroy faith in the last days? After all, Jesus put His finger on one of the signs of the end times: "Nevertheless, when the Son of Man comes, will He really find faith on the earth?" (Luke 18:8).

What happens to individuals, legislatures, even Supreme Courts, when arguments used are pretentious "lies" in respect to what they are supposed to be upholding? Why the pretense of honor, or love, or justice, when someone's freedom is limited because of his or her color or religion?

In the family, we often see a spouse pretending love, all the while destroying the mate or child with suffocating control, searing blame, or outrageous, but believable, lies. In the military, we are told that we must "waste" a village to save a country. Even the U.S. Supreme Court once approved, in the name of a free America, imprisoning Jehovah's Witnesses who chose not to salute the American flag (for religious reasons).[390] How many decades did the highest court in the United States classify Ameri-

---

389. The Diary of Georgi Dimitrov, the Bulgarian head of the Comintern, kept from 1933 to 1949. Cited in *The Wilson Quarterly*, Summer 2003, 114.

390. 1940 Minersville School District v. Gobitis 310 US 586 (1940). The Court portrayed the case as balancing conflicting claims of liberty and authority. The school's interest in creating national unity was more important than the rights of the students to refuse to salute the flag. However, the Supreme Court overruled their previous decision in West Virginia Board of Education v. Barnette, 319 U.S. 624 (1943), recognizing the fundamental right to religious liberty when it held that Jehovah's Witness schoolchildren could not be penalized when they refused to salute the American flag for religious reasons. In an opinion noted for its eloquence, Justice Robert H. Jackson wrote, "If there is one fixed star in our constitutional constellation, it is that no official, high or petty, can prescribe what shall be orthodox in politics, nationalism, religion, or other matters of opinion or force citizens to confess by word or act their faith therein."

can blacks as only two-thirds of a citizen and protected a slave-holder's ownership of slaves as personal property—in a country that told the world that "all men are created equal"?[391]

This is not the place to argue the past. We do, however, have a responsibility to discern the signs of the times, not only as citizens of the "land of the free and the home of the brave," but as students of prophecy. John the revelator tells us that, in the end time, Satan and his followers, angels and humans, will exercise all their skill in making evil so deceptive that most of the world will have "marveled and followed the beast"[392] as they behold his amazing power and authority—and most of the world will join Satan, finally, in attempting to kill those who resist their lies.

Setting up the United States

So how will Satan's lies set up the United States to be the world leader in uniting all nations under a religious authority that has universal clout and enough muscle to enforce economic hardship and persecution on those they hate? How will satanic lies become so believable that in time it can be said that "the world worshiped the beast" (Revelation 13:4)?

How?

▸ By pretense and consistent lies, though appearing to serve a noble purpose

▸ By blaming those they hate for causing the national crises

▸ By causing confusion in substituting policy for principle (the end justifies the means), substituting opinion for absolute truths, and redefining the meaning of words

▸ By employing various forms of coercion—and all to one end, the eradication of dissent and individual freedom

In 2003, during the spring war in Iraq, we had a fascinating example of how masters of evil will always find an audience who will believe them, in spite of what seems to others as undeniable reality. The Iraqi Information Minister Mohammed Saeed al-Sahaf (whom the world press came to nickname "Baghdad Bob") had been denying reports that U.S. Army and Marine forces were moving freely in the center of Baghdad, even when his listening audience could hear the coalition tanks nearby. He was assuring the Iraqi people that the Republican Guard was in control of the airport. Then he offered to take reporters to the airport to prove it! Of course, most of them had already been to the airport and had seen the coalition forces for themselves.

Day after day in early April 2003, the world awaited al-Sahaf's latest

391. Ibid. 384–391.
392. Revelation 13:3.

daily virtuoso performance." Some of his comedic propaganda included: "They say they brought 65 tanks into the center of the city. I say to you it is not true. This is part of their sick mind. There is no presence of infidels in the city of Baghdad at all." (All the while he had to speak louder because of the gunfire in the streets below his hotel.) Further, his daily ritual included, "U.S. troops were poisoned yesterday" and "U.S. troops are committing suicide."

Ted Simons commented, "We are entering an era in which the news media and the general public's adeptness at detecting and dissecting spin in public discourse is matched only by the messengers' confusion. Put simply, it's hard and getting harder, to know whom to believe."[393]

Blizzard Claims and Bias

This is just one analysis of what is behind and under the blizzard of false advertising claims, media bias, outrageous political accusations, and cheating scandals. In other words, it has become fashionable to deny truth, to scoff at any information that is contrary to personal opinion, to revise history, and to blame others for whatever happens. It clearly is a time when political correctness is legislating a new society of victims and tolerance for what once was unacceptable conduct.

In a time of moral confusion and financial crises, it would be a perfect time for certain leaders (who have made a career of beguiling others by appealing to their feelings, not their heads) to promise, in a fresh, captivating way, that they have the solution for peace, unity, and brotherhood of all mankind. This world has an uncanny ability to believe pretense!

Scapegoating

As we have been unfolding in this book, world conditions in the end time will be unprecedented. Natural disasters, economic impasse, and moral decadence will cause many to examine the causes of such unparalleled troubles—exactly as Satan has planned it: "Satan puts his interpretation upon events, and they think, as he would have them, that the calamities which fill the land are a result of Sundaybreaking. Thinking to appease the wrath of God [as they see it] these influential men make laws enforcing Sunday observance."[394]

This is a magnificent example of pretense and scapegoating—they go together! The same strategy Satan used in capturing the confused mind of one-third of heaven's angels (Revelation 12:4, 7, 8) will work famously in confusing the world that *God's loyalists are the cause* of this world's terrible troubles. Pure scapegoating!

---

393. Ted Simons, Editor-in-Chief, *Presentations Magazine*, March 2003.
394. Ellen G. White, *Last Day Events*, 129.

Scott Peck's *People of the Lie* is probably the most penetrating analysis of evil that I have ever read. For instance: "Evil was defined as the use of power to destroy the spiritual growth of others for the purpose of defending and preserving the integrity of our sick selves. In short, it is scapegoating."[395]

The world's religious leaders, self-afflicted by their endorsement of Spiritualism (blindsided by the immortal-soul notion) and their ambivalence toward the Ten Commandments, will look for the "cause" and a solution for last-day crises, including "fast-spreading corruption." Their pretense (saluting the big lie) leads to Satan's use of his second strategic level—the search for a scapegoat. The age-old phenomenon of scapegoating becomes worldwide and causes great anxiety and misery. Scapegoats are found in almost every social context: in school playgrounds, in families, in small groups, in churches, and in large organizations. Whole nations may be scapegoated. I like this technical definition:

> Scapegoating is a hostile discrediting routine by which people move blame and responsibility away from themselves and towards a target person or group. It is also a practice by which angry feelings and feelings of hostility may be projected, via inappropriate accusation, towards others. The target feels wrongly persecuted and receives misplaced vilification, blame and criticism; he is likely to suffer rejection from those who the perpetrator seeks to influence. Scapegoating has a wide range of focus: from "approved" enemies of very large groups of people down to the scapegoating of individuals by other individuals. Distortion is always a feature.[396]

Ellen White summed up the satanic strategy of scapegoating in the last generation:

> Yet this very class [religious leaders] put forth the claim that the fast-spreading corruption is largely attributable to the desecration of the so-called "Christian sabbath," and that the enforcement of Sunday observance would greatly improve the morals of society. . . . It is one of Satan's devices to combine with falsehood just enough truth to give it plausibility.[397]

What I am getting at is that a time of moral confusion and financial crises would be a perfect time for well-known leaders to promise, in fresh, captivating ways, that they have the solution for peace, unity, and the brotherhood of all mankind (where everyone's opinion and

---

395. M. Scott Peck, *The People of the Lie* (New York: Simon & Schuster, 1983), 119.

396. http://www.scapegoat.demon.co.uk.

397. White, *The Great Controversy*, 587.

lifestyle is equally as good as anyone else's). This cheap shot is common fare for most politicians—change the issue into finding a common culprit to blame. This ploy seems to dominate every newscast. Especially when government leaders have a motto: *Never let a crisis go to waste!*

Hitler knew how to use the strategy of scapegoating in the early 1930s in Germany. Scapegoats are always available—just find those who may look different or worship differently. If the majority doesn't respond immediately to pretense and scapegoating, the tyranny of the minority will always gain power and lead the way. Hitler's Germany is a perfect paradigm of how events in the last of the last generation will develop!

In 1972, Rene Girard, a French literary critic, focused on the question of the *violent* root of culture through literature, anthropology, psychology, and biblical criticism. Through a succession of books and articles, he has pursued what he calls his *idée fixe*: the way in which *scapegoats* found, preserve, and unify culture. Girard found that societies resort to acts of violence to restore order:

> By organizing retributive violence into a united front against an enemy common to all the rivals, either an external enemy or a member of the community symbolically designated as an enemy, violence itself is transformed into a socially constructive force.[398]

Girard went on to say:

> Where only shortly before, a thousand individual conflicts had raged unchecked between a thousand enemy brothers, there now reappears a true community, united in its hatred for one alone of its members. All the rancors scattered at random among the divergent individuals, all the differing antagonisms, now converge on an isolated and unique figure, the surrogate [scapegoat] victim.[399]

In the cosmic great controversy, scapegoating has been Satan's method over and over again—he rarely loses! Think of Caiaphus and Christ and Calvary. That same sinister mind will duplicate Calvary's madness in the end time, when "a true (?) community, united in its hatred for one alone of its members," declares that a member is expendable to save the larger community from pending chaos. For Jewish leaders, Jesus was expendable for the greater good!

Scapegoating becomes fully blossomed in the end time:

---

398. James L. Fredericks, "The Cross and the Begging Bowl: Deconstructing the Cosmology of Violence." *Buddhist-Christian Studies* 18 (1998), 155.

399. Rene Girard, *Violence and the Sacred* (Baltimore: The Johns Hopkins University Press, 1977), 79.

It will be declared that men are offending God by the violation of the Sunday sabbath; that this sin has brought calamities which will not cease until Sunday observance shall be strictly enforced; and that those who present the claims of the fourth commandment, thus destroying reverence for Sunday, are troublers of the people, preventing their restoration to divine favor and temporal prosperity.[400]

Confusion

The confusion Satan causes is seen everywhere, where honesty, clarity, integrity, and truth are under fire. We see it when policy is substituted for principle (such as, "the end justifies the means"), or when opinion is substituted for absolute truths.

One of the most remarkable books of the twentieth century, *1984*,[401] by George Orwell (Eric Hugh Blair), described a totalitarian state where "doublespeak" reverses language and obliterates or revises history to suit the state—where freedom of thought is allowed to the masses *because they don't think*!

Three chapters are entitled "War is Peace," "Ignorance is Strength," and "Freedom is Slavery." Freedom is the "freedom to say two plus two equals five." The Ministry of Peace is actually the Ministry of War; "joycamp" is really the labor camp—examples of words given meanings the exact opposite of what they appear to mean. Orwell got some of his inspiration from Nazi Germany and Communist Russia, which had earlier employed some of the methods of *1984*.

However, much of the book has been thought of as an overview of time to come, when the world generally will believe the Big Lie and falsify history—all leading to the attempted extinction of those guilty of thought crimes.

One of the classic confusions in language is "Sabbath," understood as Sunday. Both the late Pope John Paul II and his successor, Pope Benedict XVI, have written powerful epistles emphasizing the importance of the Christian's Sabbath worldwide—each time referring to Sunday.[402]

Western nations are wrestling with the double meaning of "diversity" and "multiculturalism." Both are code words. Instead of a healthy respect for differences that made America a different kind of nation on earth, they are like "Trojan horses" that smuggle into general language the notion of moral relativism—code names for "no such thing as right and wrong."

400. White, *The Great Controversy*, 590.
401. Published first in 1949 (hardback); later in paperback (Hammondsworth, England: Penguin Books, 1954, reprinted at least twenty-six times).
402. *"Dies Domini,"* May 31, 1998; *The Guardian*, May 30, 2005.

Remember the ridicule President Ronald Reagan received when he called the Russian empire "evil"? That was considered "judgmental"! When hate-filled, sex-saturated music and videos are the hottest items on the market, they are defended with language such as "expression of youth culture." If one speaks up with Christian love, he or she is labeled "intolerant." It seems we embrace the lies and run from the truth, all for fear of offending someone.

"Religious freedom" becomes "freedom from religion," not "freedom of religion."

"Gender classification" is artificial discrimination, a mere invention of society. To argue differently exhibits intolerance. Transvestites exalt "selfhood," confusing the vulnerable young. Pro-choice, for many, means pro-murder. "Family Health" courses are taught in very early grades to teach "lifestyles" that are most often at odds with the "family health" of the young student's family.

"Hate speech" trumps "free speech," threatening any group on the basis of race, color, or religion. In other words, any book that criticizes another's religion in the interest of historical accuracy or biblical principles subjects the author and publisher to legal action. Such litigation already exists in numerous countries today.

"Progressive" once meant growth and openness. But now it's a code word used by the defense of a client's altercation with police.[403] Or for church services that celebrated Evolution Sunday.[404]

"Progressive theologians, for example, did not attack traditional views. They used traditional terminology and concepts but infused them with new meanings. . . . But the arrival of R.H. Pierson to the Adventist General Conference presidency (1966) brought a dramatic change. The new administration concluded that the progressives threatened the very soul and mission of Adventism."[405]

In other words, some liberals preferred to see themselves as "progressives," in relation to conservatives, or traditionalists. In other words, "progressive" has been morphed into what so many describe as avantgarde, the muting of authority, the relativity of values (such as "pride in progressive values," Hollywood style), and emphasizing innovation over tradition.

"Spirituality" becomes Novocain for young and old who want the soothing "presence" of God without accepting His moral code.

Bioethics that once stressed "sanctity of life" slips into an emphasis on "quality of life." Advocacy journalism has become a modern code word

---

403. CNN, March 31, 2006.

404. *Denver Post*, February 12, 2006.

405. *Spectrum*, vol. 15, no. 2; 25, 26.

for opinion-directed news-gathering, not objective reporting. "Minority" is condemned because it is insulting and implies inferiority. "Political correctness" is a code word for shutting down freedom of speech that aims for open and frank discussion. "Freedom of expression" becomes a cover for polluting the air with profanity and pornography. "Evangelical Christian," in some minds, becomes "Religious Right." "Freedom" becomes the right to be left alone—or free to "do your own thing."

"No fault" car insurance—where both the guilty and the innocent become victims and everybody gets to collect. Words such as "overweight" and "fat" are often put in quotation marks to isolate these terms as used by intolerant outsiders who want to impose their own standards. Even "stoutness" has become a no-no. A deaf person is "hearing disadvantaged."[406]

How about the cuteness of the Planned Parenthood organization that maintains it is not an abortion provider—just a family planning agency? Or, "pro-choice" really meaning "pro-abortion."

Think of the new lingo in the business world: fired becomes "uninstalled," "unassigned," "decruited" (in England, "redundant"); bankruptcy becomes "positive restructuring."[407]

The U.S. Department of Agriculture has helped all chicken lovers: A "fresh" chicken or turkey is one that's either fresh or frozen between 26 and 32 degrees; a "hard chilled" fowl is one frozen between zero and 26 degrees. The word "frozen" can now be applied only to birds frozen below zero.[408]

Universal victimhood becomes universal innocence. Increasing numbers of juries do not feel rage but pity; they look beyond proof of guilt and focus on the disadvantages in the life of the victimizer. It seems that one can do whatever—murder, rape, arson—as long as one says he or she is sorry!

Perhaps *1984* was far more prophetic than even Orwell's most devoted followers envisioned. Language now needs a new dictionary every ten years!

The Roman Catholic Church has noticed all this! They published the *Lexicon of the Family and Life* in 2006.[409] Anticipating the publication, William Donahue, president of the New York-based Catholic League for Religious and Civil Rights, said: "The Orwellian use of language by the

---

406. John Leo, "Deaf to Good Sense," *U.S. News & World Report*, March 25, 2002.

407. *U.S. News & World Report*, February 12, 1996.

408. Ibid.

409. Joseph Meaney, ed., *Lexicon: Ambiguous and Debatable Terms Regarding Family Life and Ethical Questions*, Pontifical Council for the Family (Front Royal, VA: Human Life International, 2006).

left for their own agendas has been going on for decades." He pointed out that "elastic terms" such as "gender" and "reproductive rights" were simply code for feminist or homosexual issues and abortion, respectively. "They're sanitized, they become generic, and therefore not offensive."[410]

On January 23, 1996, Pastor Joe Wright, guest chaplain of the Kansas House of Representatives, delivered his invocation that soon rocked the nation. Paul Harvey read it on "The Rest of the Story" and received a larger response than any other he had ever aired.[411]

Instead of the usual generalities, these are the words the legislators heard:

"Heavenly Father, we come before You today to ask Your forgiveness and to seek Your direction and guidance. We know Your Word says, 'Woe to those who call evil good,' but that is exactly what we have done. We have lost our spiritual equilibrium and reversed our values. We confess:

"We have ridiculed the absolute truth of Your Word and called it Pluralism.

"We have worshipped other gods and called it multiculturalism.

"We have endorsed perversion and called it alternative lifestyle.

"We have exploited the poor and called it the lottery.

"We have rewarded laziness and called it welfare.

"We have killed our unborn and called it choice.

"We have shot abortionists and called it justifiable.

"We have neglected to discipline our children and called it building self-esteem.

"We have abused power and called it politics.

"We have coveted our neighbor's possessions and called it ambition.

"We have polluted the air with profanity and pornography and called it freedom of expression.

"We have ridiculed the time-honored values of our forefathers and called it enlightenment.

"Search us, Oh God, and know our hearts today; cleanse us from every sin and set us free.

"Guide and bless these men and women who have been sent to direct us to the center of your will. I ask it in the Name of Your Son,

---

410. *The Washington Times*, January 17, 2003.

411. *TruthorFiction*, "Kansas Prayer."

the living Savior, Jesus Christ. Amen."[412]

Not hard to stand up and say "Amen" to that prayer!

Satan is "slick," with plenty of practice in causing confusion! Remember—he is an expert at turning minds from the truth, from listening to the voice of God in the soul—anything to keep people from listening to the "everlasting gospel."

Tolerance—One of the Key Words in the End Times

"Tolerance" is an interesting word. Its first meaning is the "capacity to endure pain or hardship"; its second meaning is to "show sympathy or indulgence for beliefs or practices differing from or conflicting with one's own."[413]

In recent years, this second meaning has segued into an atmosphere that forbids open discussion of one's personal views, if those views differ from a *militant minority.* If so, those views are considered automatically intolerant! Censorship, in a backhanded way, soon trails the skirts of "tolerance." The expression of opposing views, for many, becomes "hate speech"[414]; thus, the expression of different opinions (no matter what the evidence is) reveals intolerance!

All this leads to a society so "tolerant" that a legitimate discussion regarding biblical morality would quickly move beyond free discussion to political incorrectness, to coercion and oppression.[415] In the context of the great controversy, such a strategy by Satan is exactly what might be expected in the end time, even in a land that probably has the strictest

---

412. http://www.eaec.org/desk/joe_wright_prayer.htm.

413. *Webster's Ninth New Collegiate Dictionary* (Springfield, MA: Merriam-Webster, Inc., Publishers, 1988).

414. Of course, anybody in his or her right mind is against "hate speech" that is abusive, insulting, or intimidating—often leading to violence. Some talk shows are plain shock shows, calculated to vilify and demean others. Words are like bullets and can be turned into bullets. No Christian should defend this kind of "hate speech." No Christian should ostracize gays or lesbians because their belief system contradicts what many feel is a biblical issue. Not only should Christians defend them from "hate speech," they should be defended against "hate discrimination" of any kind. Christians, like their Master, should value the person, getting beyond a person's clothing or social choices.

415. A student at Boalt Hall, the law school of the University of California–Berkeley, thinks that a long-term trend is developing, in that any dissent from the gay agenda constitutes a form of illegitimate speech: "An opinion contrary to the majority opinion at Boalt in favor of gay rights might be treated as the equivalent of racist hate speech." Or open debate on the subject "would be treated as creating a hostile work environment." Cited in John Leo, "Coercion on Campus," *U.S. News & World Report,* May 15, 2000.

"free speech" laws in the world![416] How would one have the freedom to discuss historical accuracy and biblical interpretation regarding the Sabbath-Sunday issue, in a society that forbids any negative remarks about anybody else's religion?

On February 5, 2006, the Roman Catholic Church released its "Statement on Offending Religious Sentiments," arguing, "Freedom of thought and expression cannot imply the right to offend the religious sentiment of believers." The church said that "Real or verbal intolerance . . . is always a serious threat to peace." On the face of it, this seems to promote harmony and peace. But it forces the reader to ask, "What is verbal intolerance?" When the word "sentiment" is used, we are talking about "feelings," and if anyone's feelings are offended, the discussion is a "serious threat to peace."[417] Think of Elijah on Mount Carmel!

But another side of tolerance is the post-modern flood (New Spirituality/Innovation/Emergent Church/Spiritual Formation) that sweeps away critical thinking: Everyone has the "right" to choose the "truth" that appeals to him or her, BECAUSE moral absolutes don't exist! One's personal opinion is as good or as valuable as anyone else's. In that climate, tolerance is expected in religious matters and discussions of moral values, for there is no such thing as "absolute truth"! All this, with the perfume of "political correctness."[418] Not only is tolerance expected, it will be enforced by legal means.

Ellen White could not be more relevant:

> The position that it is of no consequence what men believe is one of Satan's most successful deceptions. He knows that the truth, received in the love of it, sanctifies the soul of the receiver; therefore

---

416. "The USA, as the least-censored society in the world, has held firmly to the First Amendment and to Article 19 of the Universal Declaration of Human Rights, which has meant that attempts to make provision against hate speech have almost all been disallowed by the Supreme Court." —Ursula Owen, "The Speech That Kills," Iain Walker Memorial Lecture, Oxford University, 1999.

417. *ZENIT*, February 5, 2006, as cited in http://www.adventcry.org/archive/2005/2-19-2006.

418. The "intellectual's" ideal has been traditionally associated with a commitment to universal truths, but history shows that "they" have had difficulty living up to their ideal. Note Heidegger's Nazism in German, Lukács' Fascism in Hungary, and D'Annunzio's Communism in Italy, for starters. But since post-modernism has swept the world, including intellectuals, "the greatest cost of the demise of the intellectuals might be a lack of confidence in those universal principles. 'Now,' says McClay, 'even the public senses that there is no bearer of disinterested truth.' "—Jay Tolson, "All Thought Out?" *U.S. News & World Report*, March 11, 2002.

he is constantly seeking to substitute false theories, fables, another gospel.[419]

George Barna, founder and president of Barna Research Group, has written thirty-one books, mostly based on research related to church dynamics and spiritual growth. In his book *The Second Coming of the Church,* he reports that "Americans align themselves with values that give them control. . . . To the average American, truth is relative to one's values and circumstances. Only one out of four adults—and even fewer teenagers—believe that there is such a thing as absolute moral truth. Human reason and emotion become the paramount determinant to all that is desirable and appropriate."

He continued:

> Without absolute truth, there can be no right and wrong. Without right and wrong, there is no such thing as judgment and no such thing as condemnation. If there is no condemnation, there is no need for a Savior.

Barna quoted a twenty-four-year-old:

> "It's a pretty cool thing because there is no right or wrong when it comes to faith. You believe what you believe, for whatever reasons seem right to you, and nobody can take that away from you. And then, if you change your mind, that's not an admission of failure or being wrong, but just a change of heart or maybe a sign that you've learned or grown. It's not like math. In spiritual matters the playing field is wide open."[420]

For many, truth is what the majority thinks.

Talk about *confusion*! For a growing number, truth is whatever the majority thinks it is—or whatever some aggressive minority group might champion regardless of its merits. Allan Bloom noted in 1987 that:

> There is one thing a professor can be absolutely certain: almost

---

419. White, *The Great Controversy,* 520. Also: "By the cry, Liberality [or, tolerance, open-mindedness], men are blinded to the devices of their adversary, while he [Satan] is all the time working steadily for the accomplishment of his object. As he succeeds in supplanting the Bible by human speculations, the law of God is set aside, and the churches are under the bondage of sin while they claim to be free."—*The Great Controversy,* 522.

420. *The Second Coming of the Church* (Nashville, TN: Word Publishing, 1998), 61, 62, 75. *Newsweek,* May 8, 2000, in its cover story, "What Teens Believe," noted: "Rather than seeking absolute truths in doctrine, they cross denominational boundaries. . . . In place of strict adherence to doctrine, many teens embrace a spirit of eclecticism and a suspicion of absolute truths."

every student entering the university believes, or says he believes, that truth is relative. . . . The relativity of truth is not a theoretical insight but a moral postulate, the condition of a free society, or so they see it. . . . That it is a moral issue for students is revealed by the character of their response when challenged—a combination of disbelief and indignation. . . . The danger they have been taught to fear from absolutism is not error but intolerance. . . . The students, of course, cannot defend their opinion. It is something with which they have been indoctrinated. The best they can do is point out all opinions and cultures there are and have been. What right, they ask, do I or anyone else have to say one is better than the others?[421]

Satan obviously has done his work well! And his pitch for tolerance gathers momentum:

In 2001, more than 29.4 million Americans said they had no religion—more than double the number in 1990—according to the American Religious Identification Survey 2001 (AIRS). People with no religion now account for 14 percent of the nation, up from 8 percent . . . in 1990. . . . For them, Sundays are just another Saturday.[422]

In a nutshell, "tolerance" and "love" become interchangeable; "diversity" means everyone can express themselves except Christians, especially Christians who are faithful to the teachings of Jesus. Code words such as "sensitivity training" and "multiculturalism" reflect the lowest common denominator on which "diversity" will unite the majority. "Civility" becomes a code word for "nonjudgmentalism."

"Absolutophobia"[423] pejoratively describes those who say that some

---

421. Allan Bloom, *The Closing of the American Mind* (New York: Simon & Schuster, Inc., 1988), 25, 26.

422. "According to the World Values Survey, conducted by sociologists in 65 nations since 1981, 'We see (a religious attitude) when we ask how often people spend time thinking about the meaning and purpose of life. We see it in people's attitude toward the environment and in the growth of a worldview that sees all life as sacred and invests nature with dignity and sacred quality. . . . 'Thou shalt not pollute' is a new commandment that has snuck into the canon, even in public schools where old-fashioned moral instruction is supposedly taboo. The environmental and peace and gender-equality movements are clearly inculcating values without being specifically religious. . . . Contrary to the well-known secularization theory that God is dead and will soon drop off the consciousness map, the USA is a holdout. Spirituality is actually growing in the USA."—*USA Today*, March 7, 2002.

423. John Leo, "A No-Fault Holocaust," *U.S. News & World Report*, July 21, 1997.

behavior or ideas are just plain wrong. Campuses of America are awash with teachers and students who deny the existence of objective truth: All they can discuss is differences in perspective.

Thus, in many pulpits, as well as in academic centers, the words "judgment" and "judgmental" are suddenly condemned. After all, who has a right to "judge" anyone, if everyone has a right to his or her own opinion! For many modern pulpits, "grace" trumps "judgment"—as if those two words are antithetical!

William J. Bennett wrote:

> It is, therefore, past time for what novelist Tom Wolfe has called the "great relearning." We have engaged in a frivolous dalliance with dangerous theories—relativism, historicism, and values clarification. Now, when faced with evil on such a grand scale [September 11, 2001], we should see these theories for what they are: empty. We must begin to have the courage of our convictions, to believe that some actions are good and some evil and to act on those beliefs to prevent evil.[424]

This most brief overview of this remarkable and rapid drift from moral absolutes to a spirituality measured by feeling and opinion is chiefly due to dismay with the doctrinal confusion that abounds in Christian churches generally.

Doctrinal Confusion

But the confusion reaches beyond Christianity, when leading "conservative" rabbis representing the majority of Jews in the United States are telling their congregations that "the story of Noah was probably borrowed from the Mesopotamian epic Gilgamesh," "that the way the Bible describes the Exodus is not the way it happened, if it happened at all," that archeologists digging in the Sinai have "found no trace of the tribes of Israel—not one shard of pottery," "that the 'tales' of Genesis . . . were a mix of myth legend, distant memory and search for origins, bound together by the strands of a central theological concept." Liberal Protestants have been talking like that for more than a century—but now "conservative" Jewish leaders?[425]

Ellen White foresaw this religious crisis and nailed its cause:

> The vague and fanciful interpretations of Scripture, and the many conflicting theories concerning religious faith, that are found

---

424. "Count one blessing out of 9-11 tragedy: moral clarity," *Houston Chronicle*, October 7, 2001.

425. Michael Massing, "As Rabbis Face Facts, Bible Tales Are Wilting," http://www.nytimes.com. 2000/03/09.

in the Christian world, are the work of our great adversary, to confuse minds so that they shall not discern the truth. And the discord and division which exist among the churches of Christendom are in a great measure due to the prevailing custom of wresting the Scriptures to support a favorite theory.[426]

After years of looking at church squabbles over petty doctrinal arguments; after observing that loyal churchgoers are not much better people than non-goers; after hearing the limited gospel preached every weekend, whether in pulpits, on TV or radio, where the most they hear is a gospel of free forgiveness but not the gospel that includes responsibility and divine power to transform the life—is it any wonder that restless youth, as well as their jaded parents, are voting with their feet?[427]

On October 21, 2003, George Barna announced his update of "Americans Describe Their Views About Life After Death." After reporting divergent views, Barna pointed out that:

Americans' willingness to embrace beliefs that are logically contradictory and their preference for blending different faith views together create unorthodox religious viewpoints. . . . Millions of Americans have redefined grace to mean that God is so eager to save people from Hell that He will change His nature and universal principles for their individual benefit. It is astounding how many people develop their faith according to their feelings or cultural assumptions rather than biblical teachings.[428]

---

426. White, *The Great Controversy*, 520.

427. Barna, op. cit. After his extended research, Barna concedes that "we [Christians] think and behave no differently from anyone else." Then, on page 6, he proceeds to give examples of similarities of behavior between Christians and non-Christians: Have been divorced (among those who have been married)—Christians: 27%; non-Christians, 23%. Gave money to a homeless person or poor person in past year—Christians: 24%; non-Christians: 34%. Took drugs or medication prescribed by physician in past year—Christians: 7%; non-Christians: 8%. Watched an X-rated movie in the past three months—Christians: 9%; non-Christians: 16%; Donated any money to a nonprofit organization in past month— Christians: 47%; non-Christians: 48%. Bought a lottery ticket in the past week—Christians: 23%; non-Christians: 27%. Feel completely or very successful in life—Christians: 58%; non-Christians: 49%. It is impossible to get ahead because of your financial debt—Christians: 33%; non-Christians: 39%. You are still trying to figure out the purpose of your life—Christians: 36%; non-Christians: 47%. Satisfied with your life these days—Christians: 69%; non-Christians: 68%. Your personal financial situation is getting better—Christians: 27%; non-Christians: 28%.

428. http://www.barna.org/cgi-bin//PagePressRelease.asp? (October 24, 2003).

Control and Coercion

Where is all this pretense, scapegoating, and confusion heading? Where it always ends up—in coercion and the use of power to control or destroy the hated minority. Satan, working through world authorities, will grant "power . . . and cause as many as would not worship the image of the beast to be killed" (Revelation 13:15). In crisis, politically correct legislation will appear so timely and necessary that all offenders are worthy of death!

But all is not bleak! The great controversy between God and Satan will not go on forever! Reckoning day is just ahead! Ideas and decisions surely have consequences, and it comes down to freedom versus coercion. The Bible previews that moment when time is running out for planet Earth.

The issue comes down to when God's loyalists receive the seal of God, and those who reject God's messages receive the mark of the beast and worship its image. Two groups are finally and clearly distinguished.

God's loyalists reflect the character of Jesus; Satan's loyalists reflect his character. The last time we saw this clearly distinguished was at the Cross! Satan did his best to beat Jesus down, physically and emotionally—applying awful pressure. And he will do his best to beat down our Lord's faithful, in every way possible, when he has the greater majority of all worldly inhabitants primed to destroy those stubborn Sabbath keepers.

Satan's hate is never calm. Ultimate selfishness lashes out unrestrained. And that is exactly what we see in the biblical overview of the seven last plagues—cartoonlike pictures of unrestrained evil, selfishness, and rage. The wicked have been sheltered for years from the full venom of the dragon (Satan) by the grace of God reaching for their hearts. But after probation has closed, after each person has chosen either to worship the God of the fourth commandment or the false gods represented by Babylon, the wicked, by their own choice, no longer are protected from evil forces in the universe.[429]

As the plagues begin to fall, those who are worshiping the image of

---

429. "Unsheltered by divine grace, they have no protection from the wicked one. Satan will then plunge the inhabitants of the earth into one great, final trouble. As the angels of God cease to hold in check the fierce winds of human passion, all the elements of strife will be let loose. The whole world will be involved in ruin more terrible than that which came upon Jerusalem of old. . . . The same destructive power exercised by holy angels when God commands, will be exercised by evil angels when He permits. There are forces now ready, and only waiting the divine permission, to spread desolation everywhere."—White, *The Great Controversy*, 614.

the beast (Revelation 13:15) have further "reason" to hate God's loyalists. They have been "enraged" with the power that attended the "loud cry," and "their anger is kindled against all who have received the message." And now, "those who honor the law of God have been accused of bringing judgments upon the world and they will be regarded as the cause of the fearful convulsions of nature and the strife and bloodshed among men that are filling the earth with woe."[430] They now blame all these terrible plagues on God's faithful, as if they are responsible for what seems, to them, to be the anger of God!

This malignant rage aimed at those who fearlessly stand for freedom in a very troubled, angry world soon results in not a stiffer Sunday law, but a new way to eliminate the Sabbath keepers in their "semblance of zeal for God."[431] That new "way," unknown to the United States and so contrary to its historical principles, will be a Sabbath "decree," denouncing Sabbath keepers "as deserving of the severest punishment, and giving the people [those worshipping the beast and its image] liberty, after a certain time, to put them to death."[432]

The entire universe will see the ultimate hatred of ultimate evil once more. When the fiendish rage of Satan is focused on God's loyalists in this last hour of the end times, the universe will see again what happened at the cross—evil will again have its way, but only for a little while.

Summary

Satan has practiced his strategy for control of God's world of intelligent beings ever since his revolt in heaven. His tactics are always the same—pretense, scapegoating, confusion, and finally, control through coercion.

God's loyalists will face up to these satanic weapons as Jesus did. They will keep fresh in their minds the truth about God. They will not be distracted by evil's attempts to blame others for the "mess" evil is causing. They will keep their minds on core truths of the gospel so that ordinary ways of using language are not confused with the subtlety of "progressive" thinking. They will foresee how evil attempts to control and coerce, taking courage in the warmth of others who also see the danger.

It has never been this late before! Red Alert! The future is galloping into us! We all are living in the time when Satan's ferocity against God and His loyalists overflows all previous assaults. Let us keep our minds alert and

---

430. Ibid., 614, 615.

431. Ibid., 615.

432. Ibid.

our vision focused on the key elements of the great controversy that will soon end. The payoff is out of this world!

CHAPTER ELEVEN

THEME:

> The same optimistic fog that deluded Noah's neighbors and
> convinced them that Noah was a fanatic will be duplicated in
> the last days, just prior to the return of our Lord.

Intoxicating Optimism Dangerous to One's Health

In focusing on what could be called "last-day events," we have been tracing the religious world as it runs through the political, financial, and natural worlds—and vice versa. On one hand, we hear/see the robust song of the optimists—on the other, the doleful worries of the pessimists! Who is right?

Think of two friends on the corner of Fifth and Broadway, New York City, watching two others carrying sandwich signs. One sign says: "The world is about to end." The other: "The world will never end." Then one bystander says to the other, "One of those men is an optimist, and the other is a pessimist. But I can't tell which is which!"

Such will be the murky choices in the crescendo of last-day events, especially in the United States. And this is exactly how Satan will keep the issues confused. We have been looking at pessimistic events in the end time, such as increasing "natural" disasters; astounding financial miscalculations that shatter confidence, causing huge personal distress around the world; and overwhelming concessions to immorality, wherein nothing is right or wrong but is merely a matter of opinion.

But Satan is not dumb! He knows that pessimism often leads one to seek help from a Higher Power. Church attendance goes up in times of crisis. So he plays his optimism card!

Let's follow now the other side of his end-time strategy—the appeal of better days ahead! Facts are, that when probation closes for all living, this world will never have looked so good for most people! Even as Noah could not pierce the fog of lies that preachers, teachers, and politicians had spread in his day, so last-day heralds of Christ's soon return will meet the same optimistic fog.

Note the clarity of this statement:

> Come when it may, the day of God will come unawares to the ungodly. When life is going on in its unvarying round; when men are absorbed in pleasure, in business, in traffic, in money-making; when religious leaders are magnifying the world's progress and enlightenment, and the people are lulled in a false security—then, as the midnight thief steals within the unguarded dwelling, so shall sudden destruction come upon the careless and ungodly, "and they shall not escape" (1 Thessalonians 5:3).[433]

For a little perspective, think of the past fifty years. Think of what the transistor and microelectronics have done for almost every industry, every home. Think of computers that can make quadrillions of computations a second! Think of MRI and CT body scanners. Think too of Teflon, lasers, organ transplants, polymers, stents for blocked arteries, and mesh to repair aneurysms—or of the Salk vaccine (when was the last time you visited a polio victim in the hospital)?[434] Problems that seemed formidable only fifty years ago are now forgotten as if they had never existed—or, if remembered, only as relics of what seems to be medieval times! Now, multiply these successes by a factor of 100, and you will begin to realize what we can expect in the next few years!

And more real years for most! During the twentieth century, life expectancy grew by nearly three decades. By 2020, life expectancy (men and women averaged) will be 79.2. And while living longer, we also are doing so with lower rates of disability and poverty than previous generations.[435]

According to medical research, soon we should expect vaccines to in-

---

433. *The Great Controversy,* 38; see also 338.
434. I remember vividly my days in the Hinsdale Sanitarium and Hospital (1952), having been diagnosed with polio. All around me were iron lungs, helping other patients to breathe. Parents were not allowing children to go to swimming pools or grocery stores. It was a very stressful time for many parents. I thank the Lord for one miraculous night when the fever suddenly left, and the effects of the polio virus vanished from my body.
435. *AARP Bulletin,* December 2010, 34.

oculate against most forms of cancer, even as we have virtually freed the world of smallpox, whooping cough, and polio in the last few years (although there seems to be an uptick in the latter two lately).

The amazing speed in deciphering the entire human DNA (genome), with its sixty thousand or so genes, has been far faster and cheaper than first estimated. Genetic engineering hopes to pinpoint the faulty genes that cause many of our diseases, whether inherited and acquired. These findings not only help physicians diagnose problems even in the womb, they provide ways by which the mutated gene can be manipulated to offset the potential damage. It has been estimated that half of our drugs in the next few years could result from gene manipulation.

All the while we should remember the caution of Craig Venter,[436] famous for his role in being one of the first to sequence the human genome: "From the time of the first few discoveries of gene defects—Huntington's disease, for example—everybody thought that if you knew your genome, you would know when you would die and what you would die from. That is nonsense."[437]

Asked as to what medical benefits the Human Genome Project has contributed, Venter said: "Close to zero to put it precisely. . . . We have, in truth, learned nothing from the genome other than probabilities. How does a 1 or 3 percent increased risk for something translate into the clinic? It is useless information."

However, Francis Collins,[438] director of the U.S. National Institutes of Health, in an interview with *The Times* (British newspaper) to mark the tenth anniversary of the sequencing of the human genome, said:

> "Certainly within ten years I will be very surprised and very disappointed if most people in the developed world will not have the genomes sequenced as part of their medical record, and I would

---

436. John Craig Venter (born October 14, 1946) is an American biologist and entrepreneur, most famous for his role in being one of the first to sequence the human genome and for his role in creating the first cell with a synthetic genome, in 2010. Venter founded Celera Genomics, The Institute for Genomic Research, and the J. Craig Venter Institute, and is now working at the latter to create synthetic biological organisms and to document genetic diversity in the world's oceans. He was listed on *Time* magazine's 2007–2010 lists of the most influential people in the world. *Wikipedia.*

437. Adam Keiper, National Review Online, August 9, 2010, "The Human Genome and the Human Being."

438. Francis Collins, an American physician-geneticist, noted for his landmark discoveries of disease genes and his leadership of the Human Genome Project (HGP) and described by the Endocrine Society as "one of the most accomplished scientists of our time." *Wikipedia.*

hope it will come even sooner. . . . There would be no need to take more blood samples; it's just a click of the mouse to know whether that drug dose ought to be adjusted, or whether there is a risk of a nasty side effect."[439]

Only a few years ago, we heard talk that the general population will have gimmicks that would have the accuracy of the most advanced GPS systems used by the military. As I write, I have in front of me the December 2010 issue of *Consumer Reports*. No longer will we be excited about the marvelous GPS in our automobiles; the common cell phone will give us all the information that the most elaborate GPS system has been doing! Are you optimistic yet?

In fact, just considering the cell phone, often carried now even by children, is more than anyone twenty years ago even imagined: instant talking, messaging, and locating almost anyone in the world (if you pay for it)!

Personal Privacy Versus the Elusive Joy of Security

Most people are fascinated with the "improvements" of modern science and imagination. Novartis[440] stuck an adhesive patch onto the shoulders of patients taking the blood pressure drug Diovan; the chips sent text messages to their cell phones when it was time to take the next pill. The experiment was designed to improve "compliance."

The first chip is inside the pill being swallowed. It sends a signal to the chip in a patch on your shoulder. *If you fail to take your next pill, the shoulder chip nags you on your mobile.* After the text arrives on your phone, the message then goes "onto the Internet for caregivers to review and analyze."

Joe Jimenez, head of pharmaceuticals at Novartis, said tests using the system on patients using Diovan, a drug to lower blood pressure, had boosted "compliance" with prescriptions from 30 percent to 80 percent after six months.[441]

Digital Angel, Inc.,[442] has in the last decade encircled the world, and

---

439. Alastair Jamieson, "Gene Data for All 'Within a Decade.' " *Telegraph .co.uk*, June 24, 2010.

440. Novartis International AG is a multinational pharmaceutical company based in Basel, Switzerland, ranking number three in sales among the worldwide industry, which accounted for $36.173 billion in 2008. It currently is the sixth largest pharmaceutical company in terms of revenue ($41.5 billion in 2009). *Wikipedia*.

441. http://www.bnet.com/blog/drug-business/novartis-chip-texts.

442. Headquartered in South St. Paul, Minnesota, their products offer security for people, animals, the food supply, the government/military arena, and commercial assets. *AARP Bulletin*, December 2010, 4.

nobody has escaped its embrace. We have seen its magic on all kinds of products we buy. If you work in a receiving/shipping department, you have seen the ubiquitous RFID label (radio frequency identification).

But the capability can track more than manufactured products. *The Wall Street Journal* reported on September 29, 2010, that India's tech savvy is being put to the test, as the country embarks on a daunting mission: assigning a unique twelve-digit number to each of its 1.2 billion people!

The project, which seeks to collect fingerprint and iris scans from all residents and store them in a massive central database of unique IDs, is considered by many specialists the most technologically and logistically complex national identification effort ever attempted. One of their hopes is that unique ID numbers will help ensure that government welfare spending reaches the right people and will allow hundreds of millions of poor Indians to access services such as banking, for the first time.

However, civil liberties groups say the government is collecting too much personal information without sufficient safeguards.

The team that created the project came up with a plan to capture a mix of biometric information—digital photos, fingerprints, and iris scans—as well as names, addresses, genders, and dates of birth. Since they knew they wouldn't have a second chance to collect the data, the engineers say they erred on getting too much information, including all ten fingerprints instead of just one. The government would issue the random twelve-digit numbers by mail. Passports, driver's licenses, ration cards, and government health-insurance cards will have the numbers either printed on them or embedded electronically.

Signing up is technically voluntary, but any government agency or company will be allowed to require a unique ID as identity proof, an approach critics say amounts to a de facto mandate for people to enroll.

In addition to biometrics, residents provide an array of personal information, including their caste, religion, and cell phone number. State agencies and companies who register people can gather whatever information they deem appropriate.

Another concern is that marketers will find ways to build profiles of people based on how they use their IDs—tracking where people bank, which hospitals they check into, and who their cell phone providers are, for example: "You will basically be creating these wonderful resources for people to mine," says Sudhir Krishnaswamy, a law professor at the National University of Juridical Sciences in Kolkata.[443]

The Computer Blitz

We are living in a world when even the most educated and experienced

443. http://www.tldm.org/bible/bible.htm.

in the computer world in its early years never dreamed of what has now happened during the past fifty years. IBM's storied chairman for many years, Thomas Watson, said in 1943, "I think there is a world market for maybe five computers."[444] Rocket scientist, John van Neuman, opined in 1949, "We have reached the limits of what is possible with computers."[445] And the developer of Ethernet and other Internet-related technologies—Robert Metcalfe, said that the "Internet will catastrophically collapse in 1996."[446]

None of what follows was operating ten years ago! And five years ago we all thought that we were pushing earth's limits of possibility. But today, China grabs the supercomputing leadership spot in latest ranking of the world's top five hundred supercomputers.[447]

The Chinese Tianhe-1A system at the National Supercomputer Center in Tianjin has achieved a performance level of 2.57 petaflop/s[448] (quadrillions of calculations per second). Only a few mathematicians know what that means—all I know is that this computer is very fast.

The former number one system—the Cray XT5 "Jaguar" system at the U.S. Department of Energy's (DOE) Oak Ridge Leadership Computing Facility in Tennessee—is now ranked in second place. Jaguar achieved 1.75 petaflop/s running Linpack, the TOP 500 benchmark application.

Of the top ten systems, seven achieved performance at or above 1 petaflop. Five of the systems in the top ten are new to the list. Of the top ten, five are in the United States, and the others are in China, Japan, France, and Germany.

China is also accelerating its move into high performance computing and now has forty-two systems on the TOP 500 list, moving past Japan,

---

444. http://www.technobility.com/docs//vp-chap-02.htm.

445. http://www.iwise.com/87GBQ.

446. http://www.boerner.net/jboerner/?p=8001.

447. http://www.top500.org/ November 11, 2010.

448. *Petaflop* is a measure of a computer's processing speed and can be expressed as: A quadrillion (thousand trillion) floating point operations per second (FLOPS). Breaking the petaflop barrier is expected to have profound and far-reaching effects on the future of science. According to Thomas Zacharia, head of computer science at Cray's Oak Ridge National Laboratory in Tennessee, "The new capability allows you to do fundamentally new physics and tackle new problems. And it will accelerate the transition from basic research to applied technology." Petaflop computing will enable much more accurate modeling of complex systems. Applications are expected to include real-time nuclear magnetic resonance imaging during surgery, computer-based drug design, astrophysical simulation, the modeling of environmental pollution, and the study of long-term climate changes.

France, Germany, and the United Kingdom to become the number two country behind the United States

Forbes magazine noted that experts estimate a computer would need to execute about ten quadrillion calculations a second to approximate the activity of the human brain. Given current trends, such technology could be available for $1,000 by 2020 (prediction made in 2005).[449]

But so much is on the table as I write. New sources of energy will awesomely expand speed, especially in the ability to pull important information off the biggest databases almost instantly! Think of photonic chips that work on light rather than electricity.[450]

Creative Minds Keep Blowing Hope

Think next, of nanotechnology.[451] One nanometer (nm) is equal to one billionth of a meter, or 0.000000001 m. That requires a good microscope! Yet nanotechnology is a hot, young science that makes invisibly tiny machines and materials. Here, scientific entrepreneurs manufacture things less than 1/1,000th the width of a human hair, promising ever-smaller computers, stronger and lighter materials, even "nanobots" able to cruise through human blood vessels to treat diseases.

Nanotech will gives us the capability to resist not just liquid stains but also dirt—including dust, shed bodily tissues, and bodily oils. At least in theory, we won't need to wash clothes—just shake them out! Wonder what that will do to the appliance industry?[452]

In 2009 gene therapy got a boost from nanotech, when antitumor genes, wrapped up in a nanoparticle, were delivered directly to cancer cells.[453]

Wherever we look, pessimistic doomsayers are continually being proven wrong, at least for now. This world will soon find sources for renewable energy other than oil and gas. The so-called population explosion; the scarcity of food and world famine; the environmental hysteria, including Carl Sagan's "nuclear winter" frenzy, that some opined would create a clutch of worldwide disorders—all these dreary forecasts are being eclipsed by modern discoveries and everyday wonders. According to the experts,

---

449. *This Week,* August 19, 2005.

450. *Financial Times,* September 16, 2010.

451. "Nanotechnology, shortened to 'nanotech', is the study of manipulating matter on an atomic and molecular scale. Generally nanotechnology deals with structures sized between 1 to 100 nanometer in at least one dimension, and involves developing materials or devices within that size. Quantum mechanical effects are very important at this scale." *Wikipedia.*

452. *The Sleuth,* "The Future of Fabric," July 12, 2006.

453. *Newsmax Maxlife,* March 2010.

we can look forward to an increased cadence of startling and wonderful breakthroughs in the near future. Really, who wouldn't say that the world is getting better and better?

Think of the inventions and great improvements that are on the edge of tomorrow:

- Wolfram Alpha, revolutionary new software that may put Google in the shade and that will understand questions and give specific, tailored answers, plus a neat page of related information, all properly sourced.[454]

- Human skin turned into heart and brain cells made in a test tube, a breakthrough in stem-cell research that could end the need to clone human embryos.[455]

- Robot-driven cars on roads by 2030, in a test run by the U.S. Defense Advanced Research Projects Agency.[456]

- Frozen embryos, some waiting many years to be born; even fraternal twins born seven and a half years apart.[457]

- Lost a lung or anything else? Grow your own, regenerating your own cells that replace defective tissue—or grow new, healthy organs or limbs.[458]

- Paralyzed people controlling artificial limbs by thought alone.[459]

- Robotic aids help with common chores, even cooking dinner from scratch.[460]

- Micropolyester clothes that feel like silk, clean and wash like cotton, and are priced like, well, polyester.[461]

- Montana and North Dakota have an estimated 3.0 to 4.3 billion barrels of undiscovered, technically recoverable oil—a twenty-five-fold increase in the estimated amount of oil that can be recovered, compared to the U.S. Geological Survey's 1995 estimate of 151 million barrels of oil.[462]

- Life-altering left ventricular assist device (LVAD) mechanical pump

454. *The Independent*, May 3, 2009.

455. Ibid., November 21, 2007.

456. http://www.Breitbart.com/news/2007/2007/02/17/070218000644.7.

457. *Time*, March 2, 1998.

458. *USA Today*, February 25, 1995.

459. *The Guardian*, March 21, 2005.

460. *The Kiplinger Washington Editors*, April 22, 2005.

461. *The Sleuth*, "The Future of Fabric," July 12, 2006.

462. U.S. Geological Survey, Released April 10, 2008.

that greatly assists pushing blood through the heart.[463]

▶ Honda's Stride Management Assist is designed to help people with weakened leg muscles, such as stroke patients, to walk more freely than ever before.[464]

▶ A bion—a rechargeable battery-powered electrode about the size of a matchstick implanted in the neck—sends signals that reduce pain as much as 95 percent—for those who can't tolerate medication.[465]

▶ Televisions to be fitted in contact lenses within ten years, powered by the viewer's body heat. Channels could be changed by voice command or the wave of the hand.[466]

▶ GrapheneGate (UCLA) opens the door to smaller, faster, less toxic electronics and thus plays a key role in energy conservation and waste reduction.[467]

▶ A brilliant LED is twenty thousand times more powerful than current Xenon technology and will be installed on masts and tall buildings to warn airplanes.[468]

▶ Dark silicon (portion on transistors that is underused for lack of sufficient power) boosted on new phone chip (GreenDroid) that will enable the more widespread use of solar energy and other forms of renewable energy for battery recharging.[469]

Or, we all can get those expensive cheese sandwiches (in London) that carry a whopping price tag of £111.95, with a £5 loaf of sourdough dressed with extra virgin olive oil, then layered cheese, slices of quail's egg, heirloom black tomato, epicure apple, fresh figs, dainty mustard red frills, pea shoots and red amaranth for a salad layer and topped with edible gold dust.[470]

Alice in Wonderland Optimism

Or, we can be duped by the "college-degree scam." Sounds like progress, but misguided! Those of us who have been in the middle of it all have watched with dismay at the flagrant rejiggering of classroom grades,

463. *Newsmax Maxlife*, March 2020.

464. Ibid.

465. Ibid.

466. *Telegraph.co.uk*, February 2009.

467. *Alternative Energy Digest*, September 4, 2010.

468. Ibid.

469. Ibid.

470. http://www.dailymail.co.uk/news/article-1310805/TV-chef-Martin-Blunos-creates-cheese-sandwich-costs-incredible-110.html#ixzz18nutju6o.

from the elementary schools up through universities. We call it "devaluation" of the standard A–F. Many reasons exist, but the chief one during the past forty years is the idea that we should not embarrass or discourage anyone—losing self-worth is considered a tragedy. But what is worse, punting the child up the educational field, hoping that he or she will find it easier further down the road? Those children are suddenly face to face with reality, sooner or later—possibly when they discover that no one wants to hire them, especially when so many have a hard job reading their own diploma.

But Richard Vedder, Professor of economics at Ohio University and director of the Center for College Affordability and Productivity, pointed out that in 1992, 28.9 million college graduates were employed, and 5.1 million, about 17 percent, were in jobs the BLS (Bureau of Labor Statistics) termed "non-college level jobs." In 2008, total college graduate employment as 49.3 million and 17.4 million—35 percent—were in jobs classified as requiring less than a bachelor's degree.

Dr. Vedder called it "the single most scandalous statistic in higher education. It reveals many current problems and ones that will grow enormously as policymakers mindlessly push enrollment expansion amidst what must become greater public-sector resource limits."

Some of his observations:

The data suggest a horrible decline in the productivity of American education in that the "inputs" used to achieve any given human capital (occupational) outcome have expanded enormously. More simply, it takes 18 years of schooling (including kindergarten and the typical fifth year of college to get a bachelor's degree) for persons to get an education to do jobs that a generation or two ago people did with 12-13 years of education (graduating more often from college in four years and sometimes skipping kindergarten).

Further:

All of this supports the notion that credential inflation arises from a perceived need by individuals to demonstrate potential employment competence through a piece of paper, i.e. a college diploma.

Vedder concludes:

We are deceiving our young population to mindlessly pursue college degrees when very often that is advice that is increasingly questionable.[471]

Let's look at our education malaise from another angle: "Nearly one-

471. *The Chronicle of Higher Education*, December 22, 2010.

fourth of the students who try to join the U.S. Army fail its entrance exam, painting a grim picture of an education system that produces graduates who can't answer basic math, science and reading questions."[472]

U.S. Education Secretary Arne Duncan told the AP: "Too many of our high school students are not graduating ready to begin college or a career—and many are not eligible to serve in our armed forces, . . . I am deeply troubled by the national security burden created by America's under-performing education system."[473]

Said retired Navy Rear Admiral Jamie Barnett: "The effect of the low eligibility rate might not be noticeable now—the Department of Defense says it is meeting its recruitment goals—but that could change as the economy improves."[474]

The report by The Education Trust found that 23 percent of recent high school graduates don't get *the minimum score* needed on the enlistment test to join any branch of the military. Questions are often basic, such as: "If 2 plus x equals 4, what is the value of x?"[475]

The military exam results are also worrisome because Pentagon data shows that 75 percent of those aged seventeen to twenty-four don't even qualify to take the test, because they are physically unfit, have a criminal record, or didn't graduate high school.

"It's surprising and shocking that we are still having students who are walking across the stage who really don't deserve to be and haven't earned that right," said Tim Callahan with the Professional Association of Georgia Educators, a group that represents more than 80,000 educators.[476]

Recruits must achieve a score of at least thirty-one out of ninety-nine on the first stage of the three-hour test, to get into the Army. The Marines, Air Force, Navy, and Coast Guard recruits need higher scores. "A lot of times, schools have failed to step up and challenge these young people, thinking it didn't really matter—they'll straighten up when they get into the military," said Kati Haycock, president of The Education Trust. "The military doesn't think that way."[477]

Tom Loveless, an education expert at the Brookings Institution think tank, said the results echo those on other tests. In 2009, 26 percent of

---

472. Associated Press, Christine Armario and Dorie Turner, December 21, 2010.
473. Ibid.
474. Ibid.
475. Ibid.
476. Ibid.
477. Ibid.

seniors performed below the "basic" reading level on the National Assessment of Education Progress. He said: "A lot of people make the charge that in this era of accountability and standardized testing, that we've put too much emphasis on basic skills," Loveless said. "This study really refutes that. We have a lot of kids that graduate from high school who have not mastered basic skills."[478]

A Department of Defense report notes the military must recruit about 15 percent of youth, but only one-third are eligible. More high school graduates are going to college than in earlier decades, and about one-fourth are obese, making them medically ineligible. In 1980, by comparison, just 5 percent of youth were obese.[479]

Why This Emphasis?

Why am I making a point of all this? Because much of the present educational quandary has come half-cooked and ill advised off the tray of educational theorists over many decades. Too many want students to be measured by their intentions, not by the consequences. For a long time, I have used that legal phrase, *cui bono*—"to whose benefit." Educational theorists seem to have a new program every few years to try out on all grades from kindergarten to university graduates—skilled teachers only roll their eyes, but what can they do about it!

Educational theorists need to look at the purpose of education, and I have never seen it better said:

> Our ideas of education take too narrow and too low a range. There is need of a broader scope, a higher aim. True education means more than the pursual of a certain course of study. It means more than a preparation for the life that now is. It has to do with the whole being, and with the whole period of existence possible to man. It is the harmonious development of the physical, the mental, and the spiritual powers. It prepares the student for the joy of service in this world and for the higher joy of wider service in the world to come.[480]

In other words, the most important goal of every parent and child is to see that each student has the right choices to fulfill his or her personal needs and capabilities. Some boys should become the best auto mechanics possible in a world of incredible technology. Some girls should keep in mind the practical duties of a future home life, as well as professional horizons when selecting a career. We need to offer such pathways as will really ex-

478. Ibid.
479. Ibid.
480. White, *Education,* 13.

cite the young who either don't have the funds or personal inclinations to directly advance to four-year college or university programs. Their chosen profession will be as useful in time of need as any MD, or JD, or any other doctorate! Plus, we would have many more happy homes!

The Difference a Century Makes

▸ In 1908, average life expectancy was forty-seven years, only 14 percent of homes had a bathtub, 8 percent had a telephone, only 8,000 families had cars, there were only 144 miles of paved roads, and the maximum speed was 10 miles per hour.

▸ Average wage, 22 cents per hour; average yearly wage, $200–$400. A dentist earned $2,500; a veterinarian, between $1,500–$4,000; and a mechanical engineer, $5,000. Eighteen percent of households had at least one full-time servant or domestic help.

▸ More than 95 percent of all births took place at home; 90 percent of all doctors had no college education (and many medical schools were condemned by the government as substandard).

▸ Five leading causes of death were: #1 pneumonia and influenza; #2 tuberculosis; #3 diarrhea; #4 heart disease; #5 stroke. Only 230 murders were reported in the entire U.S.A.!

▸ Marijuana, heroin, and morphine were all available over the counter at the local corner drugstore. Back then, the ads promised: "Heroin clears the complexion, gives buoyancy to the mind, regulates the stomach and bowels, and is, in fact, a perfect guardian of health."

▸ Sugar cost 4 cents a pound, eggs were 14 cents a dozen, and most women washed their hair once a month, using Borax or egg yolks for shampoo.

▸ Canada prohibited poor people from entering their country for any reason.

▸ The population of Las Vegas, Nevada—only 30.[481]

Optimists Must Be Prepared for Disappointments

I think of the families in Westfield, Massachusetts (home of my maternal grandparents and the horsewhip industry), where hundreds had been employed for many decades and where much of their life savings was invested. Lo, the automobiles came along, horses were no longer the preferred mode of transportation, and the need for horsewhips vanished.

---

481. http://www.qondio.com/what-life-was-like-in-1908-compared-to-2008what-things-have-changed-in-100-years-in-america.

But not much lasts forever when so much is overtaken by the next new invention—jobs and investments often go into the tank.

Think of Howard Johnson, originally a six hundred-restaurant/motel chain, a star performer for many years that is going through a slow-motion death.[482]

Or Borders, a strong, pleasant bookstore fighting for its life.[483] Or AOL, nearly a decade ago, during the merger with Time Warner, worth $100 billion but today bearing a much smaller price tag.[484] Or Radio Shack, suffering from the slump in consumer electronic space, currently looking for a buyout.[485] Or U.S. Cellular, the country's sixth-largest wireless carrier, which will probably be scooped up by Verizon or AT&T.[486] Or Foot Locker, long known for its sneaker supercenters, now surpassed by casual shoe sales, closing many stores, and facing a sad end.[487]

What surprises me most is Alcoa, the aluminum manufacturer, now competing with Russia and China in an industry that exists because of heavy state subsidies—the world is awash in aluminum. Right, not much is fair in this world!

I think of the weighty predictions of *Omni*, published from October 1978 to fall 1995, that gave people a look into the world of art, science, technology, science fiction, computers, UFOs, robotics, medicine, astronomy, space, the mind, and beyond.[488] (Yet, they couldn't predict their own demise!) But millions then did believe such predictions as these:

▶ By 2001, the first anti-aging treatments will extend the human lifespan to more than a century of vigorous health.

▶ Quebec will secede from Canada by 1991; four eastern provinces will join the United States by 2004.

▶ By 2000, oil prices will plummet to between seven and nine dollars per barrel. New technologies for recovering oil from old wells will keep prices low.

▶ By 2000, Taiwan will rejoin the People's Republic of China. The two Koreas will reunite.

▶ By 2003, you will zoom from 0 to 60 miles per hour in a sleek, sporty all-electric car.

---

482. *Investing Answers*, "Names That Will Vanish by 2012." July 16, 2010.
483. Ibid.
484. Ibid.
485. Ibid.
486. Ibid.
487. Ibid.
488. *Omni*, October 1992.

▸ Colonization of the moon will begin in 2010.

▸ By 2000, your toilet will have two handles. One will release 3.5 gallons of water for solid waste; the other will release 1.5 gallons for liquid waste. (At last, something—in some places, at least—*True!*)

▸ A "Cosmic Watergate" will shock the nation. Over two hundred documents leaked to the press, will prove that the U.S. government withheld evidence of the existence of UFOs and extraterrestrial life.

▸ Genetic therapy will become commonplace by 2005.[489]

General John M. Shalikashvili, chairman, U.S.A. Joint Chiefs of Staff, said at Bradley University, Peoria, Illinois, on May 19, 1994: "With the end of the Cold War, billions of the world's citizens, most of them having never known freedom, are suddenly free to choose their own governments, to embrace the prosperity that comes from free markets, and to find new ways to create world peace. For the first time in my life, the world is not divided into armed camps on the verge of a conflict that would threaten our very existence. . . . And while dangers abound. . . . it is a remarkably better and a more hopeful world than ever in the history of mankind."[490]

Heady Optimism a Century Ago

Historians can speak to optimism as well as pessimism by just reviewing the past one hundred years. Less than one hundred years ago, optimism was in full bloom. The scientific revolution gave us a new world of medicine, communication, transportation; preachers proclaimed a new world of peace without war. But the new science led instead to weapons of mass destruction as never before seen (1914–1918).

Yet, hardly had twenty-five years passed when, after a brief hiccup of recovery, the whole world was enveloped in total war and then the mushroom shock. Lesson learned: The evils of this world will not be overcome by knowledge and reason alone.

Even the best in medical research and practice is subject to this warning from Michael S. Lauer, MD, at the world-renowned Cleveland Clinic:

One study suggests that over the space of about 10-15 years, roughly half of what you know now turns out to be wrong or obsolete. Dr. Lauer only had to look back twenty years ago: clearing blocked blood vessels was only a dream and statins did not exist and protective aspirin had barely caught on.[491]

---

489. Ibid.
490. *USA Today,* May 19, 1994.
491. *Heart Advisor,* September 2006.

Optimists Are Both Right and Wrong

So optimists are right—the world will not end in either a whimper or a bang. World nuclear powers will not incinerate the earth; we will not drown or be suffocated in our own garbage or shrivel up in mass starvation.

But optimists are also wrong—the future is not in the hands of ingenious men and women who, up to now, have always come up with the necessary solutions to "whatever" problems we may face. Technology will not cure, for example, the self-interest of relatives or neighbors, or nations, as they grab for what they have not earned, trampling others in their pursuit. Technology may recycle used glass and metals but not the rising tide of moral garbage.

Technology will not eliminate deceit and spinmeisters who make a career of repackaging morally deficient leaders. Technology, in itself, will not be able to produce trust and fairness—regardless of Hollywood's ability to substitute style for substance.

Lurking Fears That Won't Go Away

All this breathtaking technology does not lower the pervasive fear that "something is not right." Think of Wikileaks! Think of the enormous financial black hole into which almost every sovereign nation is being sucked. Think, what caused the demise of the mighty former Soviet Union? What happened is that they went broke. They didn't have the operating capital to run the huge bureaucracy that was their government, so it died without a whimper. Even with a tight money supply, the United States continues to fund other countries. We seem anesthetized to a day of economic reckoning. Commerce is the lifeblood of a country; without it, you have no army, navy, social programs, education, or healthcare.

The ultimate goal of many well-placed leaders, often behind the front page, is to bankrupt this nation in the interest of world control of all finance.

What indeed could be more suffocating than a disease-cured world, filled with computerized homes with the latest labor-saving devices for all, guaranteeing adequate food for every man, woman, and child (all very probable expectations)—if that world wallows in its comforts and sensual excesses, valuing security above freedom, while scorning the time-honored values of honesty, hard work, fidelity in marriage and concern for constitutional freedoms.

Satan's Trump Card

So, with this unprecedented "wonderful" world full of more promises than we can keep up with, Satan will try hard to keep comfortable, disease-free, over-stimulated men and women occupied and uncon-cerned *regarding real events* in these end times. Even as Noah's contem-poraries choked on the fog of optimism, so will those unprepared for the return of Jesus.

Optimism is intoxicating! The former editor of *The Wall Street Journal*, Robert Bartley, told the graduating class of Hillsdale College:

"In the new century we can, and should choose optimism over pessimism. The danger of pessimism is that it is likely to be self-fulfilling. . . . We will be plunged into paralyzing confusion unless we seize new opportunities and embrace the optimistic view that holds that problems can be solved, that progress can be made. If you, the Class of 1994, can remember this as you leave our cloister to enter the world, you will discover that the new century *is* cause for optimism."[492]

Satan's Goal: Moral Insensitivity

Jesus compared the end-time with the frightful days in which Noah lived prior to the Flood: "But as the days of Noah were, so also will the coming of the Son of Man be" (Matthew 24:37). What could Jesus have meant? What do we know about the "days of Noah"?

Very early in the history of humanity, men and women were magnifi-cent physical specimens and must have been incredibly knowledgeable in all things mechanical, medical, and philosophical—compared to us! But we read the dark side of this morning of world history in Genesis 6: "Then the Lord saw that the wickedness of man was great in the earth, and that every intent of the thoughts of his heart was only evil continually. . . . The earth is filled with violence through them" (Genesis 6:5, 13).

What happens to any of us when exposed to horror or lust or deceit for long? We all know the experience of reading or seeing on TV the stories of outrageous suicide bombers, of rampaging hurricanes and floods, of Sudanese famine, or of Mexican executions of anyone who gets in the way of drug trafficking. It may be on the first page at first, maybe, but soon we flip the pages numbly—we have seen it all before. It takes a huge disaster, and it must be closer to home, before we realize the horror of such things and stop to read beyond the headline.

The same happens with pornography. It may begin with magazines flaunted at the supermarket check-out stands. Perhaps an interesting book, true or fiction. For hundreds of thousands, a couple of pecks on the computer keyboard—and the world of hot pornography blasts one's senses. I know of a pastor's wife who became so involved with her

---

492. *Imprimis*, September 1994.

intriguing Internet obsessions that she didn't feed her children with any pattern or care for her home—nor did she mind the forthcoming divorce. But this pattern—the innocent (!) moment, the flirting kiss, the hidden magazine or website, the exciting rendezvous—leads downhill fast. Lust is always played out on a slippery slope, and no one knows that better than Satan.

No one starts out knowing the end of that first slip into moral numbness. But is there anyone alive in any country of this world who is immune to the steady tug of lust, whether promoted in most schools everywhere, or in the most degraded slums or fanciest condos, at office parties or college campuses, or wherever. Billboards, movie advertising trailers on innocent TV programs, required reading in even religious schools, immodest dress, peer pressure to engage in immoral behavior, even risqué photos in church magazines—all function on a gutter level that would not have been permitted fifty years ago. The more we are immersed in lust or horror or deceit, the less evil it becomes, even for those who choose to avoid it![493]

Why does all this need to be said? Because the numbed mind, the cavalier attitude toward evil, will find it virtually impossible either to grasp or appreciate this world's final call to "worship Him who made heaven and earth" and to join those who "keep the commandments of God and the faith of Jesus" (Revelation 14:12). That's why Noah, "a preacher of righteousness" (2 Peter 2:5), found such resistance when the world was coming to its end in his day. And why Jesus sighed, "When the Son of Man comes, will He really find faith on the earth?" (Luke 18:8).

---

493. "Vice is a monster of so frightful mien,
    As to be hated needs but to be seen;
    Yet seen too oft, familiar with her face,
    We first endure, then pity, then embrace."
    —Alexander Pope, *Essay on Man*, Epistle II, Line 217.

CHAPTER TWELVE

THEME:

> "But as the days of Noah were, so also will the coming of the Son of Man be. For as in the days before the flood, they were eating and drinking, marrying and giving in marriage, until the day that Noah entered the ark, and did not know until the flood came and took them all away, so also will the coming of the Son of Man be" (Matthew 24:37–39).

How Jesus Looked at the End of the World

Yet across the gulf of space, minds that are to our minds as ours are to those of the beasts that perish, intellects vast and cool and unsympathetic, regarded this earth with envious eyes, and slowly and surely drew their plans against us. And early in the twentieth century came the great disillusionment."[494]

So begins probably the most vivid novel ever written describing earth invasion by beings from afar. H. G. Wells' description of chemical weapons—the Black Smoke used by the Martian fighting machines to murder human beings en masse—was later a reality during the First World War, with the use of mustard gas. The Heat Ray, used by the Martians to annihilate nineteenth-century military technology, causing widespread devastation, is a precursor to the concept of laser weaponry, now widely familiar. Comparison between lasers and the Heat Ray was made as early as the latter half of the 1950s, when lasers were still in development. Prototypes of mobile laser weapons have been developed and are now being researched and tested as possible future space weapons.

Among Wells' other far-reaching ideas was the concept of an armored

---

494. H. G. Wells, *The War of the Worlds* (Book one: *The Coming of the Martians.* Chapter one: "The Eve of the War").

202 • RED ALERT: Hurtling Into Eternity

fighting vehicle, devoid of wheels and using the "musclelike" contractions of metal discs along an axis to produce movement—the modern tank.[495]

When adapted to radio on October 30, 1938, and aired over the Columbia Broadcasting System radio network, "War of the Worlds" caused enormous panic. The first two-thirds of the sixty-minute broadcast consisted of simulated "news bulletins," which suggested that an actual alien invasion by Martians was currently in progress.

The news grows increasingly ominous, as a cylindrical meteorite lands in Grover's Mill, New Jersey. A crowd gathers, and events are related by an on-site reporter. The meteorite unscrews, revealing itself as a rocket machine. Onlookers catch a glimpse of a "tentacled, pulsating, barely mobile Martian, before it incinerates the crowd with Heat Rays." The reporter's shouts about incoming flames are cut off in mid-sentence!

This section ends famously: a news reporter broadcasting from atop the CBS building describes the Martian invasion of New York City—"five great machines" wading across the Hudson River, poison smoke drifting over the city, people running and diving into the East River "like rats," others "falling like flies"—until the reporter, too, succumbs to the poison gas. Finally, a despairing ham radio operator is heard: "Calling CQ. Isn't there anyone on the air? Isn't there anyone on the air? Isn't there . . . anyone?"[496]

Amidst anxiety just prior to World War II, some listeners heard only a portion of the broadcast and took it to be a real news broadcast. Newspapers reported that panic ensued, some people fleeing the area; others thinking they could smell poison gas or could see flashes of lightning in the distance. Within a month, there were 12,500 newspaper articles about the broadcast or its impact.

Of course, it was only a radio broadcast of a famous novel. But was it far off the mark?

> There was a great earthquake, and the sun became black as sackcloth of hair, and the moon became like blood. And the stars of heaven fell to the earth as a fig tree drops its late figs when it is shaken by a mighty wind. Then the sky receded as a scroll when it is rolled up, and every mountain and island was moved out of its place. And the kings of the earth, the great men, the rich men, the commanders, the mighty men, every slave and every free man, hid themselves in the caves and in the rocks of the mountains, and said to the mountains and rocks, "Fall on us and hide us from the face of Him who sits on the throne and from the wrath of the Lamb! For the great day of His wrath has come, and who is able to stand?" (Revelation 6:12–17).

---

495. http://en.wikipedia.org/wiki/The War of the Worlds.
496. Ibid.

And that question: Who is able to stand? That question has your name on it. And mine!

The Real Invasion From Outer Space

What is going on here that sounds so ominous—and so personal! Apparently, no one is left out or left behind!

John the revelator is describing the real invasion from outer space—the awesome, climactic return of Jesus, the Crucified and Risen Christ!

Jesus, however, earlier described this invasion as a glorious event:

"Then the sign of the Son of Man will appear in heaven, and then all the tribes of the earth will mourn, and they will see the Son of Man coming on the clouds of heaven with power and great glory. And He will send His angels with a great sound of a trumpet, and they will gather together His elect from the four winds, from one end of heaven to the other" (Matthew 24:30, 31).

But the law of consequences is applied:

When the Lord Jesus is revealed from heaven with His mighty angels, in flaming fire taking vengeance . . . on those who do not obey the gospel of our Lord Jesus Christ. These shall be punished with everlasting destruction from the presence of the Lord and from the glory of His power, when He comes, in that day, to be glorified in His saints and to be admired among all those who believe, because our testimony among you was believed (2 Thessalonians 1:7-10).

What happens to everybody? The righteous living are transformed into their new glorified bodies and caught up to be with Christ. Those who chose not to submit their lives to God's wooing appeals are consumed by the glory of the Lord. The righteous dead are resurrected with glorified bodies and are raptured to be with Christ, but the unsaved dead remain dead until the second resurrection (John 5:29; Revelation 20:5, 6).

Could anything be made clearer? But listen to our Lord's encouragement: "Now when these things begin to happen, look up and lift up your heads, because your redemption draws near" (Luke 21:28).

Encouragement! That is what I have been trying to share throughout this book! When the future is galloping into us as never before, let us renew our courage, because our redemption "draws near."

We have been warned that "the final movements will be rapid ones,"[497] that "perplexities . . . scarcely dreamed of are before us,"[498] that "events of the future . . . will soon come upon [us] with blinding force,"[499] that "a storm

497. White, *Testimonies for the Church,* vol. 9, 11.

498. Ibid., 43.

499. White, *Manuscript Releases,* vol. 4, 74.

is coming, relentless in its fury,"[500] that "no one [should] feel that he is secure from the danger of being surprised,"[501] that we should be preparing for what is about "to break upon the world as an overwhelming surprise,"[502] and that we should be able to "catch the steady tread of the events."[503]

In view of what you have read in this book, is it possible that some will still say, "I never saw it coming!" Or, "Why didn't someone tell us?" That is why this book is named *Red Alert.*

But what I must insist is this: Even though we have touched on many key areas that will certainly converge on the last generation in a "perfect storm," no one knows precisely how any one of these areas—such as natural disasters, economic distress, papal influence, Sunday laws, psychic phenomena, etc.—will exactly happen in specific detail. But we can be fairly clear about the general progression of events.

We have only painted the picture of the last days as clearly as we now have information in any of these areas. I assure you, I know that I will be profoundly "surprised" at how the "rapid movements" will develop with "blinding force." But I can say without ambiguity that the coming "storm" that arises from each of the areas highlighted in this book will truly be "relentless in its fury." And together, the combined effect will catch us all with "overwhelming surprise." All of us! But the better we are prepared, the easier it will be to balance ourselves when we are surprised!

One of the clearest predictions Jesus made regarding the last generation is found in Matthew 24:14—"And this gospel of the kingdom will be preached in all the world as a witness to all the nations, and then the end will come."

We do not need a college degree to understand what our Lord is saying. Millions of Christian groups are focused on getting their message out to "all the world." I commend the energy and personal sacrifice that hundreds of thousands are devoting to their particular denomination's mission programs. Those in certain countries who resent their presence are killing many thousands of them annually. Since 1907, when the slogan was first coined by a Protestant mission board, many denominations have focused on taking the "gospel to all the world in this generation."[504]

---

500. *Testimonies,* vol. 8, 315.

501. White, *Last Day Events,* 17.

502. *Testimonies,* vol. 8, 28.

503. *Testimonies,* vol. 7, 14.

504. The World Missionary Conference (1910, in Edinburgh, Scotland), organized chiefly by Methodist layman John R. Mott, saw great promise for spreading the gospel through the expanding network of railroads. They adopted a motto: "The evangelization of the world in this generation," and let nothing stand in their way. They invited Baptists, Method-

"This" Gospel

On closer examination of our Lord's prediction, we note that He said, "*this* gospel." Even in the first fifty years after Jesus returned to heaven, Paul said that he had to contend with "a *different* gospel" (Galatians 1:6). In the approximately two thousand years since, any teenager can see that there are many gospels in the world—many, in direct contradiction to each other. What shall we make of all this?

▸ We must get back to what Jesus taught about the "good news." Remember, He was talking to His disciples before His crucifixion! There were things about "this gospel of the kingdom" that He had already been teaching His disciples, that must go to all the world before He returns.

▸ We don't need to work ourselves through the many "different" gospels in the world today, in order to find "this gospel" that must go to "all the world." Something more than repeating the name of Jesus and the fact that He was crucified are included.

▸ The recovered "everlasting gospel" is not the limited gospel that so many good and dedicated Christians have been proclaiming.

▸ We must ever keep in view that the purpose of the gospel is not only forgiveness but also restoration of everything spoiled by sin. We must unite the grace of pardon with the grace of power.

▸ We must give special attention to the "everlasting gospel" that John the revelator said would be timely and urgent in the end times: "Then I saw another angel flying in the midst of heaven, having the everlasting gospel to preach to those who dwell on the earth—to every nation, tribe, tongue, and people" (14:6).

▸ We must recognize that there is something very important about the "everlasting gospel" that has been forgotten or corrupted—that must be recovered in the last days. The "everlasting gospel" is the complete gospel that is being recovered by those who are "saying with a loud voice, 'Fear God and give glory to Him, for the hour of His judgment has come' " (14:7).

▸ The "everlasting gospel" proclaims loudly that God is our Creator and that our first act of worship is to "worship Him who made heaven and earth." The first battle in the great controversy was over worship, and the last battle in this conflict is all about worship.

---

ists, Lutherans, Episcopalians, Presbyterians, Quakers, and others to get together and talk, banning dialogue about doctrine so they wouldn't be diverted from conversation about missionary cooperation. See http://www.edinburgh2010.org/fileadmin/files. And http://peopleofpraise.org/news/?p=1.

▸ Those proclaiming worldwide this "everlasting gospel" are identified in verse 12: "Here is the patience [Greek: endurance] of the saints, here are those who keep the commandments of God and the faith of Jesus."

▸ In a nutshell: The "everlasting gospel" simply answers the questions, Who is God? What is His character? and What does God want to accomplish with His plan of salvation?

The Message of the Mission

While we have used Matthew 24:30, 31 as the launching pad for our discussion of the end of the world, Jesus did not "drop the subject" after His resurrection. In His commission to His disciples He said, "Go therefore and make disciples of all the nations, baptizing them in the name of the Father and of the Son and of the Holy spirit, teaching them to observe all things that I have commanded you; and lo, I am with you always, even to the end of the age" (Matthew 28:19, 20).

In the commission to His disciples, Christ not only outlined their work, but gave them their message. Teach the people, He said, "to observe all things whatsoever I have commanded you." The disciples were to teach what Christ had taught. That which He had spoken, not only in person, but through all the prophets and teachers of the Old Testament, is here included. Human teaching is shut out. There is no place for tradition, for man's theories and conclusions, or for church legislation. No laws ordained by ecclesiastical authority are included in the commission. None of these are Christ's servants to teach. "The law and the prophets," with the record of His own words and deeds, are the treasure committed to the disciples to be given to the world. Christ's name is their watchword, their badge of distinction, their bond of union, the authority for their course of action, and the source of their success. Nothing that does not bear His superscription is to be recognized in His kingdom.[505]

This then, is the Everlasting Gospel. It is the Gospel connected to the Everlasting Covenant. "Bind up the Testimony [Covenant] and seal the law among My disciples." (Isaiah 8:16).

"This is the testimony that must go throughout the length and breadth of the world. It presents the law and the gospel, binding up the two in a perfect whole."[506]

---

505. White, *The Desire of Ages*, 826.
506. White, *Testimonies to Ministers*, 94.

Take not the position that men can be moved by the presentation of the love of God alone. You may build ever so fine a structure, but it is without foundation. Dig deep, lay the foundation on Christ alone—a crucified Redeemer who died for the transgressor that he should not perish but have eternal life. How? Only by coming back to his allegiance to God's holy law. "Repentance toward God, and faith toward our Lord Jesus Christ." Acts 20:21.

The law and the gospel go hand in hand. The one is the complement of the other. The law without faith in the gospel of Christ cannot save the transgressor of law. The gospel without the law is inefficient and powerless. The law and the gospel are a perfect whole. The Lord Jesus laid the foundation of the building, and He lays "the headstone thereof with shoutings, crying, Grace, grace unto it." Zecharah 4:7. He is the Author and Finisher of our faith, the Alpha and Omega, the beginning and the end, the first and the last. The two blended—the gospel of Christ and the law of God—produce the love and faith unfeigned.[507]

This is no milquetoast gospel! This gospel has the meat of the Word, and power to change men and women into fit citizens of Christ's kingdom! This gospel sees the continuity of the Old and New Testaments. This gospel proclaims that "The New Testament is not a new religion, and the Old Testament is not a religion to be superseded by the New. The New Testament is only the advancement and unfolding of the Old."[508]

This gospel does not "array Christ against Christ."[509] This gospel includes the Elijah Message as referenced in Malachi 4. It includes the application of the New/Everlasting Covenant as described in Jeremiah 31:31–33, Ezekiel 36:25–27, and Exodus 34. It recognizes the New/Everlasting Covenant as "an arrangement for bringing men again into harmony with the divine will, placing them where they could obey God's law" (White, *Patriarchs and Prophets*, p. 371).

Truly, "The third angel's message comprehends more than many suppose."[510]

World Statistics

As far as I have been able to determine, the Seventh-day Adventist

---

507. White, Diary Entry for December 27, 1890—in *The Ellen G. White 1888 Materials*, 783.

508. White, *Special Testimonies to Ministers and Workers*, no. 3, 41.

509. White, *Review and Herald*, May 6, 1875.

510. White, *Review and Herald*, December 11, 1888.

Church is now in about 204 of the 233 nations recognized by the United Nations. That means that at this time, Adventists do not have any identifiable presence in about twenty-six countries, such as Yemen, United Arab Emirates, Saudi Arabia, Tunisia, Somali, North Korea, Bhutan, and Brunei.

When we look at the world field, 20 percent of Adventists are in South America; 16 percent in East Central Africa; 14 percent in Inter-America; 17 percent in South Africa/Indian Ocean; 12 percent in Southern Asia; compared to 3.5 percent in North America, and 26/100 of 1 percent in the Trans European Division (with other divisions making up the rest). Thirty-five percent of world Adventists live in Latin America, and 35 percent are in African divisions.

The ratio of Adventists to total population is interesting: Adventists are approximately 1 in 459 in the world field. In Peru, 1 in 41; in the Philippines, 1 in 111; in Brazil, 1 in 135; in the United States, 1 in 309; in India, 1 in 1,185.

What does all this mean? It means much work remains to be done. Is it an impossible task? Absolutely not! What kind of burden rested on the disciples after Jesus returned to heaven—that surely also *looked* like the impossible!

Seemed Impossible

Let's enjoy a little perspective. I admit that in 1947, when I began as a pastor in Illinois, a finished work seemed impossible—unless the Lord were to write the gospel on the clouds by day and trace it with laser beams on the sky at night. Today, after the first decade of the twenty-first century, the world is nearly saturated with many sources of communication that we didn't even dream of in 1947!

Think of the Internet (as of today)—no country's passport, visa, border patrol, etc., can successfully or for long forbid it (though some are trying). One of the biggest surprises I found in my travels in the Orient and in the "10/40 Window" was the forest of television antennae I saw—over some of the most dilapidated shanties. Add to the Internet both FM and shortwave radio (AWR)—and one can blanket the world without fear of border patrols!

In many, if not most, of the twenty-six countries where Adventists have no identifiable presence, these modern communication marvels *are* present. Many of our Adventist media, such as *Amazing Facts, It Is Written, The Voice of Prophecy, The Quiet Hour,* and others are blanketing most of these countries, even as we write. Written requests for Bible school lessons require a constant expansion of staff and space. These Adventist outreaches are even carrying on live Internet conversations with people who wouldn't dare attend a public meeting.

Bottom line: The Adventist challenge is not *how* we are to reach honest seekers for truth. The highest challenge is, *what kind of gospel* are they hearing? *Above all other items on the Adventist agenda should be a constant review of what kind of gospel we are proclaiming!* How different is the Adventist gospel from that of our Roman Catholic friends, who devote much energy and funds in their missionary outreach? We say, the Adventist gospel is different in every way!

What about our Baptist friends, or Pentecostal friends? They too have an enormous missionary program that in many countries is far more advanced than is ours. How different is the Adventist gospel, compared to that of Baptists and Pentecostals?

What about the worldwide expansion of mega-churches, such as Rick Warren's Saddleback Church, or Bill Hybels' Willow Creek? How different is the Adventist gospel? And in what respects? Or amidst the tsunami of the New Spirituality/Innovation/Emergent Church/Spiritual Formation movement that is flooding most all denominations—how does "this gospel" that Jesus and Paul proclaimed compare with this new force?

The only way Christ's prophecy will be fulfilled is when Adventists, embracing the responsibility of proclaiming the "everlasting gospel," truly do just that!

Good Witnesses

But there is another aspect of Matthew 24:14 that we must constantly remember: only good "witnesses" can tell the truth about the gospel. This connection between God's commission to the church—that the Christian's reflection of His character and principles would be His "witness" to the world, and that the return of Jesus depends on when this "witness" has been faithfully completed—is neatly summarized in these words:

It is the darkness of misapprehension of God that is enshrouding the world. Men are losing their knowledge of His character. It has been misunderstood and misinterpreted. At this time a message from God is to be proclaimed, a message illuminating in its influence and saving in its power. His character is to be made known. Into the darkness of the world is to be shed the light of His glory, the light of His goodness, mercy, and truth. . . . Those who wait for the Bridegroom's coming are to say to the people, "Behold your God." The last rays of merciful light, the last message of mercy to be given to the world, is a revelation of His character of love. The children of God are to manifest His glory. In their own life and character they are to reveal what the grace of God has done for them. The light of the Sun of Righteousness is to shine forth in good works—in words of truth and deeds of holiness.[511]

This is an amazing statement. Frankly, it's very unambiguous! It simply amplifies our Lord's prediction: "This gospel of the kingdom will be preached in all the world as a *witness* to all the nations, and then shall the end come" (Matthew 24:14).

Just two examples of many I could use to illustrate the awful misrepresentation God is getting in these so-called "modern times." Think of the attempted assassination of Congresswoman Gabrielle Gifford and the murder of a federal judge on January 8, 2011, in Tucson, Arizona.

Within hours, the pastor of Westboro Baptist Church (WBC), the Topeka church known for its inflammatory anti-gay protests, announced plans to picket the funerals of the six people gunned down.

Why? In a flier posted on its Web site, the controversial church said this: "THANK GOD FOR THE SHOOTER—6 DEAD!" And: *"God appointed this rod for your sins! God sent the shooter!"*

The flier claims that the shooting of both a House member and a federal judge is God's punishment for judicial and Congressional action against the WBC.

> God sent the shooter to *shoot you! And He's sitting in Heaven laughing at you!* Your federal judge is dead and your (fag-promoting, baby-killing, proud-sinner) Congresswoman fights for her life. God is avenging Himself on this rebellious house! *WBC prays for your destruction—more shooters, more dead carcasses piling up, young, old, leader and commoner—all.* Your doom is upon you![512]

My second illustration of how God has been so terribly misunderstood: My long-time friend Oliver Jacques told me about a patient that his physician father had been helping during America's Great Depression in the 1930s. The struggling father with eleven children complained to Dr. Jacques that his wife was expecting again. Then he cried, "How could God do this to me!"

Before the end of time, God will have a people who will tell *the truth* about God in such a way that many confused men and women will gladly surrender their doubts and fears. And that is the whole point of what Jesus is saying: He wants intelligent, faithful witnesses who can rightly represent God in a world that has been terribly darkened with Satan's lies.

Think about it: Witnesses in any court must not repeat hearsay! They

511. White, *Christ's Object Lessons*, 415, 416.

512. http://www.Huffingtonpost.com (January 11, 2011).

can speak only of what they personally know. God's faithful ones in the end times will be personal witnesses to what the gospel has done for them and what it will surely do for all those who also "come and see."

Could it be said any clearer:

All who receive Christ as a personal Saviour are to demonstrate the truth of the gospel and its saving power upon the life. God makes no requirement without making provision for its fulfillment. Through the grace of Christ we may accomplish everything that God requires. All the riches of heaven are to be revealed through God's people. "Herein is My Father glorified," Christ says, "that ye bear much fruit; so shall ye be My disciples." John 15:8.[513]

God waits for His professed people to step up to their responsibilities and give those who will listen the true story of His side of the controversy with evil. Until that is faithfully done, God will continue to restrain Satan from having his last hurrah in the ultimate demonstration of his plan for our world, once and for all (Revelation 7:1–4). We call that awful time of Satan's unrestrained governance the "seven last plagues."

Imagine that! Jesus is waiting to return; God is holding back the "the seven last plagues," waiting and pleading for men and women like you and me. Why? So that He can write His signature on our forehead, that we can be trusted in what we say about Him and how we represent Him.

If Jesus Won the War, Why Are We Still Fighting?

Have you ever heard anyone cry out: "If there is a God in heaven, and if He is the 'Almighty' and has a 'compassionate heart,' then why doesn't He stop the suffering which is in the world today?"

I surely have! I have heard others cry: "Why doesn't He use His almighty power to put an end to the sorrow that fills the hearts of so many people?"

"Why so many bald-headed children dying from cancer? If the Almighty really does care for the human race, then why is He so strangely silent about mankind's cruel and crippling problems?"

"Why doesn't He do something about them? And, above all else, why doesn't He answer my prayers?"

---

513. *Christ's Object Lessons*, 301; "The world today is in crying need of a revelation of Christ Jesus in the person of His saints. God desires that His people shall stand before the world a holy people. Why?—because there is a world to be saved by the light of gospel truth; and as the message of truth that is to call men out of darkness into God's marvelous light is given by the church, the lives of its members, sanctified by the Spirit of truth, are to bear witness to the verity of the messages proclaimed" (*Testimonies to Ministers*, 458).

These are not unusual questions! Ask a mother or father who gets a flag at their son's military burial ceremony! Ask a husband who watches his wife slam the door and leave for another. Or the wife who bore a man's children, only to have him chase a younger woman!

Really now, if Jesus won the war with Satan on the cross, why are we still fighting? How many more famines, wars, floods, tornadoes, pestilences, etc., must He wait for, before He pulls the curtain down? Or does He care that much?

The Big Question Remains: Why Doesn't Jesus Return?

If anyone asks, "When will Jesus return?" turn to Revelation 7 and answer: "When God finds enough people He can stamp with His seal of approval!"

In other words, God is holding back the satanic fury of the seven last plagues. Why? He is waiting for His people to catch on as to the purpose of the gospel and to act accordingly. He is waiting for people He can seal with His approval, as His forever endorsement—people He can finally use in completing the gospel commission of Matthew 24:14. These will be people who have our "Father's name written on their foreheads . . . and in their mouth was found no guile for they are without fault before the throne of God" (14:1, 5). But there is more: These are last-day witnesses to the power and purpose of the gospel; God Himself will testify to their faithfulness, and "they shall see His face, and His name shall be on their foreheads" (22:4).

Jesus will return when the controversy between good and evil has been clearly won in the last generation, when the "sheep and the goats" are clearly visible, once and for all time. He won't dilly a day—He will come as soon as He can say, without being contradicted: "He who is unjust, let him be unjust still; he would is filthy, let him be filthy still; he who is righteous, let him be righteous still; he who is holy, let him be holy still" (Revelation 22:11).

In other words, He is waiting until His loyal followers indeed are the overcomers in the controversy with Satan—living exactly as Satan has said was impossible. So many still believe that great lie that God's Holy Spirit cannot keep a person from caving into Satan's temptations!

After all, there is no mystery about those to whom God will entrust eternal life. We are not left to subjective guessing! There really is an object standard:

> For the grace of God that brings salvation has appeared to all men. It teaches us to say "No" to ungodliness and worldly passions, and to live self-controlled, upright and godly lives in this present age, while we wait for the blessed hope, the glorious appearing of our great God and Savior, Jesus Christ, who gave himself for us to

redeem us from all wickedness and to purify for himself a people that are his very own, eager to do what is good (Titus 2:11–14, NIV).

He who overcomes shall inherit all things, and I will be his God and he shall be My son (and daughter). But the cowardly, unbelieving, abominable, murderers, sexually immoral, sorcerers, idolaters, and all liars shall have their part in the lake which burns with fire and brimstone, which is the second death (Revelation 21:7, 8).

For all those reading these pages, what a privilege, what a responsibility, what a future!

Gloomy Moments

In 1857, two editorials appeared in *Harper's Weekly*, a widely read periodical:

It is a gloomy moment in history. Not for many years—not in the lifetime of most men who read this paper—has there been so much grave and deep apprehension; never has the future seemed so incalculable as at this time. In our own country there is a universal commercial prostration and panic and thousands of our poorest fellow-citizens are turned out against the approaching winter without employment, and without the prospects of it. In France the political caldron seethes and bubbles with uncertainty; Russia hangs as usual, like a cloud dark and silent upon the horizon of Europe; while all the energies, resources and influences of the British Empire are sorely tried, and are yet to be tried more sorely . . . .

It is a solemn moment, and no man can feel an indifference— which happily, no man pretends to feel—in the issue of events. Of our own troubles no man can see the end. They are fortunately, as yet mainly commercial, and if we are only to lose money, and by painful poverty to be taught wisdom—the wisdom of honor, of faith, of sympathy, and of charity—no man need seriously to despair. And yet the very haste to be rich, which is the occasion of this wide-spread calamity, has also tended to destroy the moral forces with which we are to resist and subdue the calamity.[514]

The sun is setting—the air is chill—health is failing; there are no stars—there is only universal ignorance, regret, grief, and despair. It is easy enough to say that we are in the woods, it is easy to see that we are—for a time at least—lost; it is not difficult to know that we came in of our own accord.[515]

---

514. *Harper's Weekly*, October 10, 17, 1857.
515. Ibid.

With minor editing, these words could easily be mirrored in magazines and newspapers throughout the world—especially today. Living in 1857 with its financial troubles was tough, but they had no idea of the enormous convergences of last-day troubles we have been discussing in *Red Alert*. The day is fast coming when we all will be writing similar words for ourselves but with far more reason—"the sun is setting, the air is chill."

I found Pope Benedict XVI's message to the world on Good Friday, April 14, 2006, strangely echoing our *Harper's Weekly* editor:

"Lord, we have lost our sense of sin. Today a slick campaign of propaganda is spreading an inane apologia of evil, a senseless cult of Satan, a mindless desire for transgression, a dishonest and frivolous freedom, exalting impulsiveness, immorality and selfishness as if they were new heights of sophistication. . . .

"Lord Jesus, our affluence is making us less human, our entertainment has become a drug, a source of alienation, and our society's incessant, tedious message is an invitation to die of selfishness."[516]

Evil Will Not Triumph!

I think of those ghastly shrieks of the al Qaeda terrorist, as he steered United Airlines Flight 93, on September 11, 2001, into southwestern Pennsylvania: "Allah Akbar! Allah is the greatest!" How evil can evil get? We haven't seen anything yet!

For those who have found their hope, courage, and joy in the "everlasting gospel," the darkening twilight of these last days only makes the return of their Lord that much nearer! Their trust and faith is not in themselves but in their Lord, who showed them how to live and how to die.

When I first heard about *laminin,* that important protein that looks like a cross, I turned it over as junk science, something that some overeager preacher had cooked up for effect.

But I couldn't get rid of the possibility that it may be true! Both Snopes and TruthorFiction now say that it is all true—that the "laminin" substance looks like a cross (in the electron microscope), and it indeed is in a family of proteins that "hold us together." Wikipedia describes them as "an integral part of the structural scaffolding of basement membranes in almost every animal tissue." In other words, they are cell-adhesion molecules—they hold one cell of our bodies to the next cell. Without laminin, we would literally fall apart![517]

Ah, that is the way I think about the thoughtfulness of our Creator God, our coming Lord Jesus. Paul pointed this out in Colossians

516. http://www.timesonline.co.uk/tol/news/world/europe/article705540.ece.
517. http://www.truthorfiction.com/rumors/l/laminin.htm.

1:17, speaking of Jesus: "He is before all things, and in Him all things consist." The Greek here means "hold together," "to cohere." The power that holds the whirling galaxies and keeps heavenly bodies in their courses with awesome mathematical accuracy, the power that holds together the particles within the atoms—nature or mankind—is our Coming Lord's power. He created them and maintains them! Laminin is one way He does it.

Get the message! That wonderful, pervasive power that holds everything in the immense universe together is the same power that will hold your hand and your heart today—and every day until that awesome Power returns to resurrect loved ones and to change our lousy bodies into something that will last forever! Believe it, love it, live it!

Ted Turner's Sign-Off Tape

Not everyone has this truth and faith. Ted Turner is best known for founding TBS and CNN and for his $1 billion pledge to the United Nations. He also is America's largest private landowner, owning more than two million acres (greater than Delaware and Rhode Island combined), including fourteen ranches in six states. One of his interesting quotes is: "I'd rather go to hell. Heaven has got to be boring."

But with all his wealth and prestige, he is known too for his doom and gloom. When he launched CNN in 1980, he said: "We gonna go on air June 1, and we gonna stay on until the end of the world. When that time comes, we'll cover it, play 'Nearer, My God, to Thee' over footage of a waving American flag." Turner ordered the tape locked away until it was determined that the world was about to end.

One source said, "It was like a sign-off tape that you often see in the middle of the night—but to Ted, was a sign-off forever."[518]

I remember a speaking appointment in Corpus Christi, Texas, a few years ago. During some free time, my wife and I visited the USS *Lexington*, anchored in the harbor. It is the fifth ship in U.S. history to have that brave name. The fourth was lost in the Battle of the Coral Sea (May 1942) after a brilliant and heroic effort that helped stop the advance of the Japanese toward Australia. As soon as this news hit America, the next aircraft carrier being built was named the *Lexington*, which also soon saw gallant action in the Pacific.

On December 4, 1943, a Japanese bomber disabled this new *Lexington* on a moonlit night off Tarawa. The skipper, Captain Felix Stump, went to the ship speaker system so that all aboard could hear him: "This is the captain speaking. We have taken a torpedo hit in our stern, and the rudder seems badly damaged. *Each man must do his job calmly and*

---

518. http://www.timemachinego.com.

efficiently. Don't worry. That's my job. I got you here, and I'll get you out and home." Marvelous story of how they limped home!

But there's more to the story. More than 95 percent of those on board had never been on the open sea before. They were not seasoned sailors and pilots. Citizen sailors and pilots they were, recently assembled and trained but unsure of themselves. On that moonlit night, they were an easy target, but the captain kept maneuvering the ship to face into the moonlight so that the *Lexington* would not give the bomber or submarine a broadside silhouette—all the time changing his speed and direction.

On the way back to Pearl Harbor with that disabled rudder, the Admiral of the fleet radioed to Captain Stump, "That was wonderful seamanship, Captain." The Captain replied, *"Thank you, sir, my crew was magnificent!"*

Those words swept through the crew: They were "magnificent" in the eyes of their captain! The sailors wrote home about their captain. When they limped back to Pearl, they didn't need the serenade of the Navy Band to make them feel that they were heroes. They had already heard the commendation of their captain. Knowing their captain for what he was kept them unafraid—kept them doing their duty. They could trust their captain, because he got them there, and he would get them home.[519]

One of these days, a wonderful group of people will, in a way, limp into the Harbor after the worst time of trouble ever to hit people on this earth. And they will hear their Captain say: "Well done, good and faithful servants. . . . Enter into the joy of your lord" (Matthew 25:21).

And then He will turn to the unfallen worlds and to the unfallen angels and wave His hand over the veterans from earth. And He will say, "My crew was magnificent!"

Here were the people upon whom God risked His integrity and government. In a very special way, the rest of the universe that had been watching Laboratory Earth will stand and salute these veterans of a very costly war! And then they will turn to their Captain of the universe and fall on their knees in a sob that will echo from galaxy to galaxy—a sob of relief and gratitude and love! The risk was worth it. O "Lord God Almighty! Just and true are Your ways, O King of the saints!" (Revelation 15:3).

---

519. Written on a plaque displayed in the *Lexington* in retirement at Corpus Christi, Texas.

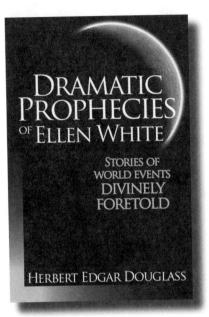

Dramatic Prophecies of Ellen White

Whether writing about war, segregation, spiritualism, healthful living, or the great controversy, God's messenger boldly spoke unpopular truths to those who needed to hear them. Today we need to listen once again. Herbert Douglass has skillfully compiled an arresting variety of examples of messages that were ridiculed at the time they were spoken, but were proved true in retrospect. This book will rekindle your faith in the Spirit of Prophecy and inspire you to look carefully at those predictions yet to be fulfilled.

Paperback, 192 pages
ISBN 13: 978-0-8163-2192-6
ISBN 10: 0-8163-2192-2

Paperback, 224 pages
ISBN 13: 978-0-8163-2156-8
ISBN 10: 0-8163-2156-6

Paperback, 160 pages
ISBN 13: 978-0-8163-1967-1
ISBN 10: 0-8163-1967-7

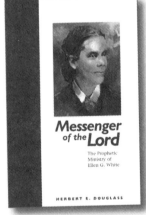

Hardcover, 512 pages
ISBN 13: 978-0-8163-1622-9
ISBN 10: 0-8163-1622-8

Pacific Press®
Publishing Association
"Where the Word Is Life"

Three ways to order:

1 Local	Adventist Book Center®
2 Call	1-800-765-6955
3 Shop	AdventistBookCenter.com

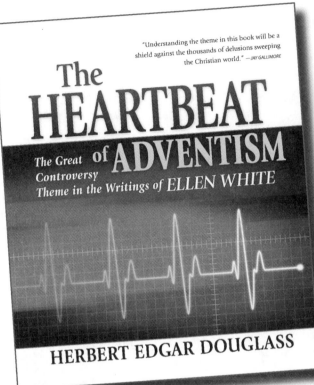

"Understanding the theme in this book will be a shield against the thousands of delusions sweeping the Christian world." —*JAY GALLIMORE*

The
HEARTBEAT of ADVENTISM

The Great Controversy Theme in the Writings of ELLEN WHITE

HERBERT EDGAR DOUGLASS

The Heartbeat of Adventism

An invaluable resource and study tool providing the opportunity to study the important theme of the great controversy as it is unfolded throughout the prophetic ministry and writings of Ellen G. White. It will provide readers with the big picture from which to frame their quest for truth.

Hardcover, 422 pages
ISBN 13: 978-0-8163-2458-3
ISBN 10: 0-8163-2458-1

"What a book this is! Understanding the theme in this book will be a shield against the thousands of delusions sweeping the Christian world; especially the many forms of seductive spirituality. Because the fog of war surrounds the great controversy, this book will give the reader instant tests to discern truth from error."–JAY GALLIMORE, PRESIDENT, MICHIGAN CONFERENCE OF SEVENTH-DAY ADVENTISTS

"Dr. Douglass has provided the reader with a study tool that is both useful, as well as timely, providing the opportunity to study this important theme with new and fresh relevance."–JIM PEDERSEN, PRESIDENT, NORTHERN CALIFORNIA CONFERENCE OF SEVENTH-DAY ADVENTISTS

"An invaluable resource for greater insight and understanding of the great controversy theme. . . . It is a volume that ought to be in every school and personal library."–JACK BLANCO, PROFESSOR EMERITUS, SOUTHERN ADVENTIST UNIVERSITY

Pacific Press®
Publishing Association
"Where the Word Is Life"

Three ways to order:

1	Local	Adventist Book Center®
2	Call	1-800-765-6955
3	Shop	AdventistBookCenter.com

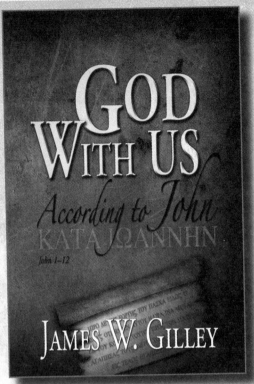
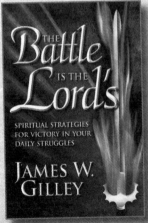

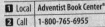

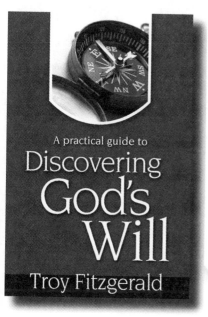

A practical guide to Discovering God's Will
by Troy Fitzgerald

Does finding God's will for your life seem like a game show in which you must choose door A, door B, or door C? Is God hiding necessary information from you? Or are you hiding from God? Troy Fizgerald, PhD, shares his conviction that you can know God's will and live happily in it. He challenges us to live each day as Abraham—traveling to the Promised Land—only by faith. That's great advice for Christians of any age.

Paperback, 144 pages
ISBN 13: 978-0-8163-2180-3
ISBN 10: 0-8163-2180-9

20 Questions
God Wants To Ask You
by Troy Fitzgerald

The questions God asks of us help us know what's on His mind and heart. They provide opportunities for us to learn to discover what God would have us be and do. Sometimes we think that God exists merely to answer our questions when we are perplexed— "Why, God, why?" we shout. In this book, it will be God asking the questions: "What is that in your hand?" "Who do you think I am?" or "What are you doing here?" Using stories and examples, the author will help you prayerfully consider and answer these questions for yourself.

Paperback, 192 pages
ISBN 13: 978-0-8163-2275-6
ISBN 10: 0-8163-2275-9

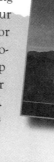
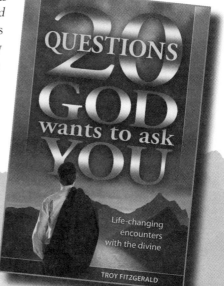

Pacific Press®
Publishing Association
"Where the Word Is Life"

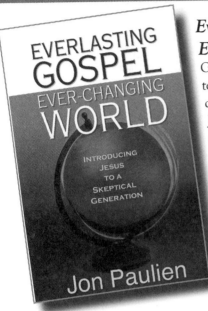
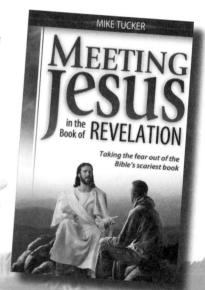

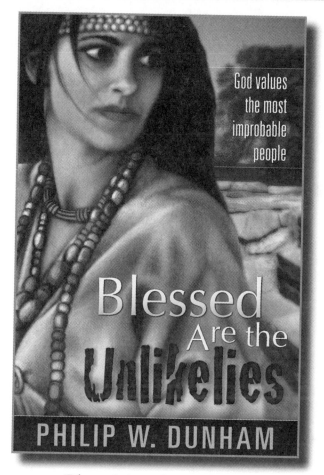

Caught Between Two Worlds

Pastor Karl Haffner reminds us that Peter's words were written as encouragement and instruction for a people surviving unbelievable hardships and trials. This is a timely message for God's people today. For whenever trouble stares us in the face—and it will—we need to know for certain that even though we're caught between two worlds, there is hope: a Living Hope.

Paperback, 144 pages
ISBN 13: 978-0-8163-2404-0
ISBN 10: 0-8163-2404-2

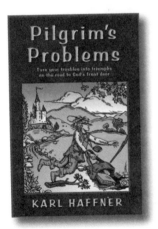

Paperback, 144 pages
ISBN 13: 978-0-8163-2022-6
ISBN 10: 0-8163-2022-5

Paperback, 128 pages
ISBN 13: 978-0-8163-1840-7
ISBN 10: 0-8163-1840-9

Paperback, 144 pages
ISBN 13: 978-0-8163-2150-6
ISBN 10: 0-8163-2150-7

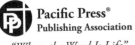

Pacific Press®
Publishing Association
"Where the Word Is Life"